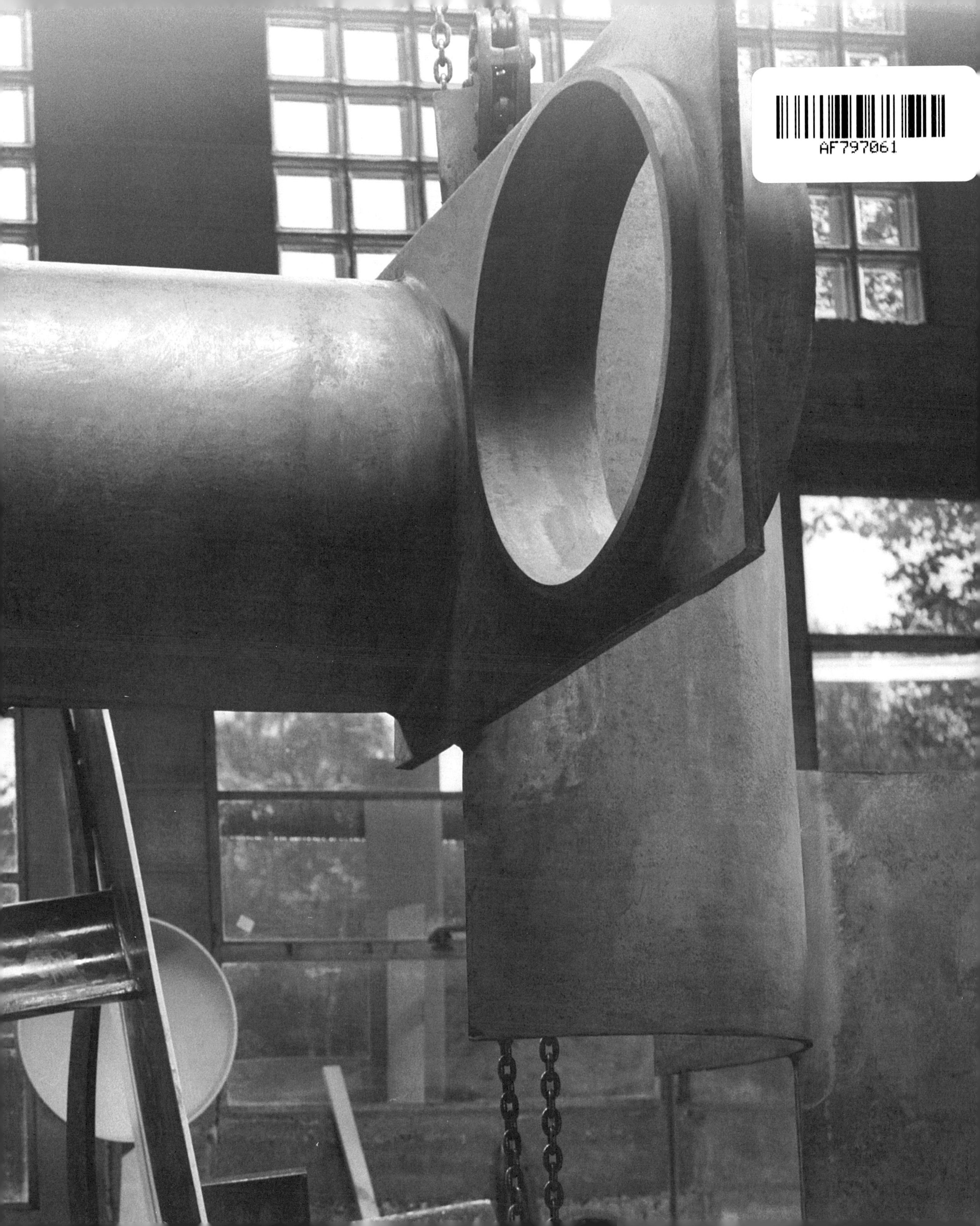

David Smith

Cubes and Anarchy

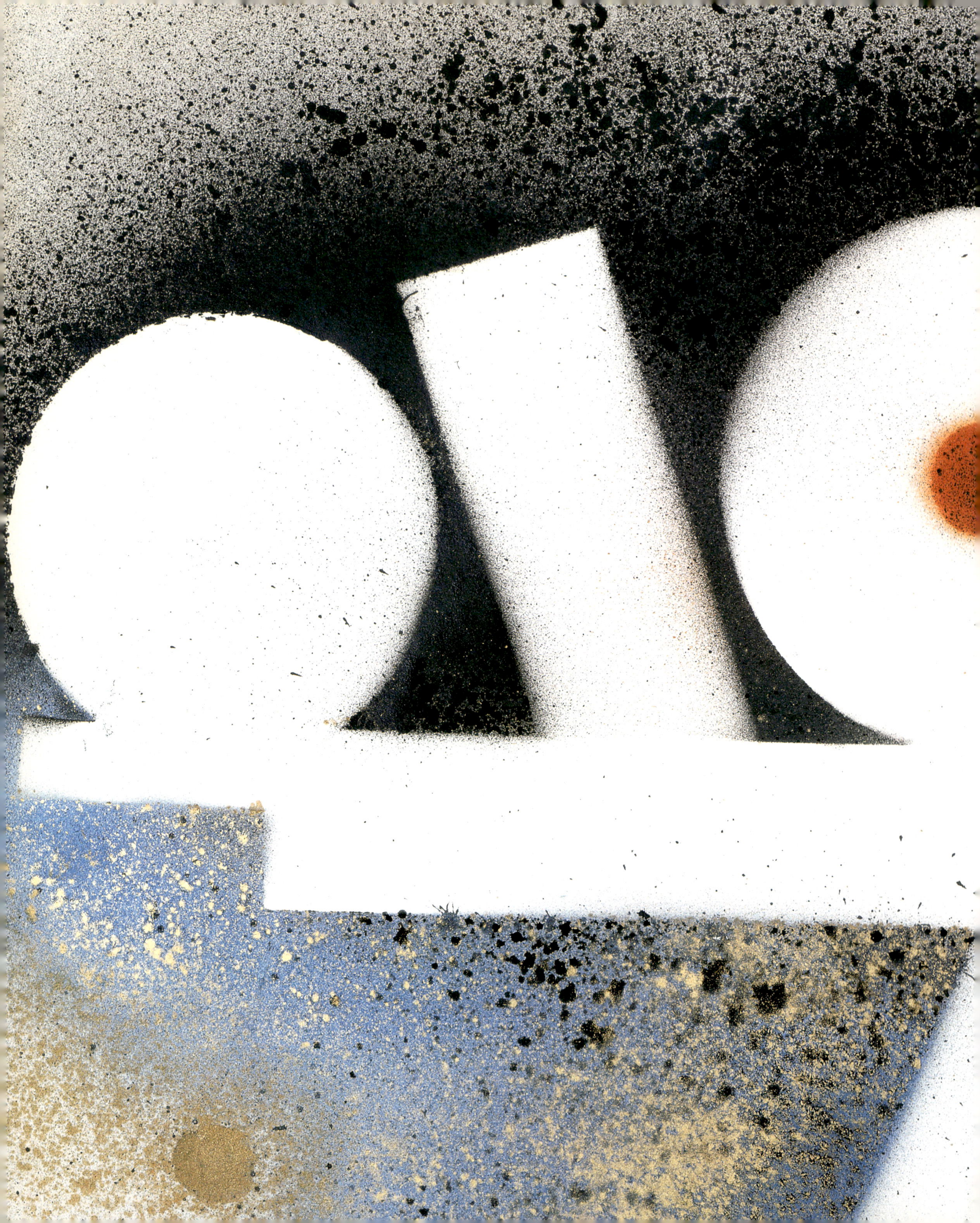

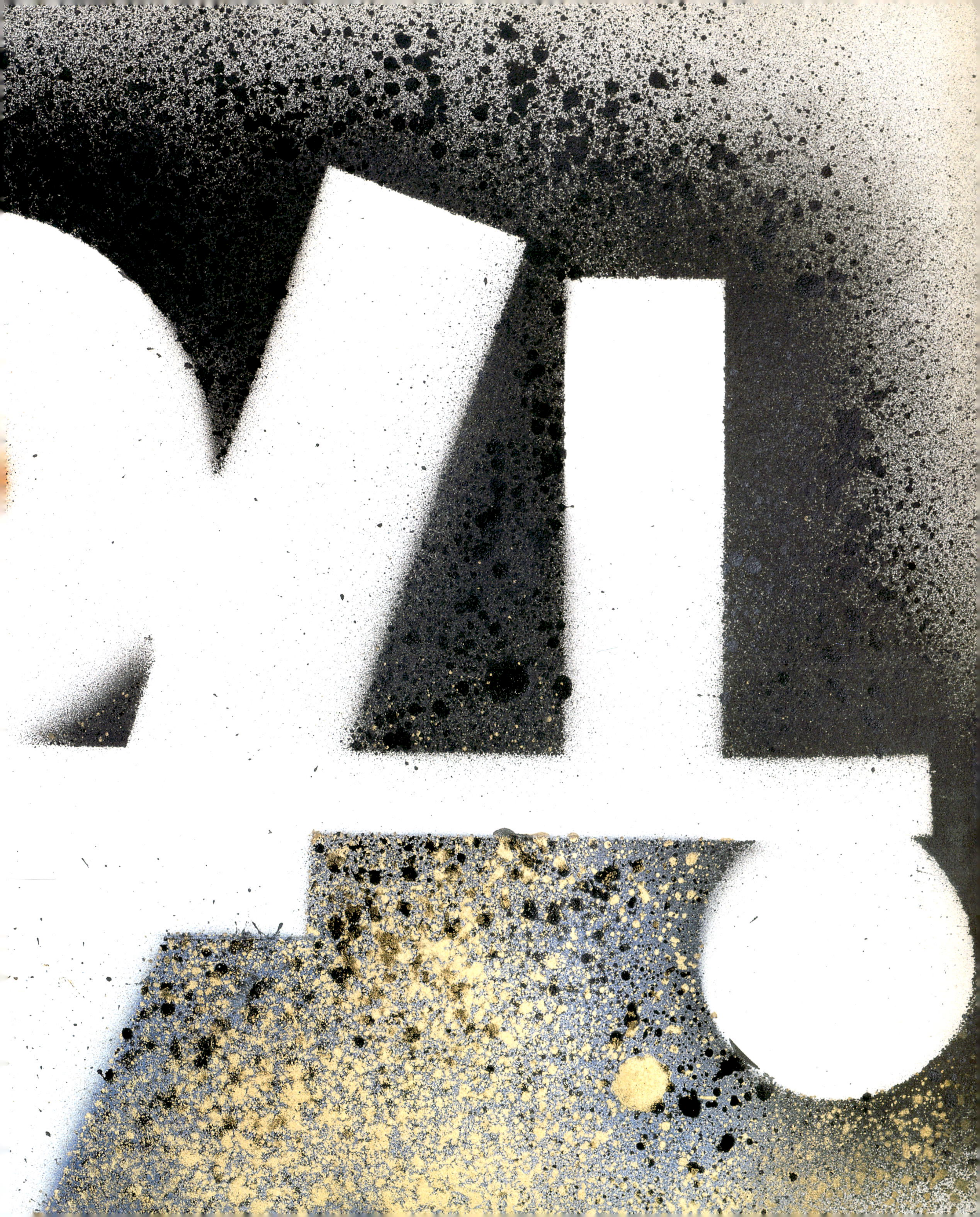

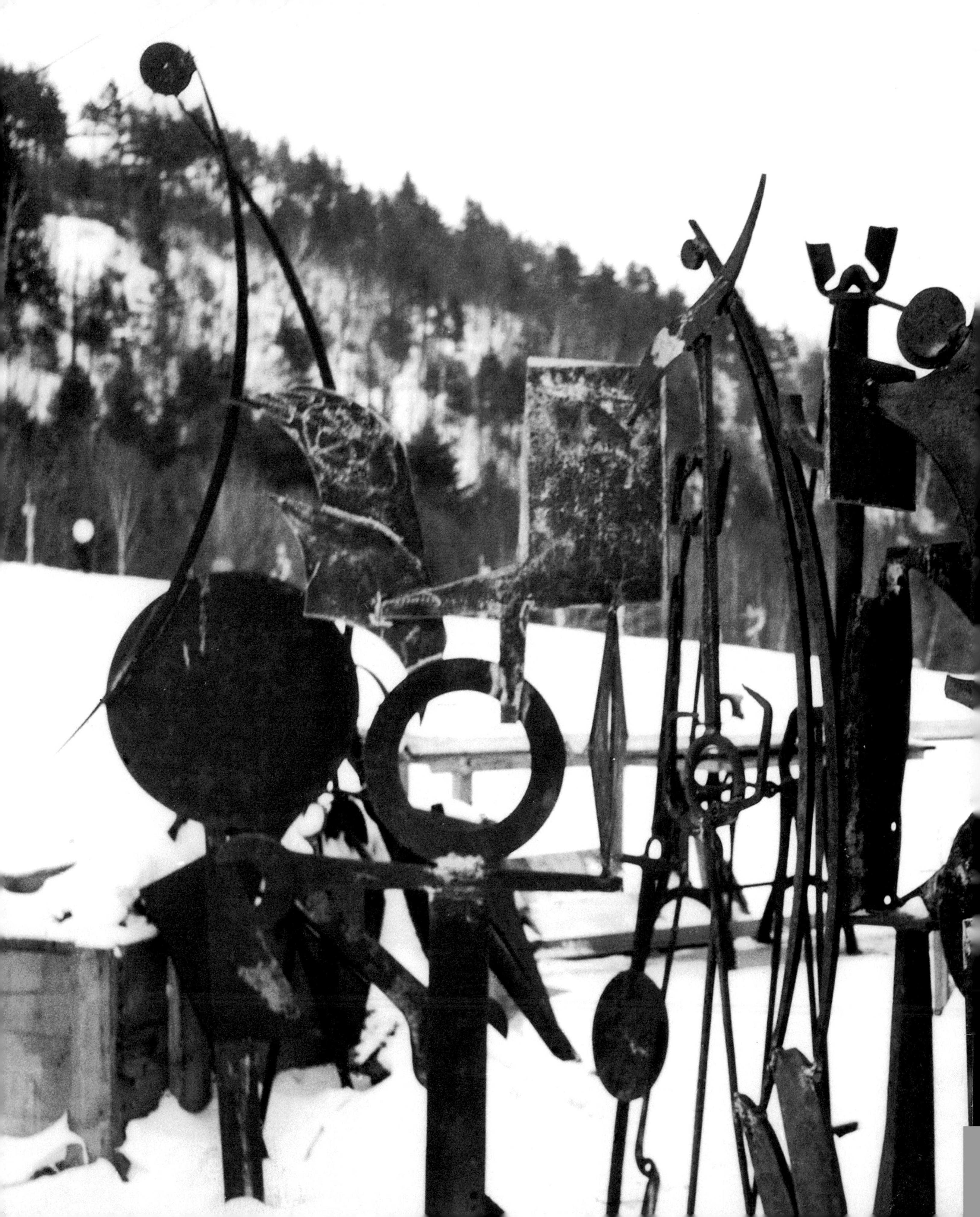

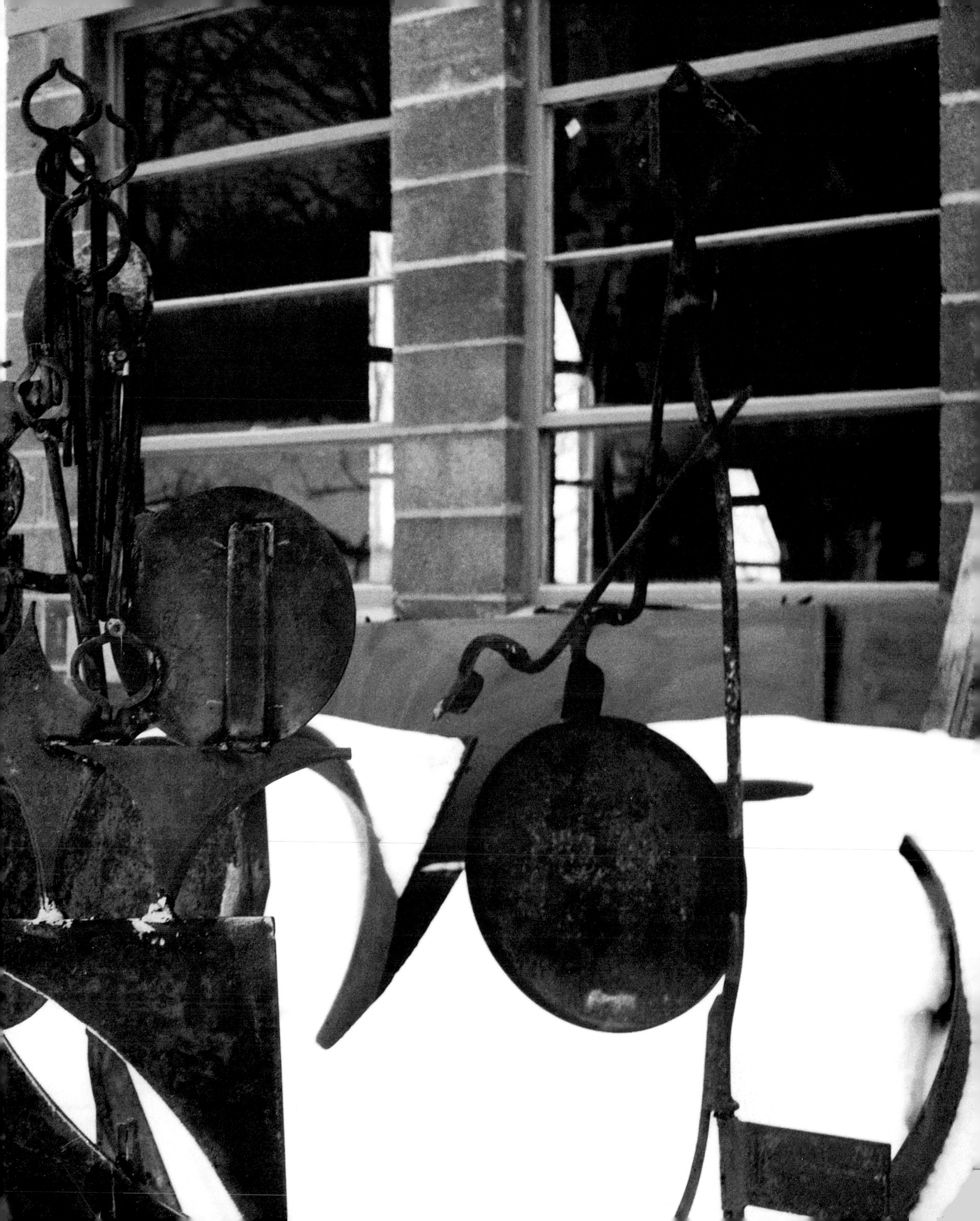

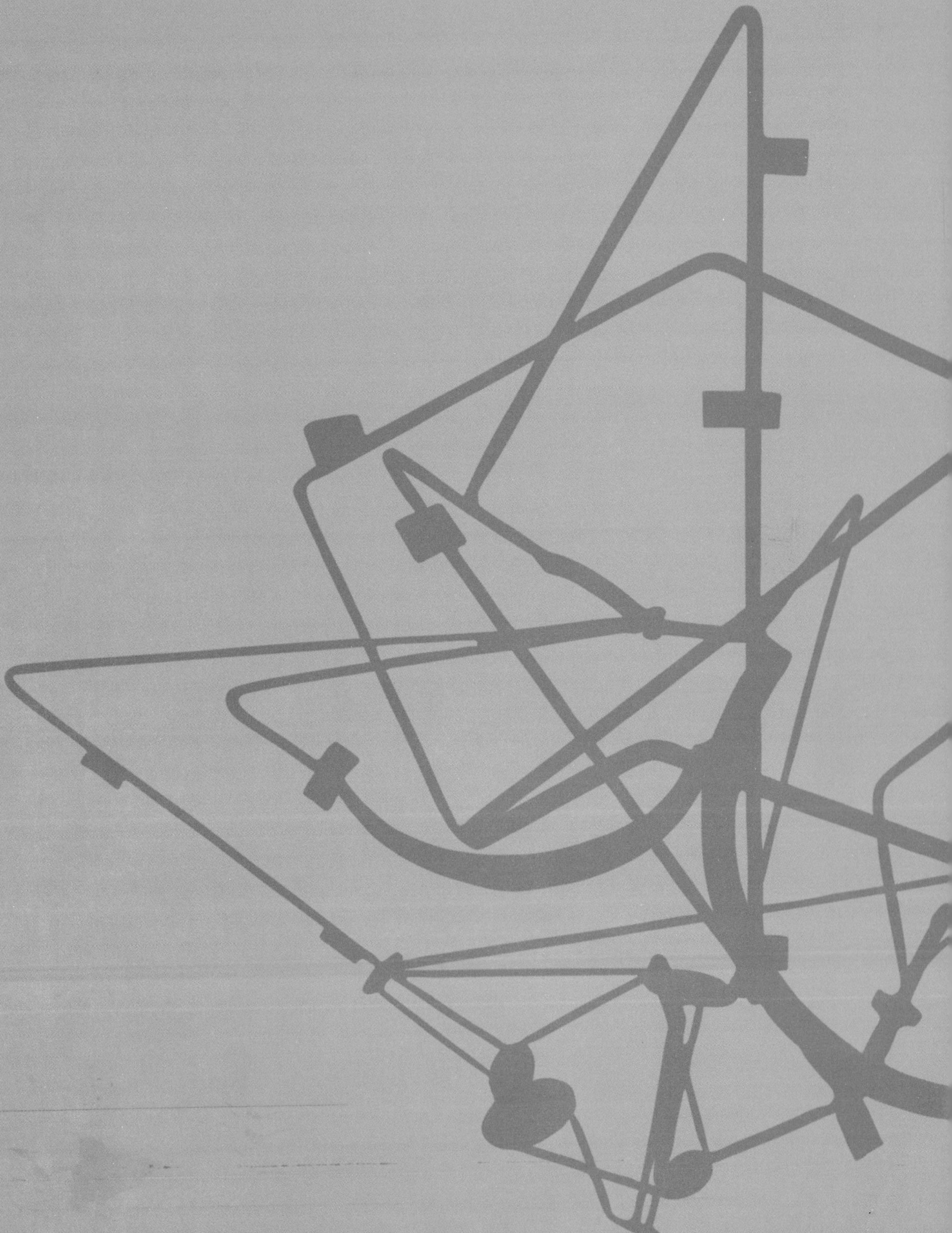

David Smith

Cubes and Anarchy

Carol S. Eliel
with contributions by
Christopher Bedford
Alex Potts
Anne M. Wagner

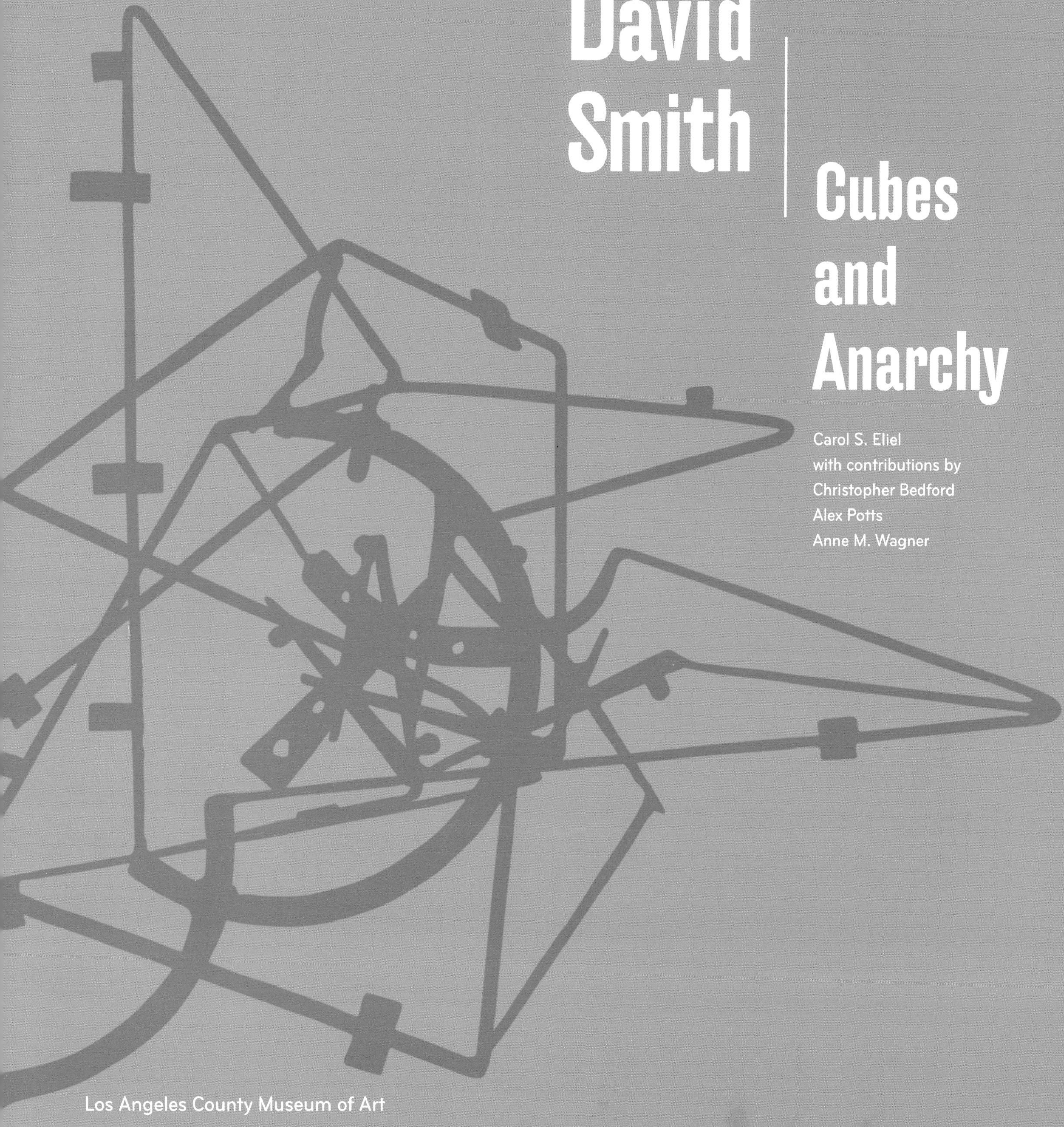

Los Angeles County Museum of Art

DelMonico Books • Prestel
Munich • Berlin • London • New York

This catalogue was published on the occasion of the exhibition *David Smith: Cubes and Anarchy*, on view from April 3 through July 24, 2011.

This exhibition was organized by the Los Angeles County Museum of Art and was made possible by Alice and Nahum Lainer, the National Endowment for the Arts, Gagosian Gallery, and the Steven F. Roth Family Foundation. Additional support was provided by the Steaven K. and Judith G. Jones Foundation, Myron Laskin, Agnes Gund, Dorothy R. Sherwood, Terri and Michael Smooke, the Dedalus Foundation, Ellie and Mark Lainer, and the Lipman Family Foundation.

NATIONAL ENDOWMENT FOR THE ARTS

This exhibition was supported by an indemnity from the Federal Council on the Arts and the Humanities.

The catalogue was supported in part by Contemporary Collectors–Orange County.

Los Angeles County Museum of Art
5905 Wilshire Boulevard
Los Angeles, CA 90036
lacma.org

and

DelMonico Books, an imprint of Prestel
Prestel, a member of Verlagsgruppe Random House GmbH

Prestel Verlag	Prestel Publishing Ltd.	Prestel Publishing
Königinstrasse 9	4 Bloomsbury Place	900 Broadway, Suite 603
80539 Munich	London WC1A 2QA	New York, NY 10003
Germany	United Kingdom	Tel 212 995 2720
Tel 49 89 242908 300	Tel 44 20 7323 5004	Fax 212 995 2733
Fax 49 89 242908 335	Fax 44 20 7636 8004	sales@prestel-usa.com
prestel.de		prestel.com

Library of Congress Cataloging-in-Publication Data

Eliel, Carol S., 1955-
David Smith : cubes and anarchy / Carol S. Eliel ; with contributions by Christopher Bedford, Alex Potts, Anne M. Wagner. -- 1st ed.
p. cm.
Published on the occasion of an exhibition held at the Los Angeles County Museum of Art, Apr. 3-July 24, 2011.
Includes index.
ISBN 978-3-7913-5121-6
1. Smith, David, 1906-1965--Exhibitions. 2. Geometry in art--Exhibitions. I. Smith, David, 1906-1965. II. Bedford, Christopher. III. Potts, Alex. IV. Wagner, Anne M. V. Los Angeles County Museum of Art. VI. Title. VII. Title: Cubes and anarchy.
N6537.S616A4 2011
730.92--dc22
2010041926

For the Los Angeles County Museum of Art
Head of Publications: Nola Butler
Editor in Chief: Thomas Frick
Editor: Jennifer MacNair
Designer: Paul Wehby
Production Manager: Karen Knapp
Supervising Photographer: Peter Brenner
Rights and Reproductions: Piper Severance
Editorial Assistant: Monica Paniry
Proofreader: Dianne Woo
Indexer: Kathleen Preciado

Printing and binding: CS Graphics, Singapore

Cover: *Star Cage* (detail), 1950, Frederick R. Weisman Art Museum, University of Minnesota, Minneapolis; endpapers: *Untitled* (*Zig III* with *Black White Backward*[?], *Ninety Father*, *Ninety Son*, and *Black White Forward*, Bolton Landing workshop) (detail), c. 1961, The Estate of David Smith; pp. 2–3: *Untitled* (detail), 1963, Jon and Mary Shirley; pp. 4–5: *Untitled* (*Voltri-Boltons* at Bolton Landing) (detail), 1963, The Estate of David Smith; p. 10: *Zig III* (detail), 1961, The Estate of David Smith, courtesy Gagosian Gallery; pp. 12–13: Dan Budnik, *David Smith Welding* Primo Piano II *in His Bolton Landing Workshop* (detail), 1962

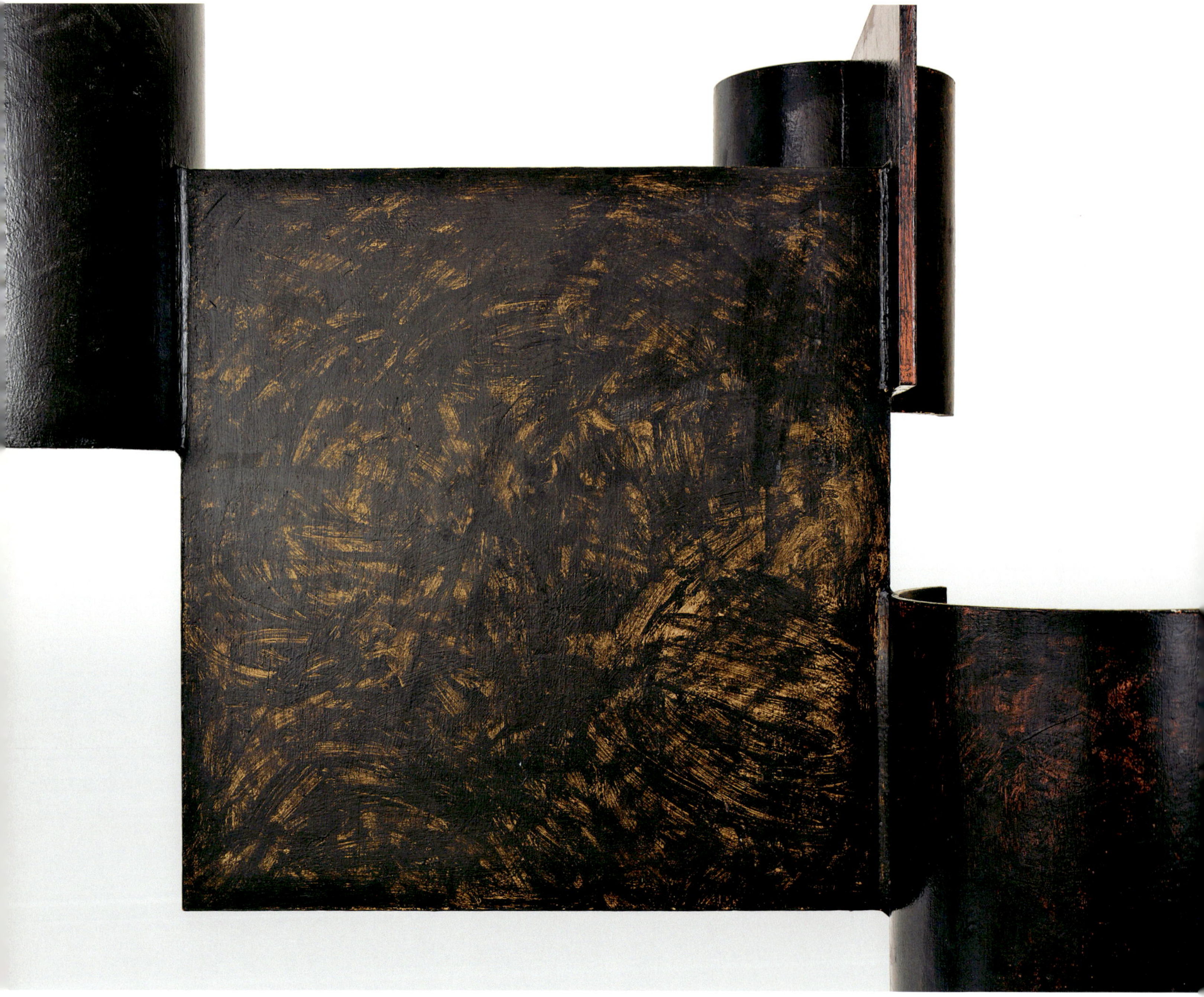

Foreword

David Smith is widely acknowledged as the greatest American sculptor of the twentieth century. He created sculptures that Donald Judd described as "some of the best in the world," yet there has not been an exhibition of Smith's work on the West Coast since a memorial show here at the Los Angeles County Museum of Art in late 1965. And there has never before been a major thematic exhibition devoted to Smith at any institution. LACMA is thus proud to present *David Smith: Cubes and Anarchy*, which considers the entirety of the artist's career while focusing on the theme of geometry in his work.

As organizing curator Carol S. Eliel reveals in her enlightening essay, geometry is a leitmotif throughout Smith's oeuvre. His fascination with the subject arose out of his self-definition as a working man and his interest in international constructivism. From his earliest small-scale sculptures to his last monumental works, what Smith called "basic geometric form" was a powerful touchstone for the artist.

Mounted just seven months after our opening on Wilshire Boulevard, LACMA's 1965 memorial exhibition of Smith's work signaled our commitment to modern and contemporary art. Now, at another moment of transformation, the museum is particularly pleased that *David Smith: Cubes and Anarchy* is the first show of modern or contemporary art to be presented in the Lynda and Stewart Resnick Exhibition Pavilion, which opened in the fall of 2010. With more than one hundred works, the exhibition is both revelatory and visually seductive.

No major Smith exhibition could be organized without the support of The Estate of David Smith, and we are grateful for its enthusiasm and generosity throughout the process. LACMA likewise wishes to thank the many museums and individuals (listed on p. 170) who kindly agreed to lend significant works from their collections. We are also deeply thankful to all those who helped sponsor the exhibition and catalogue (challenging economic times notwithstanding): Alice and Nahum Lainer, the National Endowment for the Arts, Gagosian Gallery, the Steven F. Roth Family Foundation, the Steaven K. and Judith G. Jones Foundation, Myron Laskin, Agnes Gund, Dorothy R. Sherwood, Terri and Michael Smooke, the Dedalus Foundation, Ellie and Mark Lainer, the Lipman Family Foundation, and Contemporary Collectors–Orange County. We are grateful as well to the Federal Council on the Arts and the Humanities for providing the indemnity.

This project has come to fruition thanks to the energy, scholarship, and tireless determination of curator Carol S. Eliel, who conceived and oversaw every aspect of the exhibition and catalogue. The results of her efforts are entirely worthy of the incomparable David Smith.

Michael Govan
CEO and Wallis Annenberg Director
Los Angeles County Museum of Art

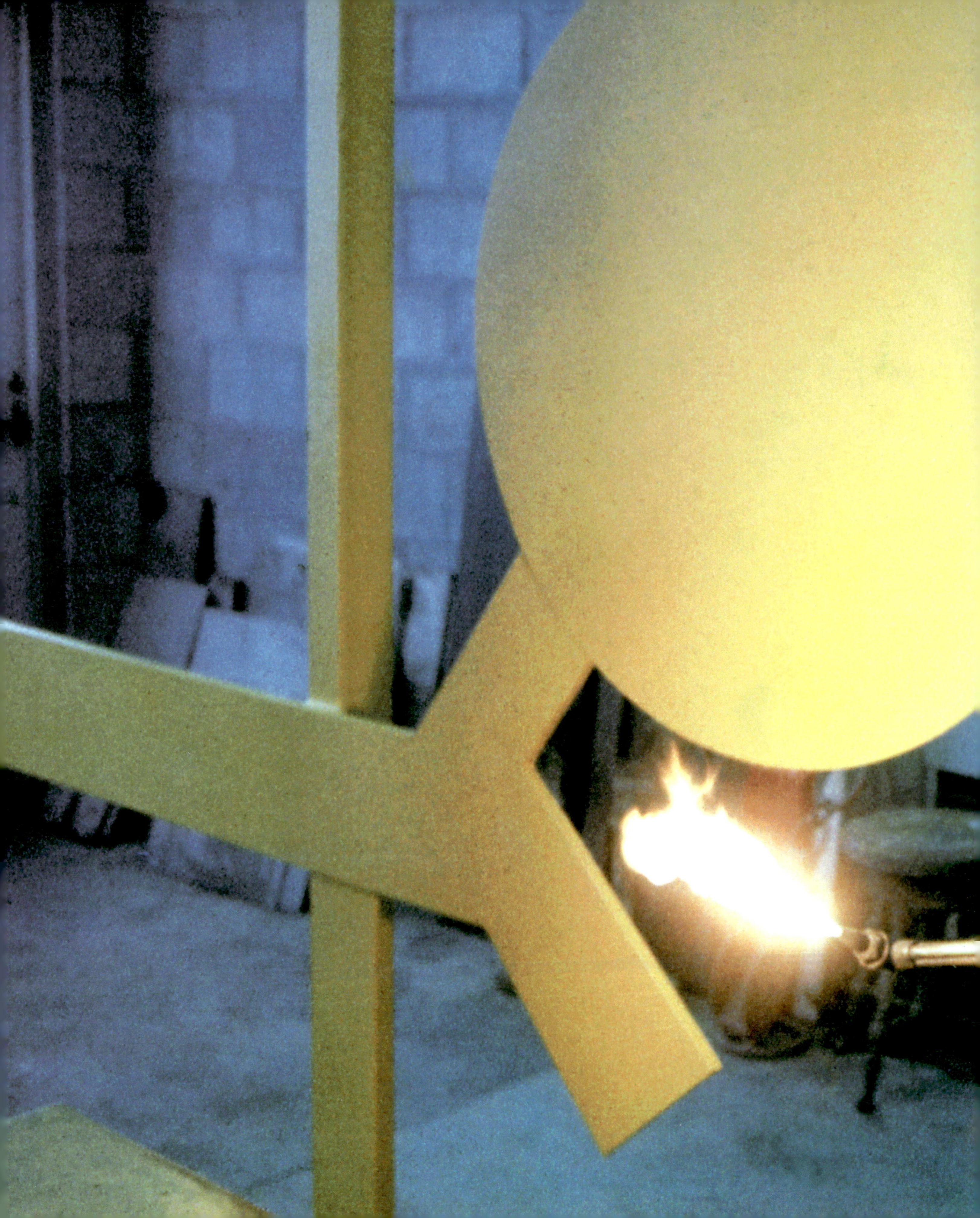

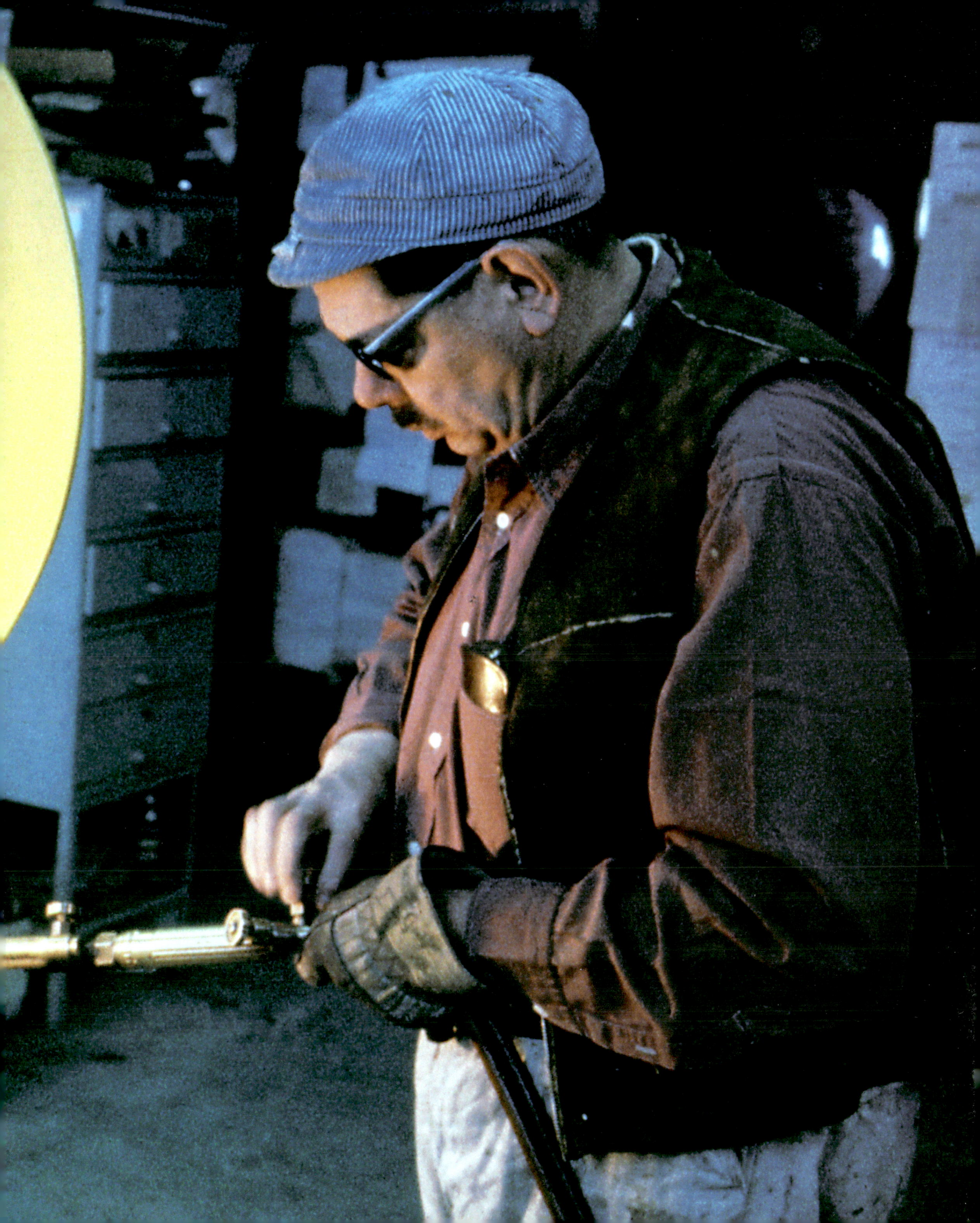

Geometry in David Smith

Carol S. Eliel

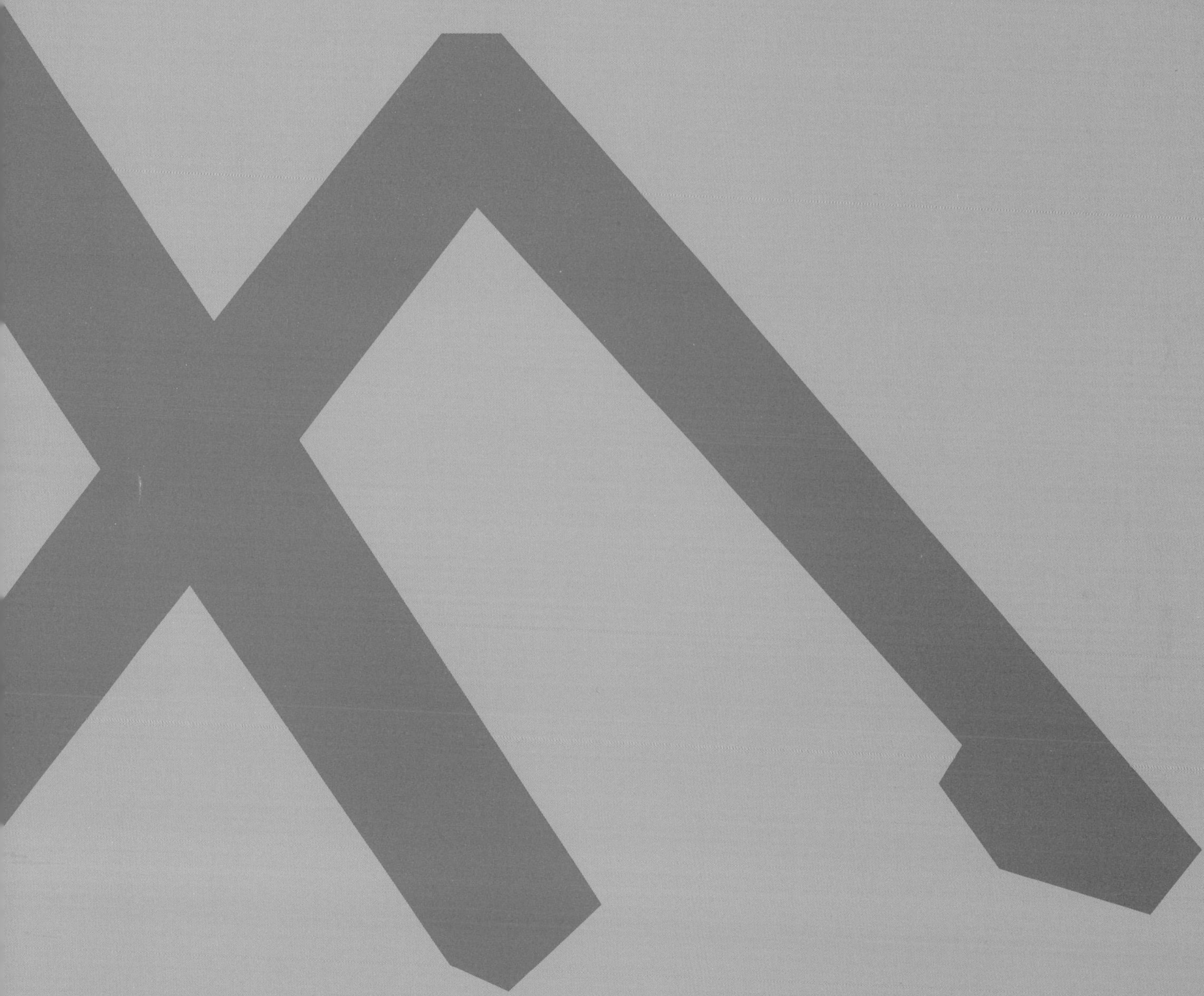

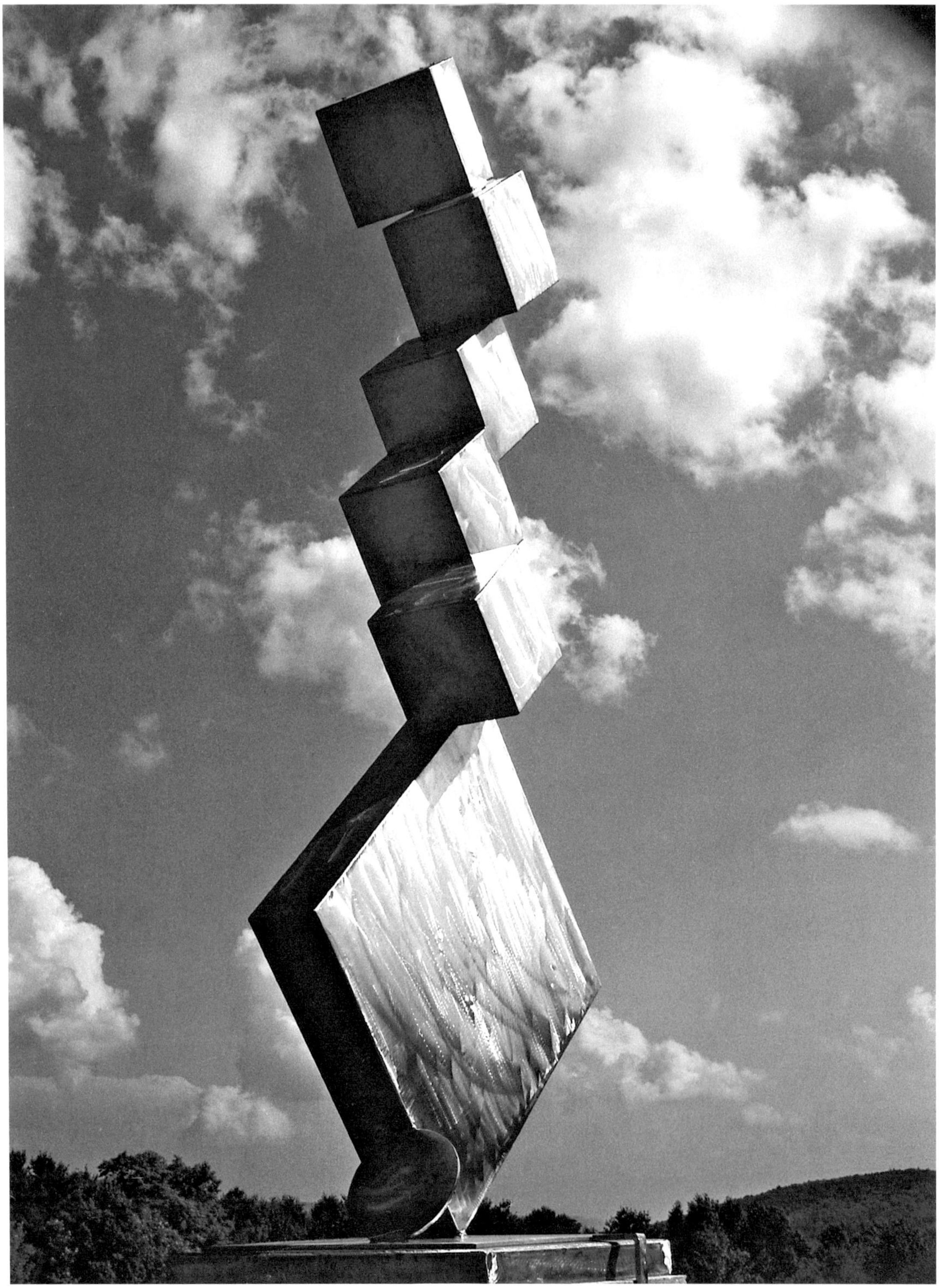

Fig. 1 | Cubi I, 1963, Detroit Institute of Arts, photo by David Smith

Widely heralded as the greatest American sculptor of the twentieth century, David Smith has been presented in numerous exhibitions over the years as a counterpart to the abstract expressionist painters or as a draftsman in space. Most scholarship has adhered to a Smith teleology that begins with the fluid, three-dimensional "drawings in space" of the sculptor-who-developed-out-of-surrealism and ends with the hard-edged forms from the 1960s of the sculptor-who-foreshadowed-minimalism. This essay—in conjunction with *David Smith: Cubes and Anarchy*, the first major thematic exhibition of his work—reveals instead a sculptor whose self-constructed identity as part of the working class motivated him to adopt the geometric forms and utopian aspirations of the international constructivist avant-garde from the very first years of his career in the 1930s until his untimely death in 1965.

To mention the theme of geometry in Smith's sculpture has been to conjure up images of his *Cubis* of the 1960s, among his last and without a doubt his best-known works (figs. 1, 2). These late sculptures, however, do not represent a new chapter in Smith's work but rather stand as final confirmation of a strong and career-long interest of the artist. Geometry is a leitmotif throughout his oeuvre; not only did his self-definition as a laborer inform his artistic vocabulary but, for Smith, labor and geometry were essentially entwined.

Smith himself acknowledged his lifelong interest in geometry. In a 1964 interview with the writer and critic Thomas B. Hess, Smith—looking back on what would tragically turn out to be almost his entire career—spoke of his fascination, starting as early as the 1930s, with found objects that have what he called "basic geometric form." "I find many things," Smith explained, "but I only choose certain ones that fit a niche in my mind, fit into a relationship I need, and that relationship is . . . of a geometric nature."[1]

In a slide lecture on his work just eleven days before his death on May 23, 1965, Smith again emphasized the fundamental role that geometry played in his work. Speaking of three recent sculptures in the form of a gate (see p. 118), the artist tellingly revealed, "These don't vary from just . . . squares, rectangles, and cylinder forms."[2]

Smith's biography has been recounted before,[3] but certain aspects are worth reviewing in the context of his self-inclusion in the working class and his interest in geometric form. Born in Decatur, Indiana, on March 9, 1906, Smith was the son of an engineer-inventor and the great-grandson of a blacksmith. Throughout his life Smith defined himself as a man of the people, a man of working-class stock who came

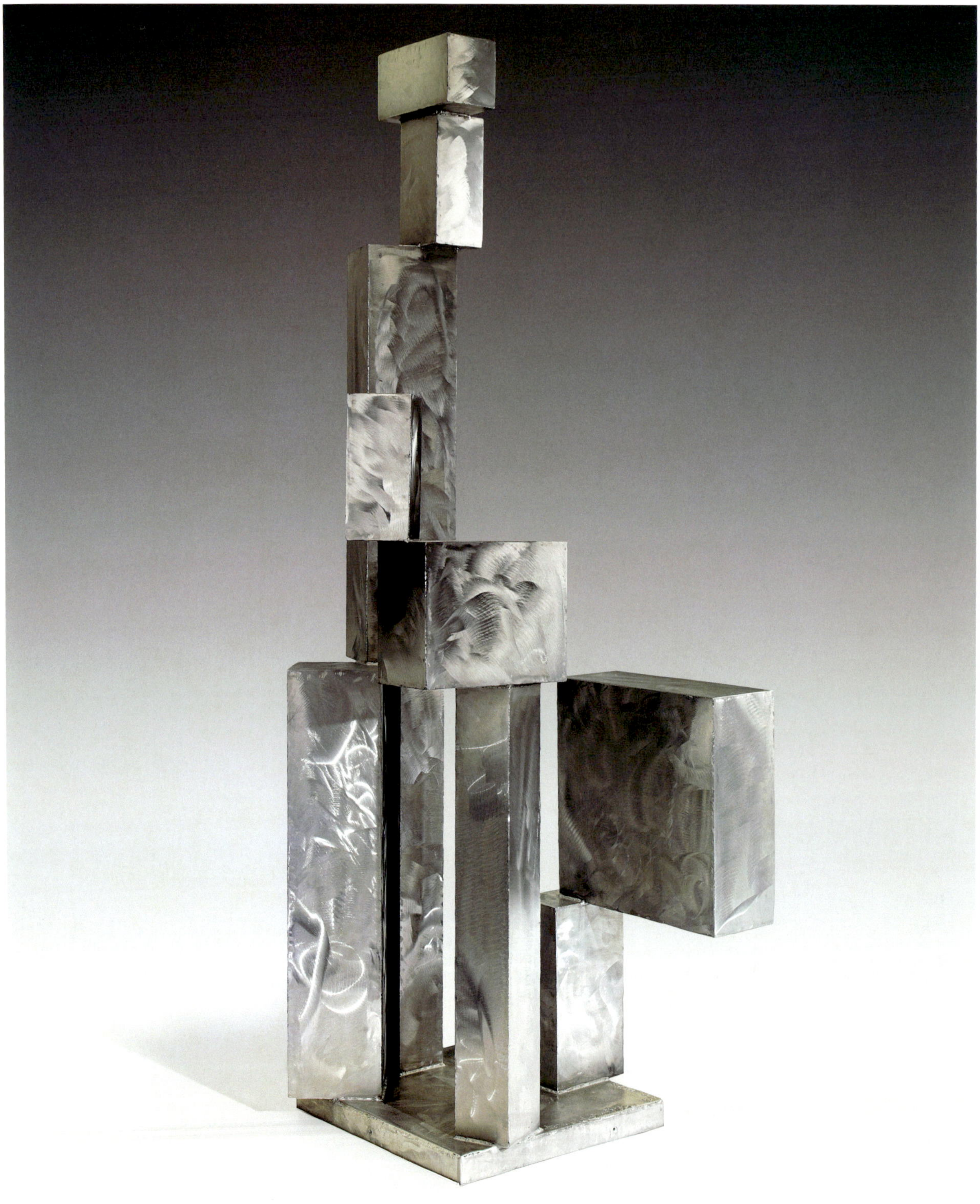

Fig. 2 | Cubi VIII, 1962, Meadows Museum, SMU, Dallas

from "early settlers . . . pioneer people who were scared for survival . . . [T]his reinforced my consciousness of the Depression."[4] When prodded in an interview to admit that even during the Depression his family had resources, Smith interrupted his interlocutor to reaffirm that "my father was a working man,"[5] as if to underscore his own proletarian bona fides. He did not want to be seen as bourgeois—as he might have been considered by the time of this interview (1964)—but rather as proletarian.

Smith had an early, almost innate, interest in machines and the mechanical. "When I was a kid, I had a pretty profound regard for railroads . . . I used to hop trains, ride on the tops of boxcars," he recalled. "We used to play on trains and around factories. I played there just like I played in nature, on hills and creeks . . . In fact, I've always had a high regard for machinery. It's never been an alien element, it's been in my nature."[6]

During the summer of 1925, after studying art for a year at Ohio University, Smith worked at the Studebaker automobile factory in South Bend, Indiana,[7] where he was a "riveter on frame assembly [and] worked on lathe—soldering jig—spot welder."[8] Around 1940 Smith wrote in some detail about his Studebaker experience (and the time immediately prior to it) in one of his notebooks, providing insights into both his understanding of the relationship between his factory work and his art, and his interest in the basic—even geometric—forms found in the industrial workplace:

> Between periods of trying to get an art education in three mid-western colleges I worked as a telephone lineman, stringing cable, laying cable, potting lead for joints, etc. I used to dig holes in the ground . . . After four months in Department 346 at the Studebaker plant, alternating on a lathe, spot welder, and milling machine, I was transferred to 348 on frame assembly. This was worked on a group plan, payment made to 80 men in proportion to the completed frames which were riveted and assembled on an oval conveyor track. It was necessary for each man to be able to handle at least six operations. Riveting, drilling, stamping, etc., all fell into my duties . . .
>
> The objects I worked with in the factory were abstract. They were always functional pieces having relationships, but were not objects of realism. Gears, crossmembers, brackets, the triangle in a circle spare tire carrier, etc., were all abstracted parts.[9]

Smith specifically connected the geometries of the factory environment (ovals, triangles, circles) with industrial labor itself (welding, milling), the same kinds of labor he later would make use of as an artist to create sculptures of iron and steel.

Although his work for Studebaker has been described by art historians as "little more than a convenient, good-paying job for a college student," it was Smith's "first experience of factory labor . . . and had a lasting impact on his identification with the working man." The Studebaker job likewise allowed Smith later in life to justify "having been a metalworker first and an artist second, establishing a chronology that mirrored his priorities in defining himself."[10] His practice as an artist would be based on this understanding of himself—indeed, on his willful self-definition—as a member of the working class.

After another brief college enrollment (this time at the University of Notre Dame, in South Bend like Studebaker), Smith moved east: first to Washington, D.C., and then, by the fall of 1926, to New York City. He soon met the artist Dorothy Dehner, who introduced him to the Art Students League, where both his artistic and political education began in earnest. At the league, Smith studied first with John Sloan, a leading member of the Ashcan school known for evincing his support of the working classes through his paintings. In a typewritten autobiographical chronology found in Smith's files after his death, Smith wrote, "From Sloan—got a certain amount of feeling—of knowing the artist's position as a rebel or as one in revolt against status quo—heard about cones and cubes and Cézanne from him."[11] Sloan clearly provided Smith with a model of the proletarian (or at least proletarian-leaning) *artiste engagé*. As Dore Ashton has noted, Smith's training with Sloan "not only brought [Smith] into the modern art world but also into the world of political commitment. He always recalled that from Sloan he had gotten 'cubes and anarchy.'"[12] It is telling that Smith himself verbalized this connection between geometry in art and political engagement at a moment around 1950 when he was looking back on and assessing his career to that point.

Another of Smith's teachers at the Art Students League, the Czech-born modernist painter Jan Matulka, opened Smith's eyes to the artistic avant-garde of the 1910s and 1920s. Matulka introduced his student to the work of Pablo Picasso as well as that of Vasily Kandinsky, Piet Mondrian, and the Russian constructivists.[13] As Smith explained more than thirty years later, "It was from [Matulka] in 1928 that for the first time I learned of . . . constructivism. Then the world . . . opened for me."[14]

Picasso's work in iron—traditionally an industrial rather than an artist's material—was of particular import to the young American: "[When] I first saw . . . his iron construction . . . I realized that I too knew how to handle this material."[15] He also realized that Picasso collaborated closely with the sculptor Julio González in this medium.[16] Smith would refer to his debt to, and respect for, González for the rest of his life. "I had seen the Picasso-González iron constructions of 1931 in the magazine *Cahiers d'Art*," Smith wrote in 1953. "This was the liberating factor which permitted me to start with steel which before had been my trade, and had until [then] only meant labor and earning power . . . My first steel sculptures were made in 1933."[17]

Smith was especially attracted to González's leftist views. Long after González's death in 1942, Smith tried to learn more about the Catalan-born sculptor, who—like Smith—had learned to weld in an automobile factory.[18] In a 1955 letter to his friend the painter Herman Cherry, Smith asked him to speak to the composer Edgar Varèse about González on Smith's behalf: "Does Varèse have any memory of political relationships . . . etc.—González was republican in the Spanish [Civil] War, his affinities were working class. I just wanted to know if he had mentioned anything very direct."[19] Smith also closely queried Jean Xceron, another friend and fellow artist, about various aspects of González's life and personality in a letter from the same moment.[20]

González is the only artist on whom Smith—a relatively prolific writer for a visual artist—ever published a monographic article.[21] In his text, which appeared in *Art News* to coincide with a 1956 exhibition of González's sculpture at the Museum of Modern Art, Smith quite specifically drew parallels between the older artist and himself, recognizing the relationship and importance of traditional "labor" to the art of both men:

> When a man is trained in metal-working and has pursued it as labor with the ideal of art represented by oil painting, it is very difficult to conceive that what has been labor and livelihood is the same means by which art can be made. (Perhaps I am basing this more on sympathy than fact in González's case, because it is a reconstruction of my own experience. Before I had painted very long I ran across reproductions . . . of González's and Picasso's work which brought my consciousness to this fact that art could be made of iron. But iron-working was labor, when I thought art was oil paint.)[22]

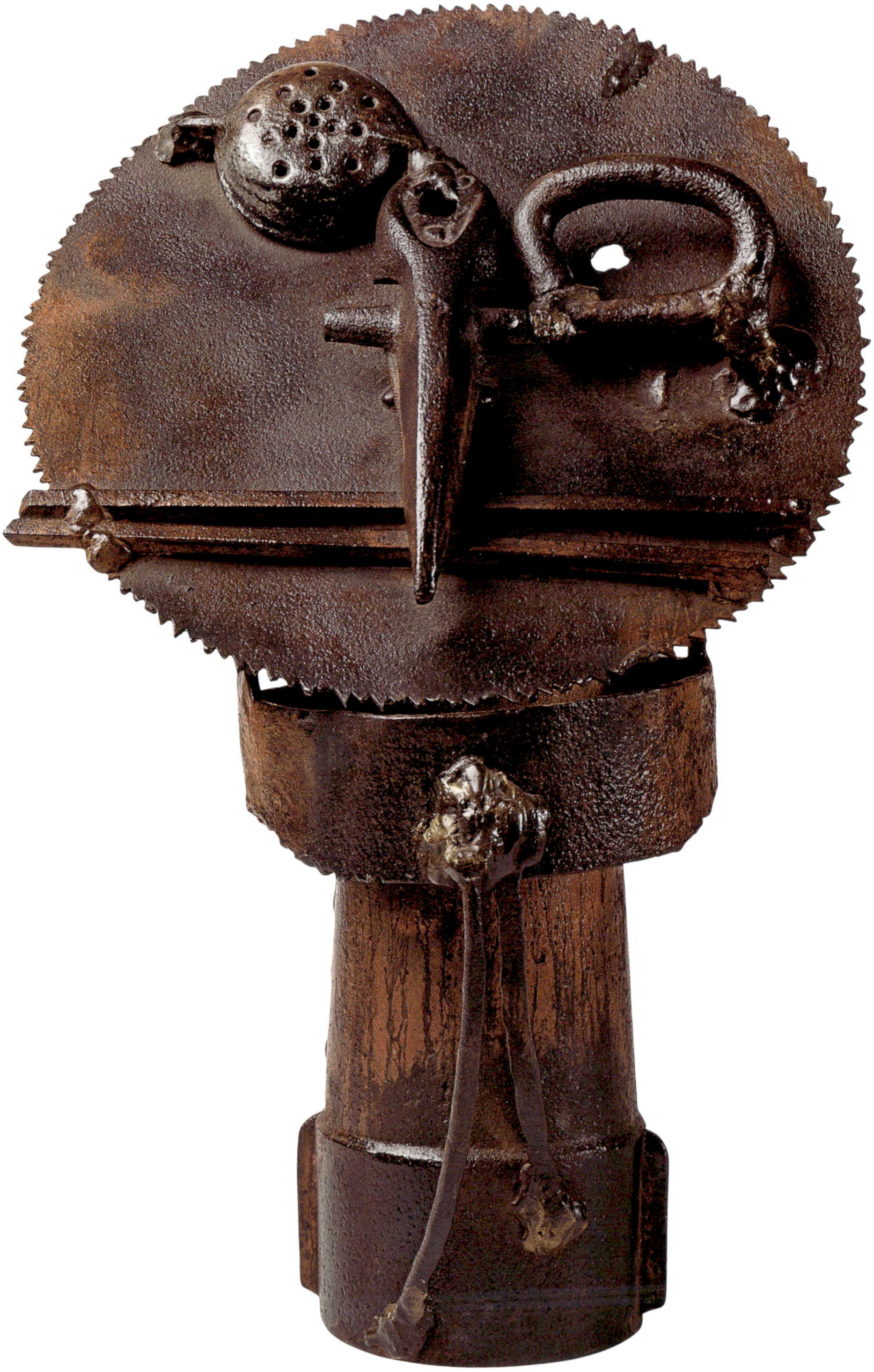

Fig. 3 | Saw Head, 1933, The Estate of David Smith, courtesy Tate, London

González had been a member of the Cercle et Carré (Circle and Square) group in Paris, which in the late 1920s and early 1930s promoted geometric constructivism through both an exhibition and a periodical of the same name. Smith noted that although González was not particularly social, he had nonetheless attended weekly meetings of the Cercle et Carré artists in the studio of the Uruguayan painter Joaquín Torres-García.[23] Smith went on to elucidate the importance of this artistic circle to González and, by extension (given the parallels he had drawn between the Catalan-born artist and himself), to his own work. In fact, John Graham—who also participated in the Parisian soirées in Torres-García's studio and was an important early link to the European avant-garde for Smith—would in 1934 give Smith a small head by González (fig. 4), reinforcing these connections.

Smith had met Graham, a Russian émigré painter and writer who frequently traveled from his then-base in New York to Paris, in 1930. It was at Graham's home that Smith first saw reproductions of González's welded metal sculptures in a 1929 issue of *Cahiers d'art*,[24] and where he would have seen three actual sculptures by González that Graham had acquired around 1927–28,[25] including the head Graham later gave to Smith. The young American doubtless had González in mind when he welded his own *Saw Head* (fig. 3) in 1933. In this early sculpture, Smith already combined a worker's tool (the saw) and methods (welding) with his interest in found geometries (the circular blade). *Saw Head* thus stands as a harbinger of his career-long interests and commitments.

Smith began making such welded metal sculptures by the fall of 1933, having purchased a welding suit and an oxyacetylene torch,[26] garb and a tool that would traditionally belong to a laborer rather than an artist. Around this time he also became involved with artists' collectives and shortly thereafter began to participate in events sponsored by the Artists Union, although it is not clear when Smith officially joined the group.[27] The Artists Union was affiliated with other labor groups in New York in the 1930s, supporting workers' rights and joining in the annual May Day parade. Smith later described this very matter-of-factly: "We marched in May Day parades and we supported all the humane causes."[28] As Dorothy Dehner (by late 1927 married to Smith) later said, "It was positively disgraceful not to. It was an obligation, it was showing our colors, so to speak."[29] Smith was an active participant in this world, the nexus of art and labor. According to Dehner, "I remember one day David came home from work and he said—this was in the very early days of our marriage—there's going

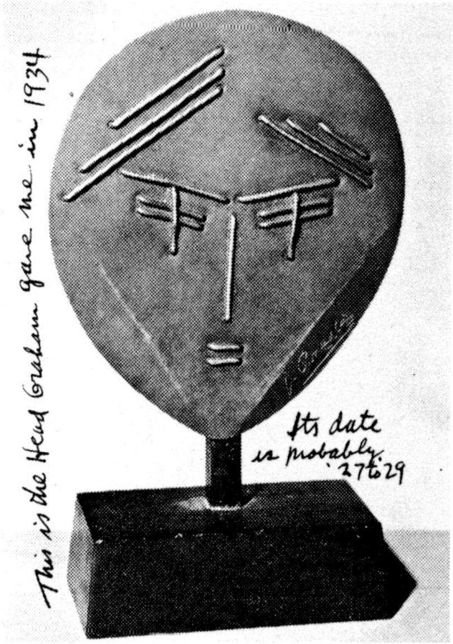

Fig. 4 | Photograph of Julio González, **Mask**, c. 1927–28. As noted in Smith's handwriting on the photo, John Graham gave this sculpture to Smith in 1934.

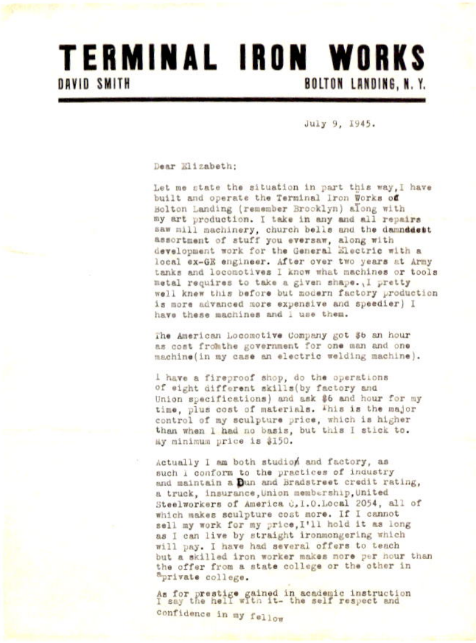

TERMINAL IRON WORKS

DAVID SMITH BOLTON LANDING, N. Y.

July 9, 1945.

Dear Elizabeth:

Let me state the situation in part this way, I have built and operate the Terminal Iron Works of Bolton Landing (remember Brooklyn) along with my art production. I take in any and all repairs saw mill machinery, church bells and the damndest assortment of stuff you eversaw, along with development work for the General Electric with a local ex-GE engineer. After over two years at Army tanks and locomotives I know what machines or tools metal requires to take a given shape. (I pretty well knew this before but modern factory production is more advanced more expensive and speedier) I have these machines and I use them.

The American Locomotive Company got $6 an hour as cost fromthe government for one man and one machine(in my case an electric welding machine).

I have a fireproof shop, do the operations of eight different skills(by factory and Union specifications) and ask $6 and hour for my time, plus cost of materials. This is the major control of my sculpture price, which is higher than when I had no basis, but this I stick to. My minimum price is $150.

Actually I am both studio and factory, as such I conform to the practices of industry and maintain a Dun and Bradstreet credit rating, a truck, insurance, Union membership, United Steelworkers of America C.I.O. Local 2054, all of which makes sculpture cost more. If I cannot sell my work for my price, I'll hold it as long as I can live by straight ironmongering which will pay. I have had several offers to teach but a skilled iron worker makes more per hour than the offer from a state college or the other in a private college.

As for prestige gained in academic instruction I say the hell with it- the self respect and confidence in my fellow

Fig. 5 | Terminal Iron Works letterhead

to be a Socialist meeting tomorrow at noon and he was going with a friend . . . We became gradually and very deeply involved ourselves [in] the Artists Union and the Artists Congress."[30] As Smith later wrote, "I generally am with all artists of conviction."[31] He also said that "art is always an expression of revolt and struggle. Progressive man and progressive art are identified with this struggle. That is our history as artists."[32]

Two statements Smith made at two different moments, each a time when it may have been politically risky for him, underscore his self-identification with the working class. In February 1940, as war raged in Europe and America's role on the international stage was hotly debated, Smith spoke at the Forum on Abstract Art held by United American Artists (another left-leaning, pacifist artists' group). He argued that "the problems of the abstract artist in a democratic society are common with those of men of good will. He rejects participation in the present imperialist war, and acknowledges his position with organized labor—to keep America out of war, for art and peace can only exist together."[33] Later, in connection with a 1952 show of Smith's work at the Walker Art Center in Minneapolis, the museum's registrar used a standardized form to request biographical and other information from the artist. Under the heading "Favorite Subject Matter," Smith wrote "Karl Marx,"[34] a brave (and potentially foolhardy) statement to make during the height of the Red-baiting years in the United States, when careers were destroyed for far less. (He luckily suffered no repercussions from his response.) Smith aligned himself with socialism until his death, however, reinforcing these inclinations in a 1964 interview with the critic Thomas B. Hess:

> Hess: But isn't your work unique in that it seems to consider a large . . . social role?
>
> Smith: I think I'm an idealist.
>
> Hess: What's the idea? Are your totems for . . .
>
> Smith [interrupting Hess]: . . . a true *socialist* society.[35]

Even in the mid-1960s, during the height of the cold war, Smith was not only willing but eager to take a radical leftist stance.

Smith's very workspaces brought together his interest in industrial materials and techniques, his view of himself as a laborer, and his art. In 1934, inside the gates of Brooklyn's Atlantic Avenue Ferry Terminal, he had come across "two Irishmen, Blackburn and Buckhorn, [who] owned the works, a series of buildings on the Brooklyn waterfront . . . Blackburn was a big gentle ironmonger . . . Buckhorn was white-collar."[36] Smith established his studio alongside these men (as well as other waterfront workers)—he later referred to the "nice 'Fraternity' down there"[37]—and called it Terminal Iron Works. Even when he moved his main studio to his Bolton Landing property (in the Adirondacks of upstate New York) in 1940, he retained the industrial-sounding name (fig. 5). Moreover, he literally capitalized on the fact that his artist's studio sounded like a manufacturing enterprise, as the name made it easier for him to obtain bank loans.[38] Indeed, Smith did understand his studio to be a small factory: "The equipment I use and my supply of materials come from factory study, and duplicate as nearly as possible the production equipment used in making a locomotive."[39]

Others also perceived Smith's workspace in industrial terms. The writer and curator Frank O'Hara described the Bolton Landing studio as a "very efficient factory set-up . . . There is a profusion of parts waiting to be assembled, of pulleys and vises and welding equipment."[40] The critic Hilton Kramer some years later described Terminal Iron Works as Smith's "workshop" (as opposed to studio), "a fully equipped welding shop, with industrial tools, factory lights, and a supply of raw materials (mostly stainless steel, cast-iron, and bronze components, and some silver), the atmosphere being that of a small-town factory in which some gadget is produced . . . *A machine shop in a landscape.*"[41]

Smith not only identified himself as a laborer throughout his career but also on occasion sought factory work, even after he had established himself as an artist. From 1942 to 1944, in order to earn the money required for various renovation and construction projects at Bolton Landing, Smith worked as a welder at the American Locomotive Company (ALCO) in Schenectady, New York.[42] He joined Local 2054 of the Congress of Industrial Organizations' (CIO) United Steelworkers of America, welding stainless-steel armor plate on M7 destroyer tanks for the army as well as assembling locomotives.[43] Ironically, for an artist who had previously stated that "art and peace can only exist together," it was Smith's job as a welder at ALCO—producing matériel for the war effort, no less—that provided him with a draft exemption.[44]

Smith deliberately retained his union membership for years after leaving his job at ALCO. Toward the end of the 1940s he said, "By choice I identify myself with working men and still belong to Local 2054 United Steelworkers of America."[45] Smith later would assert explicitly the parallels between the working methods of factory workers and artists, explaining that as an artist he had "learned from

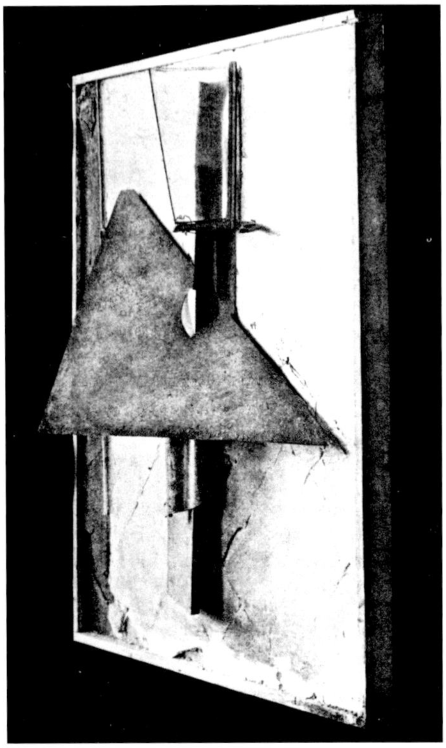

Fig. 6 | Vladimir Tatlin, **Selection of Materials**, 1914, iron, plaster, glass, and tar, location unknown

working in factories . . . that people who make things—whether it's automobiles, ships, or locomotives—have to have a plentiful supply of materials . . . I don't resent the cost of the best material or the finest tools and equipment. Every labor-saving machine, every safety device I can afford, I consider necessary."[46] Yet he found it hard to reconcile his utopian societal aspirations as an artist with the realities of a working-class existence: "I belong [to the steelworkers' union] by craft—yet the subject of aesthetics introduces a breach," he said. "I suppose it is because I believe in the future [in] a working man's society and in that society I hope to find a place. In this [i.e., current] society I find little place for identify[ing] myself economically."[47] Although Smith saw himself as both an artist and a worker simultaneously, he struggled to find comfortable common ground between those two roles in the social and economic structure of the time.

In a 1952 radio talk, Smith forged a logical connection between the modern factory and avant-garde artistic practice:

> American machine techniques and European cubist tradition, both of this century, are accountable for the new freedom in sculpture-making. Sculpture is no longer limited to the slow carving of marble and long process of bronze. It has found new form and new method. Here I am talking about direct metal construction. Contrary to the carving-away technique of classical sculpture, the new method is to assemble the whole by adding its unit parts. The building up of sculpture from unit parts, the quantity to quality concept, is also an industrial concept, the basis of automobile and machine assembly in the steel process.[48]

Coming full circle, Smith connected his interest in the modern material of steel with his interest in geometry. "The metal possesses little art history," he said. "Its associations are primarily of this century, it is structure, movement, progress, suspension, cantilever, and at times destruction and brutality . . . Yet its mill forms of geometry, planes, hard lines are all constant within my time."[49]

When we explore Smith's work itself, his connections to modernism's utopian constructivist impulses—especially the exaltation of geometry and embrace of technology—are even more apparent. As mentioned before, Smith in the late 1920s had seen reproductions of work by Piet Mondrian and the Russian constructivists (among others) in European magazines; their works also were exhibited publicly in

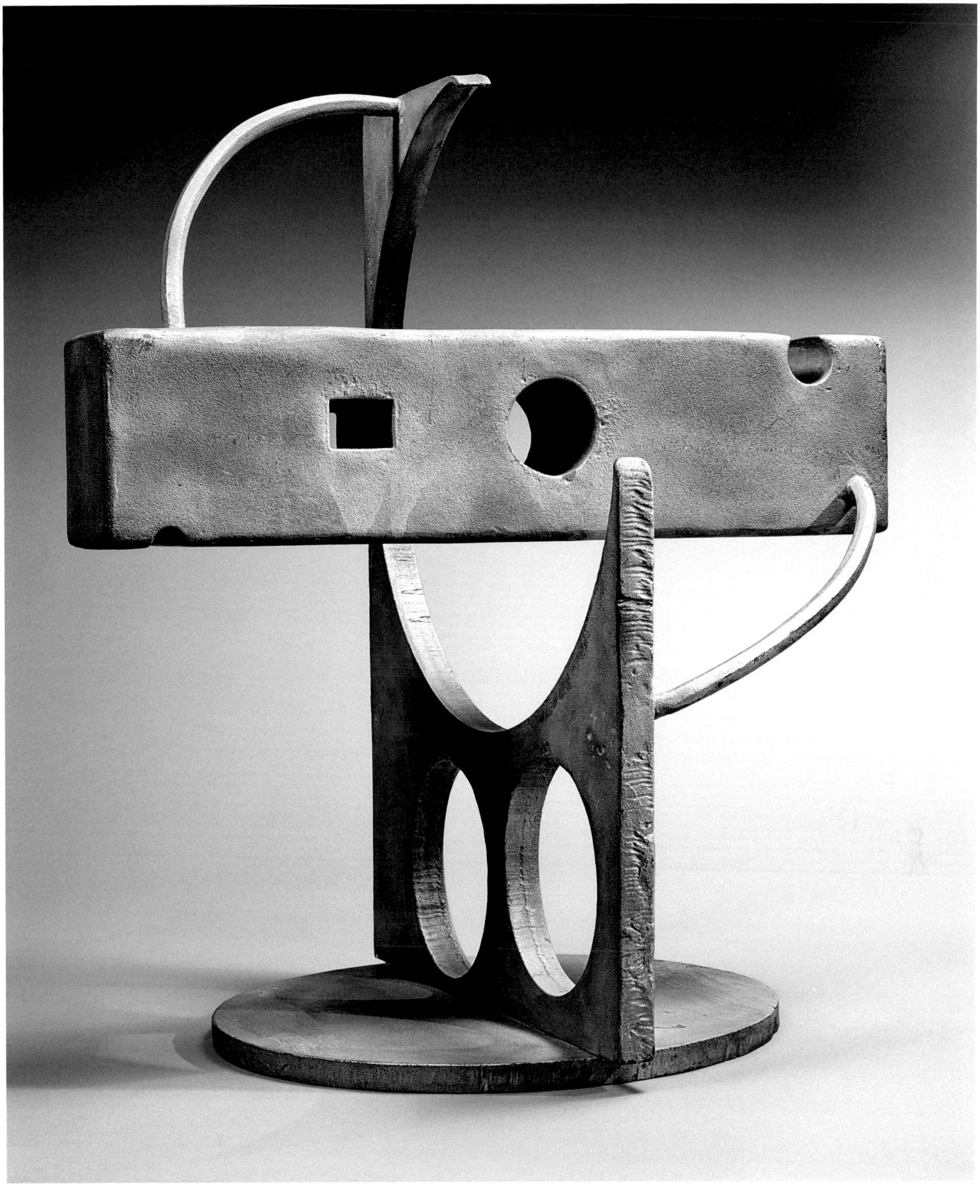

Fig. 7 | Suspended Cube, 1938, private collection, courtesy The Estate of David Smith

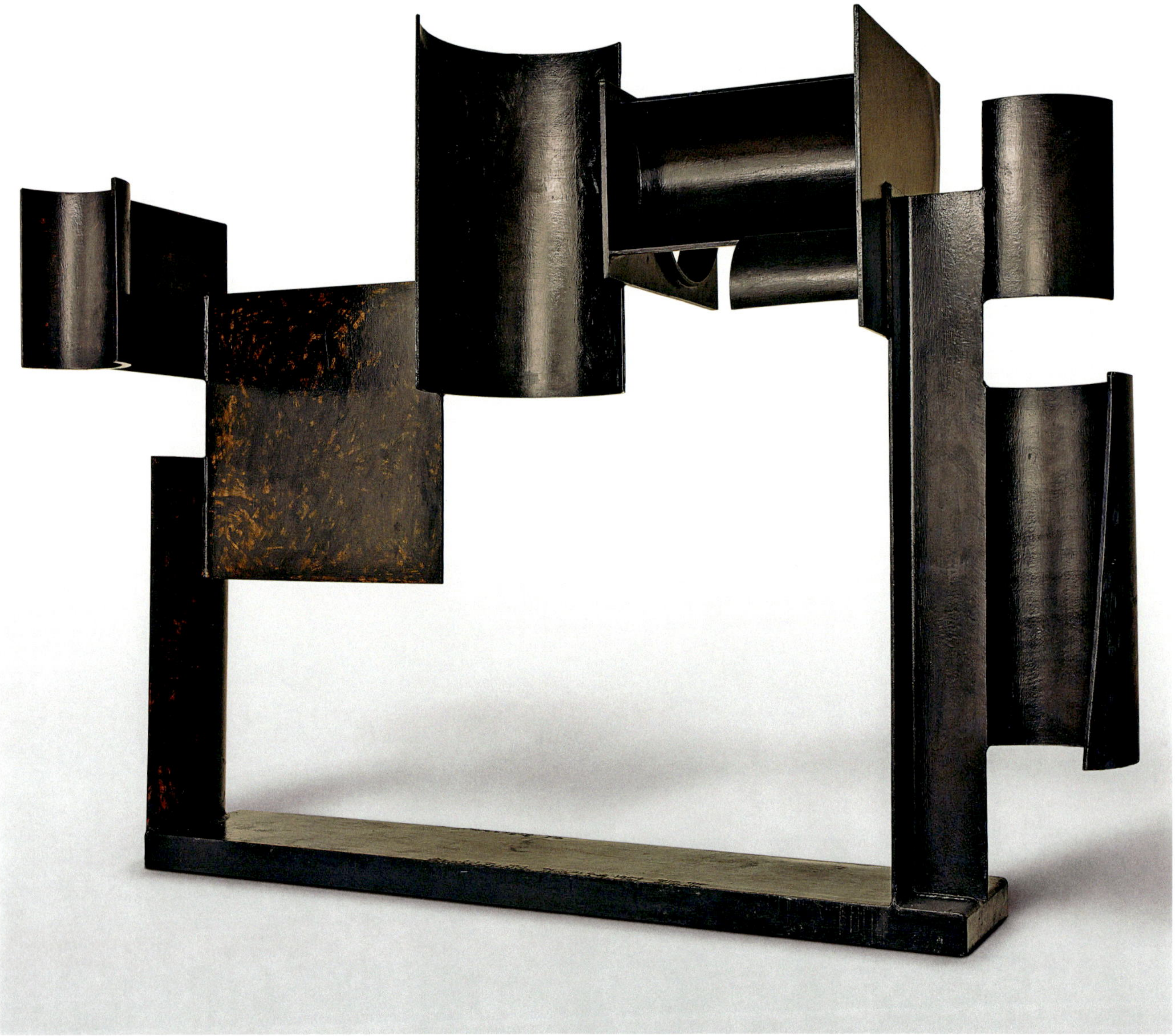

Fig. 8 | Zig III, 1961, The Estate of David Smith, courtesy Gagosian Gallery

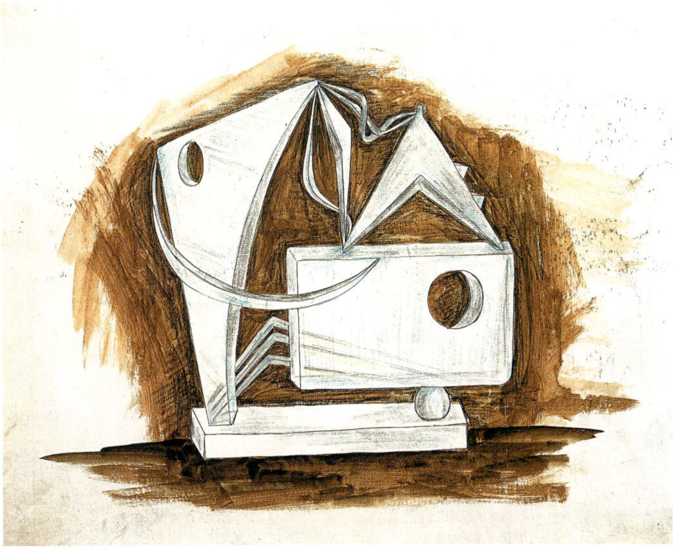

Fig. 9 | **Untitled**, c. 1937–38, Whitney Museum of American Art, New York

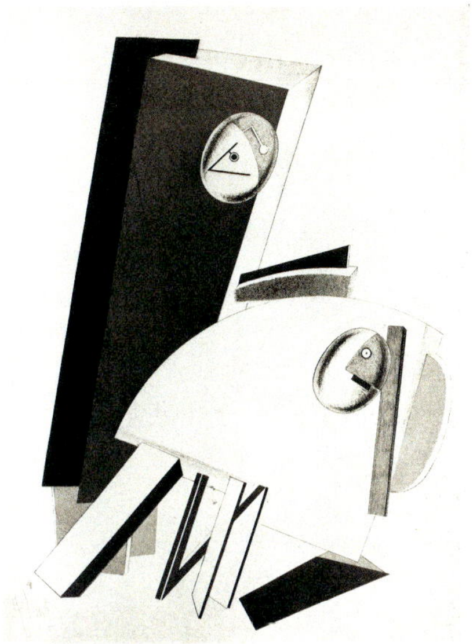

Fig. 10 | El Lissitzky, **Cowards**, 1914–15, character drawing for the opera *Victory over the Sun*, reproduced in the catalogue accompanying *Exhibition of Contemporary Art of Soviet Russia: Painting, Graphic, Sculpture*, Grand Central Palace, New York, February 1929

New York in those years. Because Smith spoke and read only English, he ignored the texts in these periodicals, focusing instead on the images. "I learned the world from seeing before I ever learned the world from words. So my world was the Dutch movement de Stijl; it was Russian constructivism; it was cubism," he explained. "They were all so new and so wonderful."[50] Just as Smith learned about Picasso's and González's use of welded iron through these publications, he also learned about the Russian constructivists' use of industrial materials: "I had seen iron work in the Russian constructivists—Rodchenko and Malevich and . . . Tatlin, and I'd seen reproductions of their work . . . in German magazines."[51]

Smith thus would have known about Vladimir Tatlin's counter-reliefs such as *Selection of Materials* (1914, fig. 6). Indeed, their influence can be seen in Smith's geometric sculptures and drawings of the later 1930s, including *Suspended Cube* and *Untitled* (figs. 7, 9). (He also could have known drawings by El Lissitzky such as *Cowards*, included in the 1929 contemporary Soviet art exhibition in New York and reproduced in the accompanying catalogue [fig. 10].)[52] Smith would have been particularly fascinated by Tatlin's wall sculptures, which had emerged organically out of two dimensions, much as Smith's own early sculptures had (fig. 12).[53] Smith's much later *Zigs* (figs. 8, 13) similarly pay homage, now on a monumental scale, to Tatlin's counter-reliefs (fig. 11).

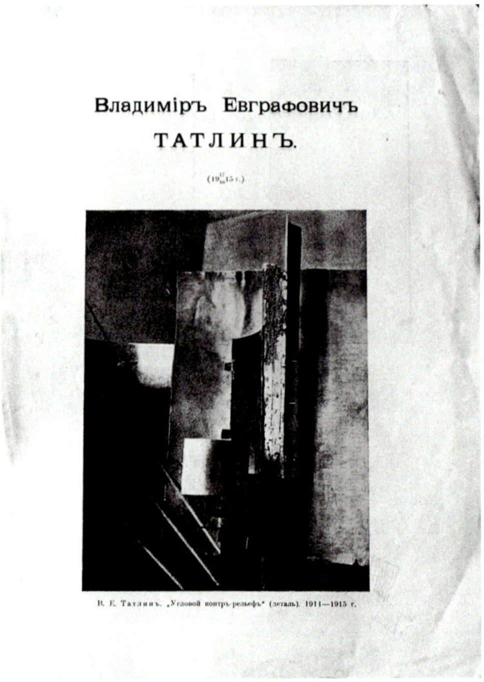

Fig. 11 | Vladimir Tatlin, **Corner Counter-Relief**, 1914–15, metal, wood, and wire, State Russian Museum, St. Petersburg, as illustrated on the cover of the booklet *Vladimir Evgrafovich Tatlin*, October 1915

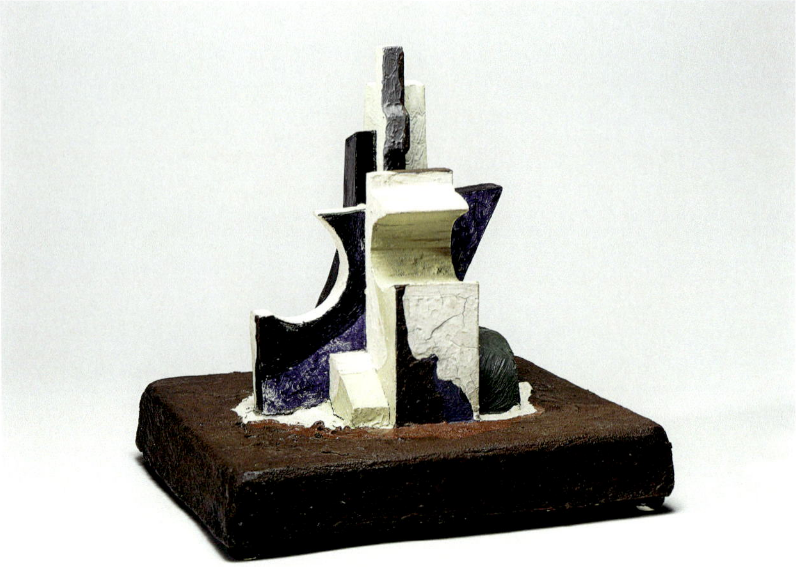

Fig. 12 | **Construction**, 1932, The Estate of David Smith

Like Smith, Tatlin was the son of an engineer (a railway engineer, no less). He sought to integrate art and life in service to the masses and believed an artistic vocabulary of abstract geometries best suited this aim. Smith's statement from 1952 about his own work could easily have been made by Tatlin or any of the other Russian constructivists: "Since impressionism the realities from which art has come have all been the properties of ordinary men, the still life has been from the working man's household, the characters, environment, landscape, have been of common nature; the bourgeois or upper class reality and [grand] pretension have not been the realities which the artist's eye have transformed. The controls of my art are not outside the daily vision of common man."[54]

A sheet in one of Smith's early sketchbooks (fig. 14) depicts a homunculus pieced together from geometric shapes. Similarly abstracted human figures are found in Tatlin's costume designs (fig. 16), which critics have described in purely geometric terms: "*Laughter*'s mask was a cylinder rounded at both ends, the openings for the eyes were two straight lines, the 'stubby' nose formed a perfect triangle and its laughing mouth a wide semicircle."[55] Across the top half of Smith's sketchbook page, his handwritten text also evokes the enduring power of geometry: "I have erected a solid . . . the structure within which I live, die, and weigh all else."

Fig. 13 | **Zig IV**, 1961, Lincoln Center for the Performing Arts, Inc., New York

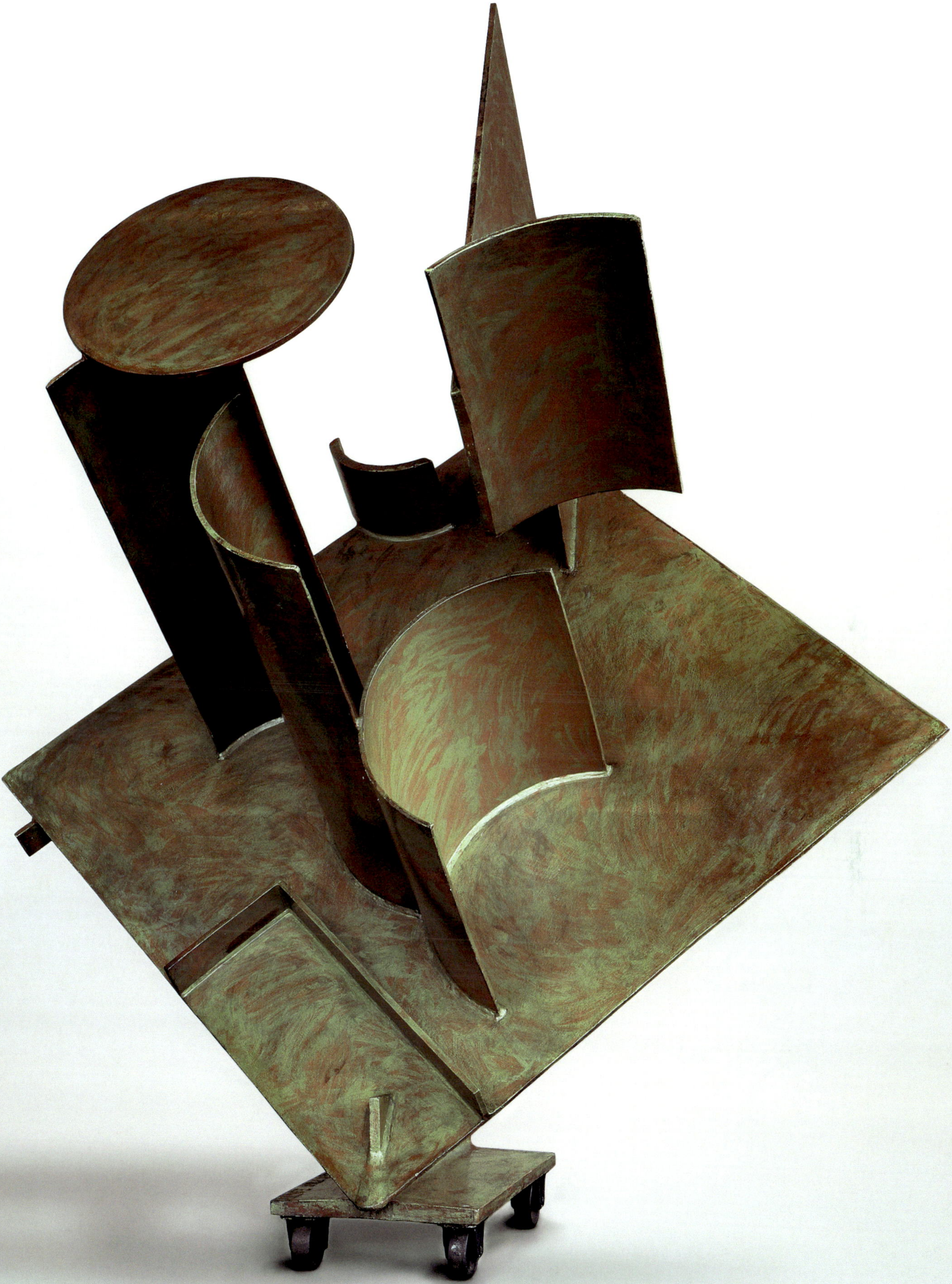

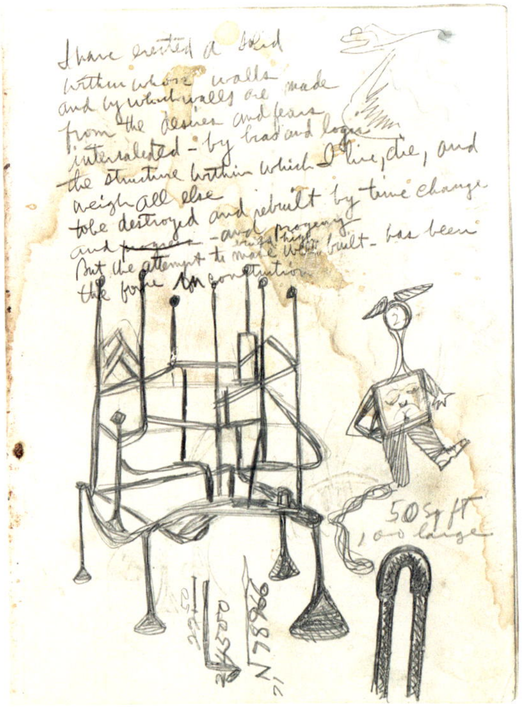

Fig. 14 | Page from Sketchbook #23, 1933–45, The Estate of David Smith

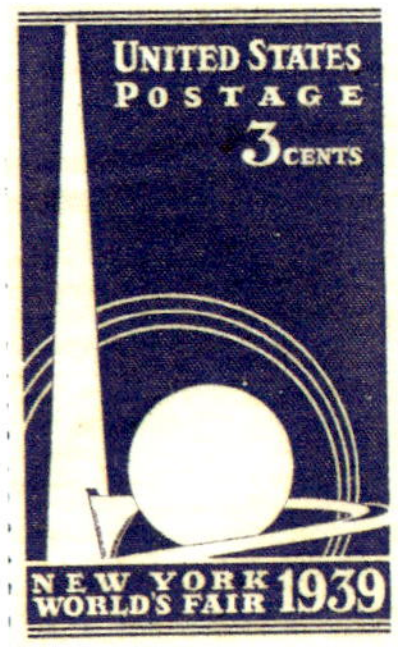

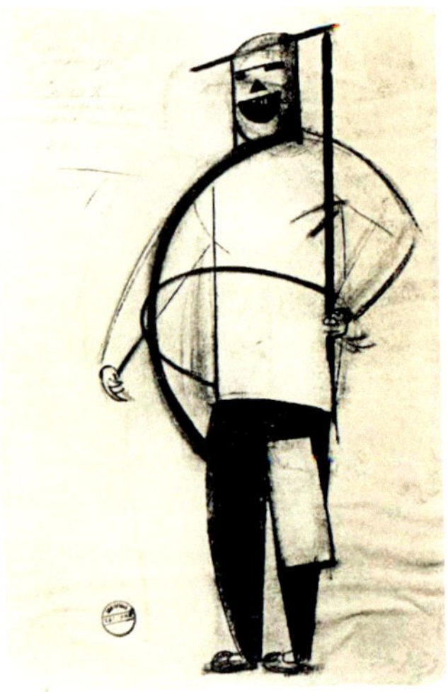

Fig. 15 | U.S. postage stamp depicting Wallace Harrison's Trylon and Perisphere, symbols of the 1939 New York World's Fair

Fig. 16 | Vladimir Tatlin, **Laughter**, 1923, costume design for Velimir Khlebnikov's play *Zangezi*, charcoal on paper mounted on cardboard, 21 1/2 x 14 3/4 in. (54.6 x 37.6 cm), Bakhrushin Theater Museum, Moscow

The idealistic concepts embedded in geometric form can be seen in Smith's sculptures and related drawings of the late 1930s as well. In June 1938, Smith's dealer Marian Willard suggested to the architect Wallace Harrison, designer of the Trylon and Perisphere symbols of the 1939 New York World's Fair, that Smith create a sculpture (never commissioned) for one of the exposition's buildings.[56] The fair itself had populist and utopian goals. A statement issued by the fair's Committee on Theme declared that "the New York World's Fair is planned to be 'everyman's fair'—to show the way toward the improvement of all the factors contributing to human welfare. We are convinced that the potential assets, material and spiritual, of our country are such that if rightly used they will make for a general public good such as has never before been known."[57]

The fair's purely geometric Trylon and Perisphere, so popular they were depicted on a U.S. postage stamp (fig. 15), symbolized these lofty aspirations. Smith presumably already knew of Harrison's emblems when he created *Blue Construction* (fig. 17) in 1938. An elegant and seemingly magically balanced play on the Trylon and Perisphere motifs, this sculpture was subsequently exhibited at the 1939 fair and lauded by the press for its "distinguished abstraction" and "strong linear forces."[58] Smith's use of sheet steel with a baked-enamel finish for *Blue Construction* underscores his desire to combine perfect geometries with industrial materials and techniques (this was also a tenet of Russian constructivism, which sought to blur the distinctions between art and manufacturing).[59] Several related sketchbook drawings, as well as other sculptures from the same period (figs. 18–20), suggest Smith's ongoing fascination with these forms, a fascination that would remain clearly evident in Smith's work into the 1950s (figs. 21, 22).

Like the Russian constructivists, the modernist sculptor Constantin Brancusi provided Smith with a model of an avant-garde artist interested in geometric forms whose aesthetic also had populist roots (in his case, Romanian folk art and architecture).[60] Smith was surely aware of Brancusi from very early in his artistic career. Brancusi exhibited publicly in New York in late 1926 and again in 1933; and in 1928—just as Smith was coming of age as an artist—federal customs courts ruled in the artist's favor in *Brancusi v. United States*.[61] Living in New York at the time, Smith could hardly have avoided reading about this case, which was heavily covered in both the art press and the general press.[62] Published descriptions of Brancusi's work and methods

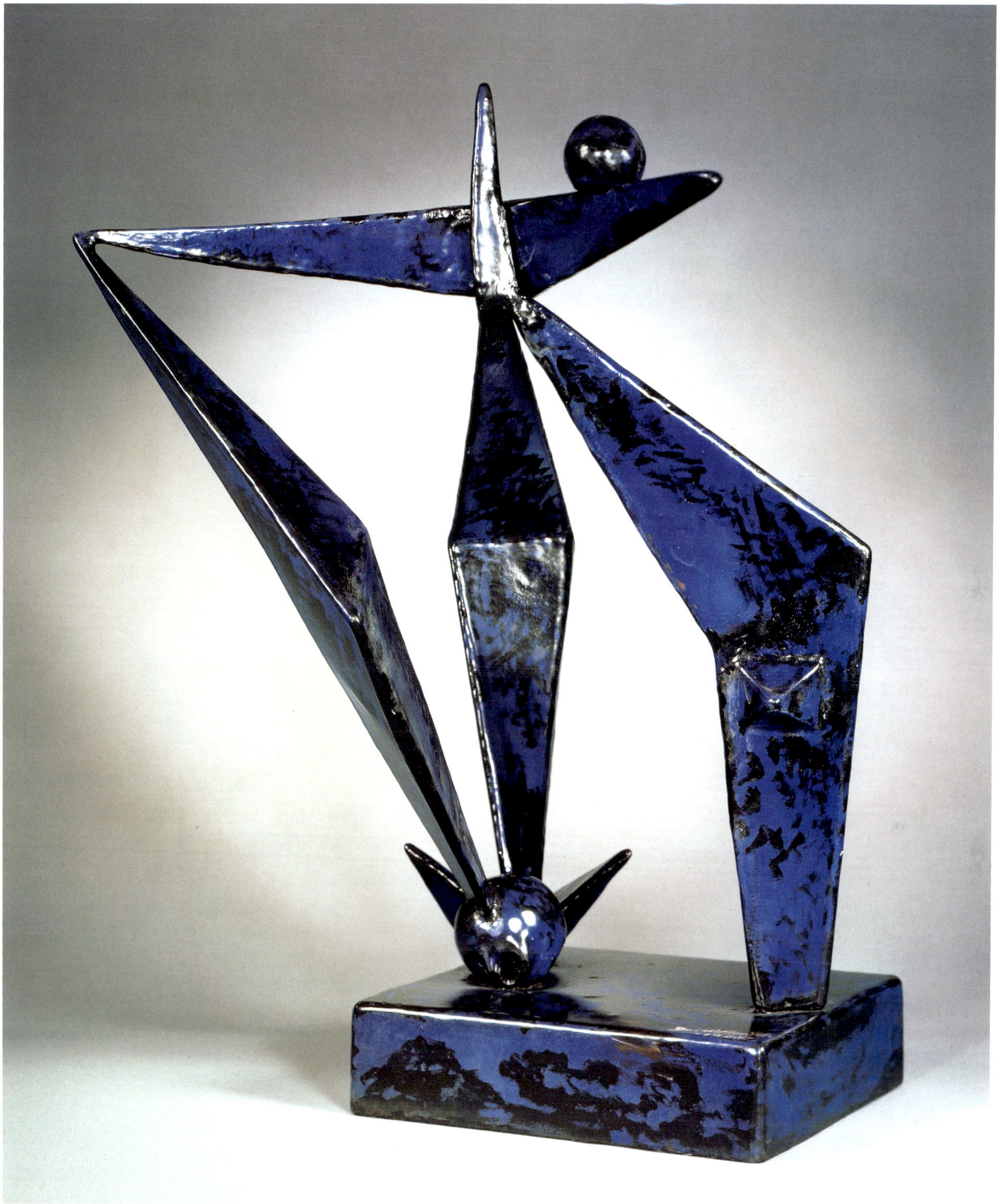

Fig. 17 | Blue Construction, 1938, The Estate of David Smith, courtesy National Gallery of Art, Washington

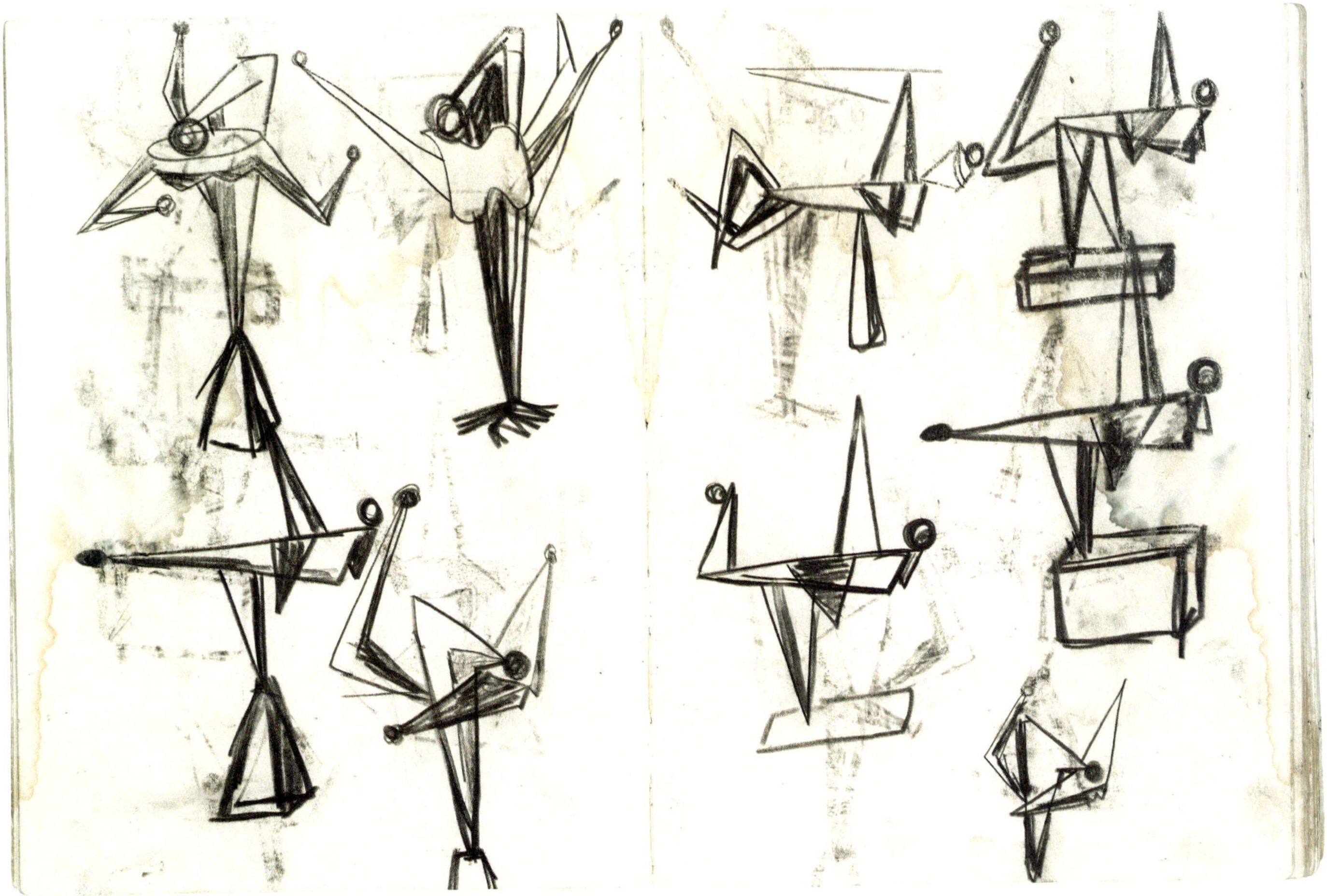

Fig. 18 | Spread, c. 1938, from Sketchbook #23, 1933–45, The Estate of David Smith

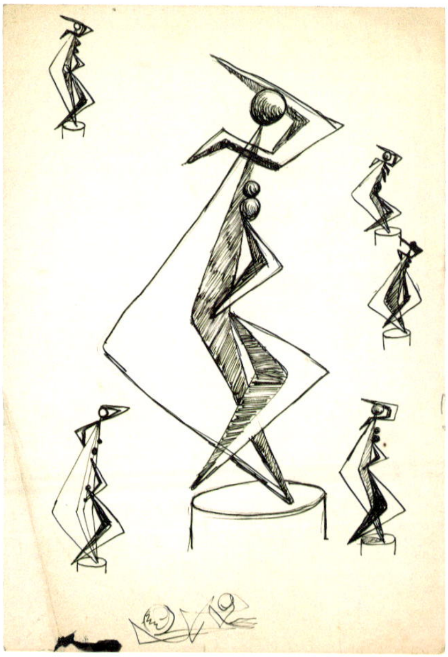

Fig. 19 | Untitled, c. 1938, The Estate of David Smith

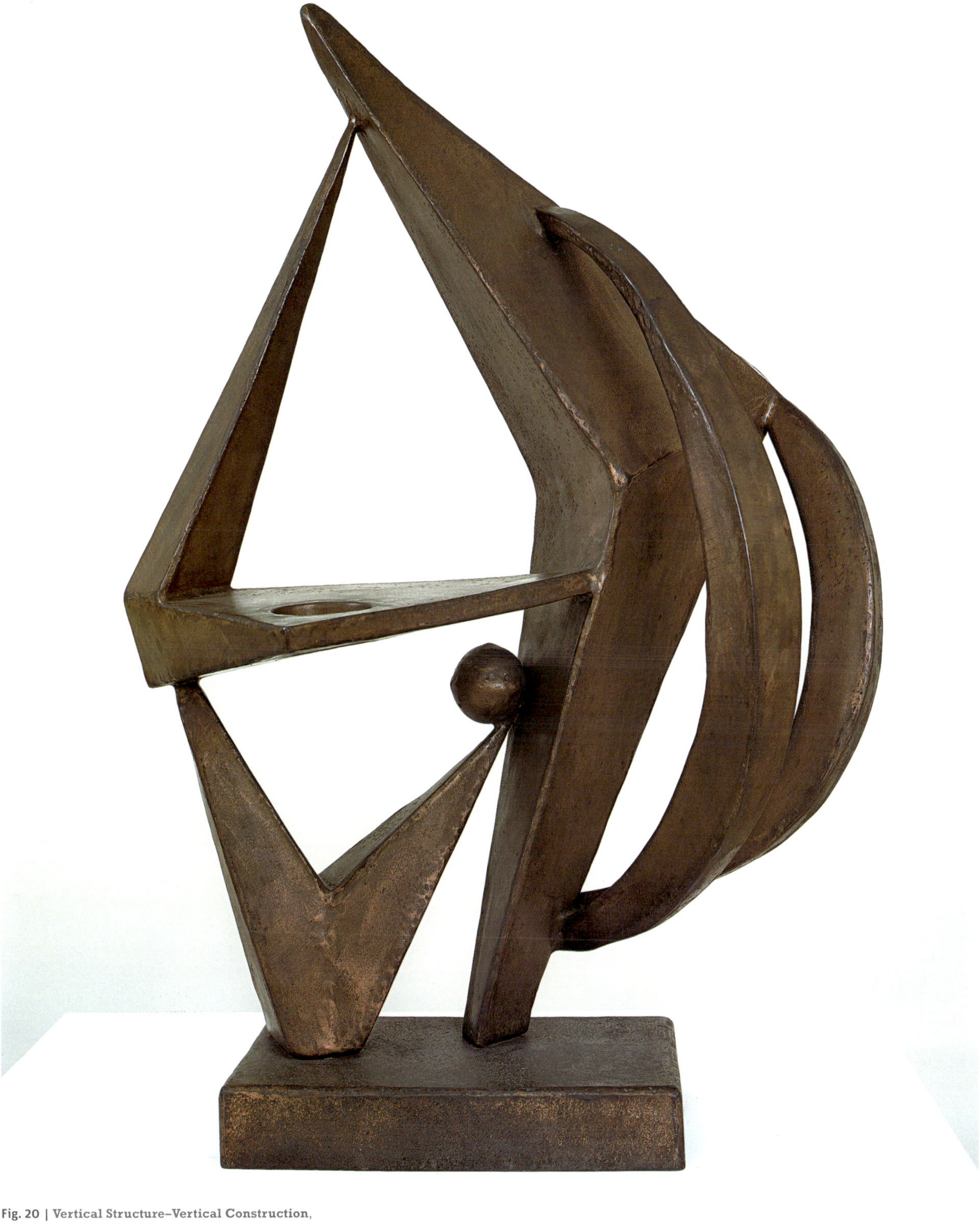

Fig. 20 | Vertical Structure–Vertical Construction, 1939, The Estate of David Smith, courtesy Museo Nacional Centro de Arte Reina Sofía, Madrid

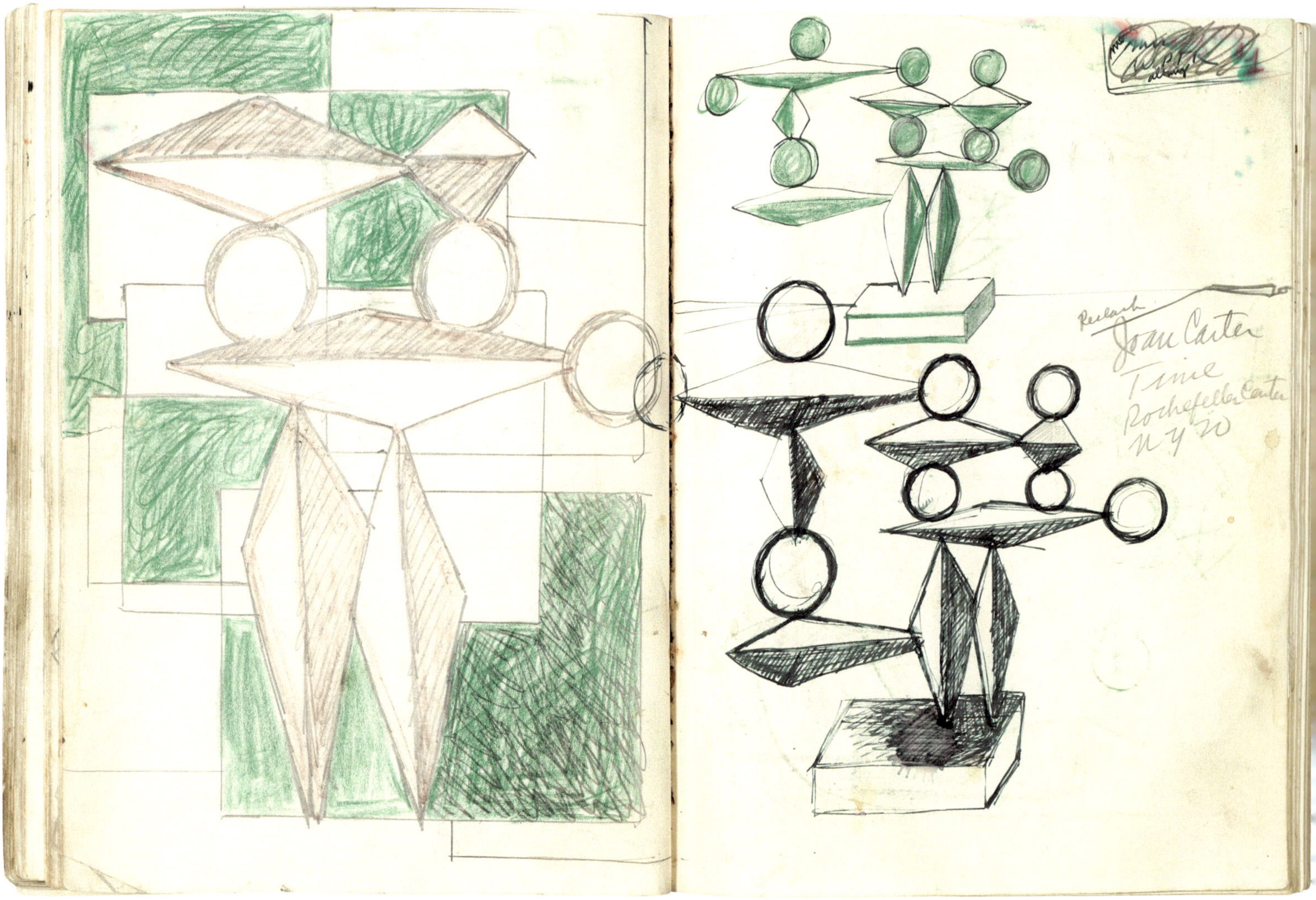

Fig. 21 | Spread, c. 1951, from Sketchbook #41, 1944–54, The Estate of David Smith

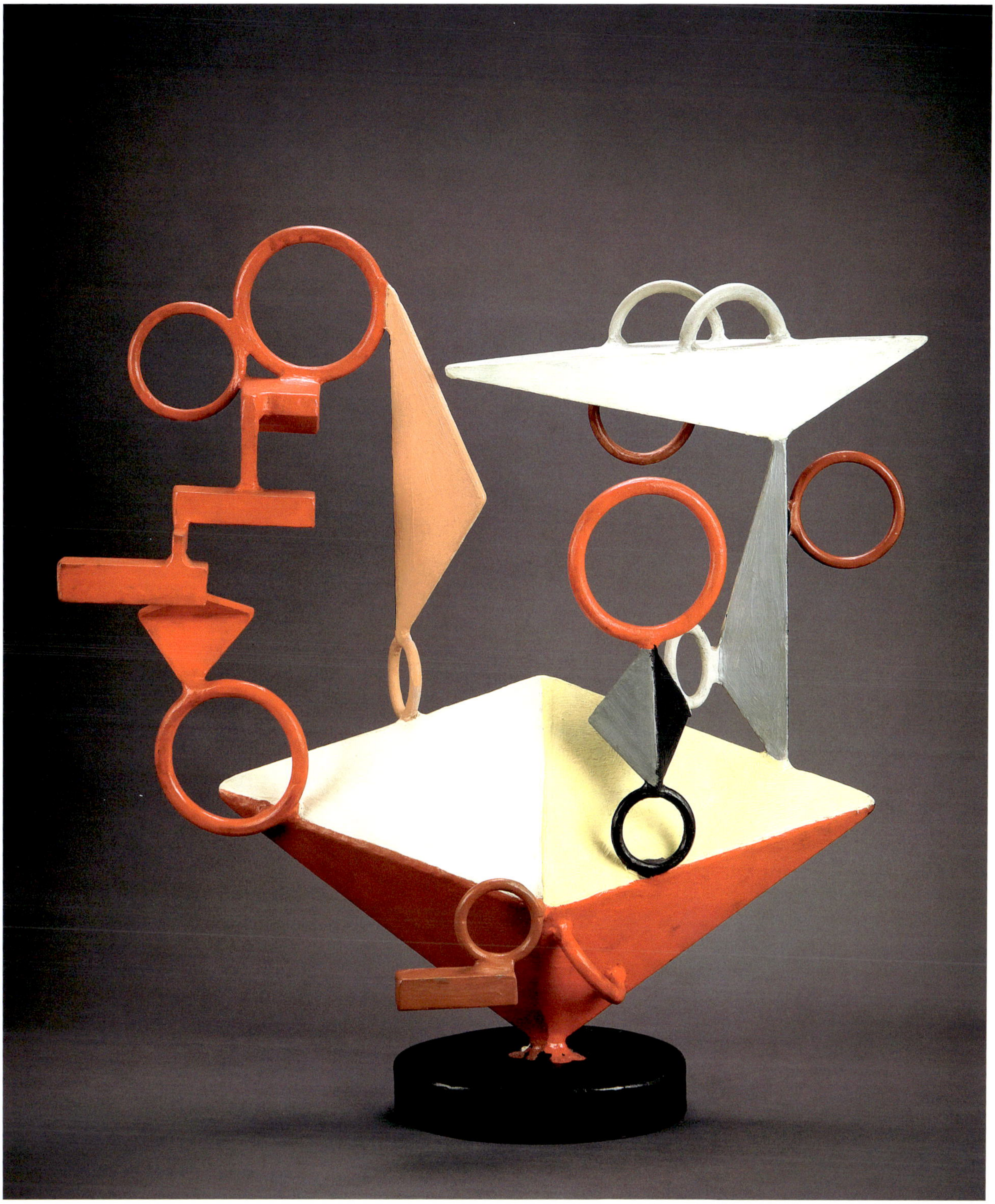

Fig. 22 | Big Diamond, 1952, Memorial Art Gallery of the University of Rochester

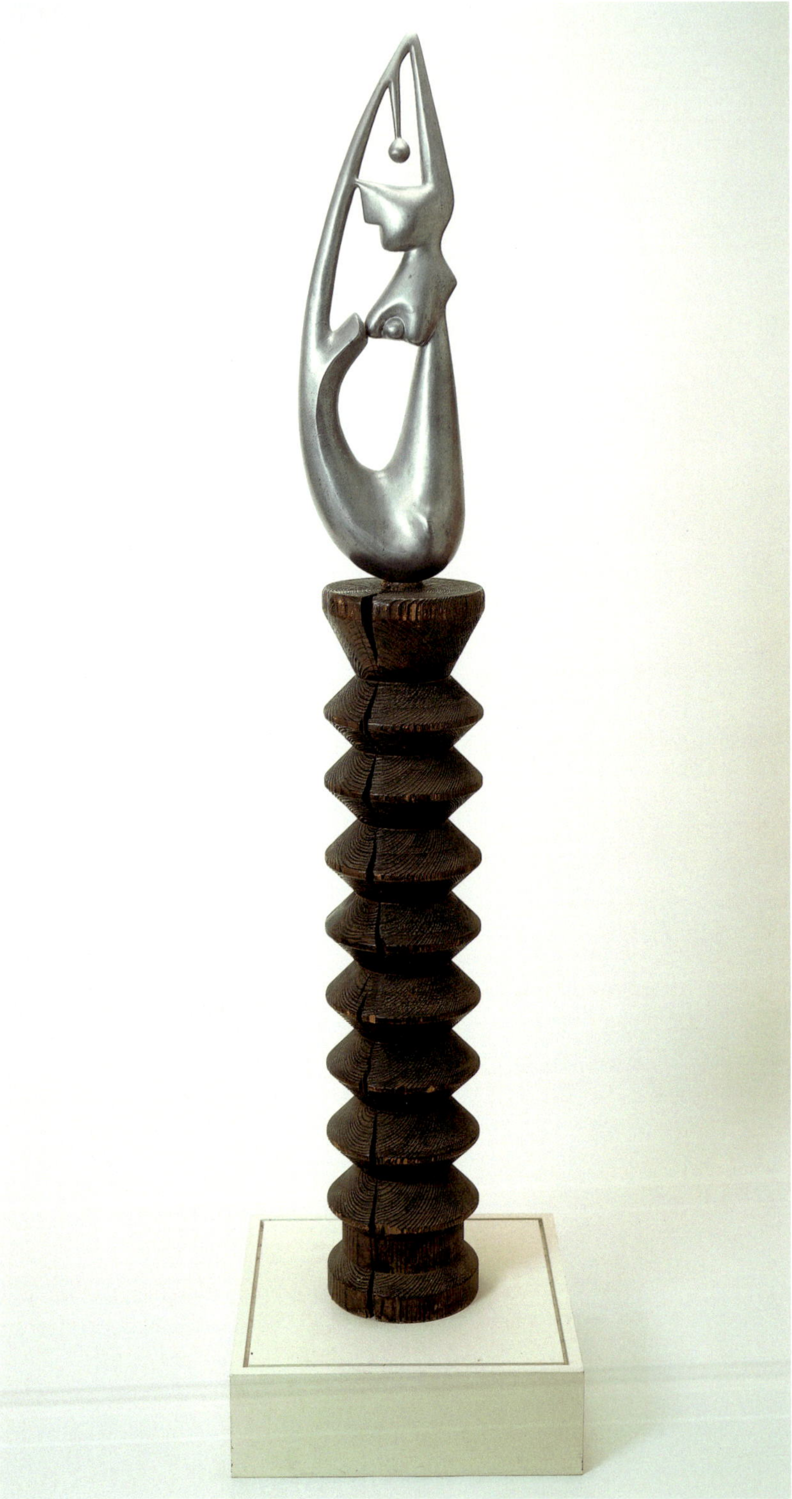

Fig. 23 | Growing Forms, 1939, University of Michigan Museum of Art, Ann Arbor

would have resonated with Smith as well. The catalogue text of his 1933 New York show called Brancusi's sculptures "a production" and adopted "the engineers' terminology" to explain his process.[63]

Smith later acknowledged that he considered Brancusi among those who created "the greatest sculptures."[64] Brancusi's handmade, rough-hewn wood bases—the aspect of the Romanian's sculpture that most emphatically reflects both his populist and geometric qualities—particularly influenced the younger artist. In the wood base of *Growing Forms* (1939, fig. 23), Smith refers directly to the repeating geometries of Brancusi's *Endless Column*, the earliest extant version of which had been on public view in New York as early as 1926 (fig. 24).[65] Smith again alludes to Brancusi's bases in an untitled drawing of 1946 (fig. 26). In the bottom right corner of this gouache, we see Smith's depiction of a distinctly Brancusi-esque base, now supporting three clean rectangles rather than the sinuous curves of Brancusi's *Bird in Space* sculptures (fig. 25). Smith repeats a similar base, again with rectangular geometries on top, in blue in the upper right corner of the same sheet. Essentially the same base reappears in three dimensions in Smith's *The Hero* (1951–52, fig. 27). Here, the series of forms atop the base (rectangular torso, triangular breasts, lozenge-shaped head) makes up an abstracted human figure identified specifically as a *hero*, asserting a link between the figure's geometries and a perfectible world.[66]

This notion of the idealized human figure created from clean geometries stayed with Smith until the end of his life, as seen in the graceful pirouette of *Cubi V* (1963, fig. 28) or the powerful stride of *Cubi XXIII* (1964, fig. 30). This connection between pure forms and utopian aspirations in Smith's work is underscored by his clear references to Russian constructivism (figs. 32–33) in numerous works, including *Three Planes* (1960–61, fig. 29), as well as his many spray drawings of the 1960s (fig. 31). Smith also associated the red, white, and black palette with romantic notions of the mechanical and the industrial. As he described it, "The beauty of the ballet of a white-to-red-to-black sheet [of steel] in a fast-rolling mill at different speeds running back and forth billowing steam with the quenches is a memory for me of automation."[67]

Smith likewise looked to Piet Mondrian—in particular his geometric forms, his use of primary colors along with black and white, and his impulse toward both literal and metaphorical purity—as a source of inspiration for his own work. As mentioned before, Jan Matulka

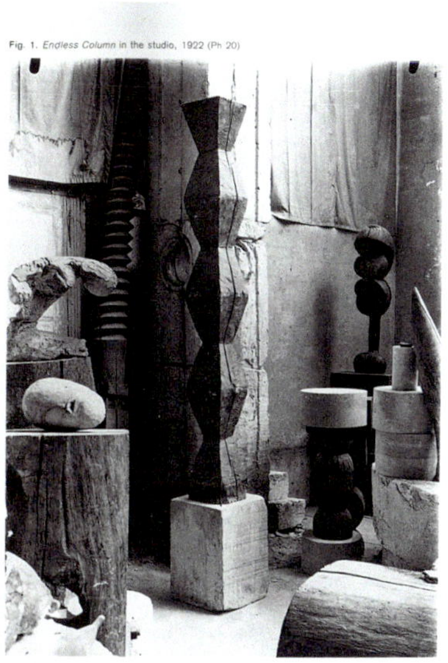

Fig. 24 | Constantin Brancusi's 1922 photograph of his studio, including **Endless Column** of 1918. A detail of this image (showing only the column itself) was reproduced in the catalogue of Brancusi's 1926 exhibition at the Brummer Gallery in New York.

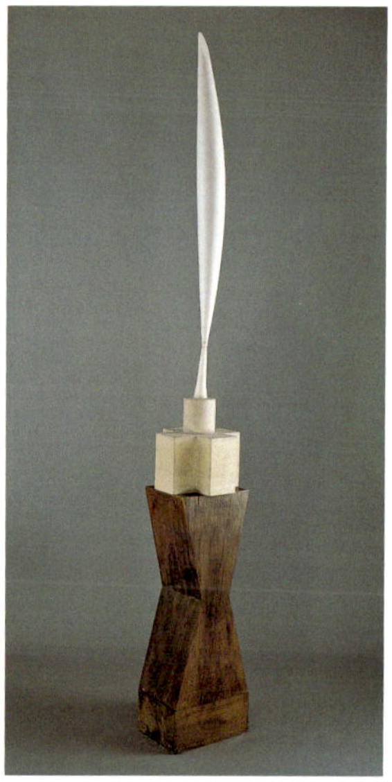

Fig. 25 | Constantin Brancusi, **Bird in Space**, 1925, marble, stone, and wood, 136 1/8 in. (345.8 cm) high, National Gallery of Art, Washington, gift of Eugene and Agnes E. Meyer. This work was exhibited at the Brummer Gallery in New York in 1926.

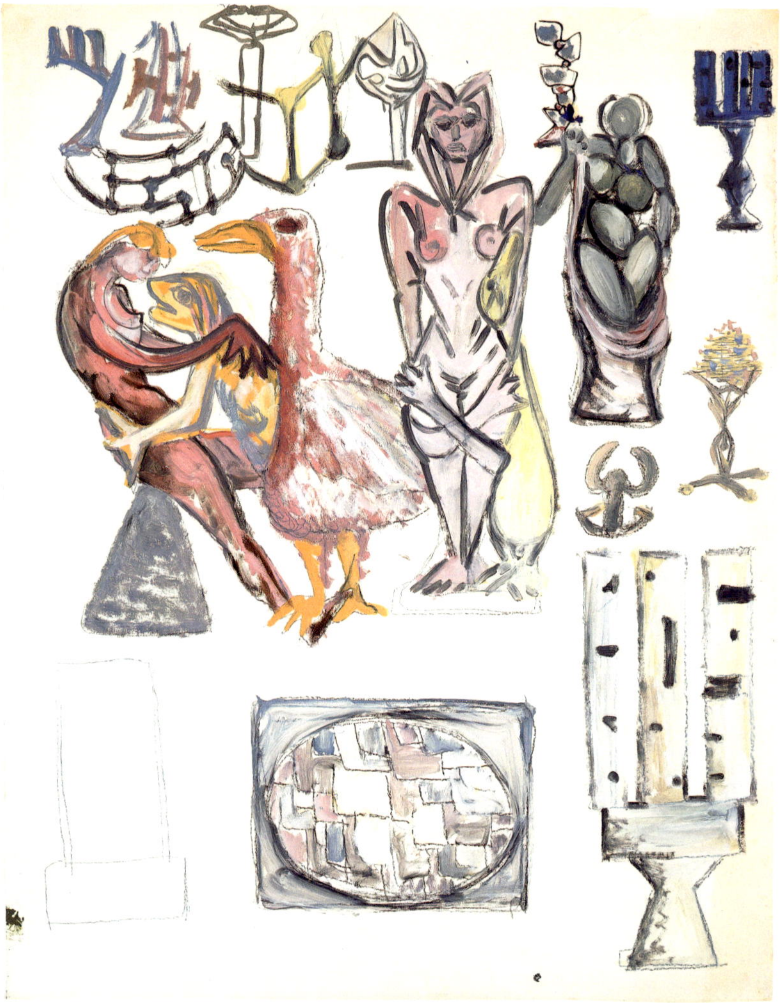

Fig. 26 | Untitled, 1946, The Estate of David Smith

introduced Smith to Mondrian's work, which the American sculptor also saw as early as the late 1920s in A. E. Gallatin's collection in New York. In sketchbook and other drawings of the 1940s and 1950s (figs. 26, 34–36), Smith makes specific reference to Mondrian's *Pier and Ocean* images of the mid-1910s, which were exhibited in New York at both the Valentine Gallery and The Museum of Modern Art in the early and mid-1940s (fig. 37). One of these drawings (fig. 35) suggests a formal connection between Mondrian's imagery and Smith's *17 h's* of 1950 (fig. 34). Although other drawings by Smith from the 1950s refer less overtly to Mondrian, they are nonetheless infused with Mondrian's sense of geometry and purity (fig. 38).

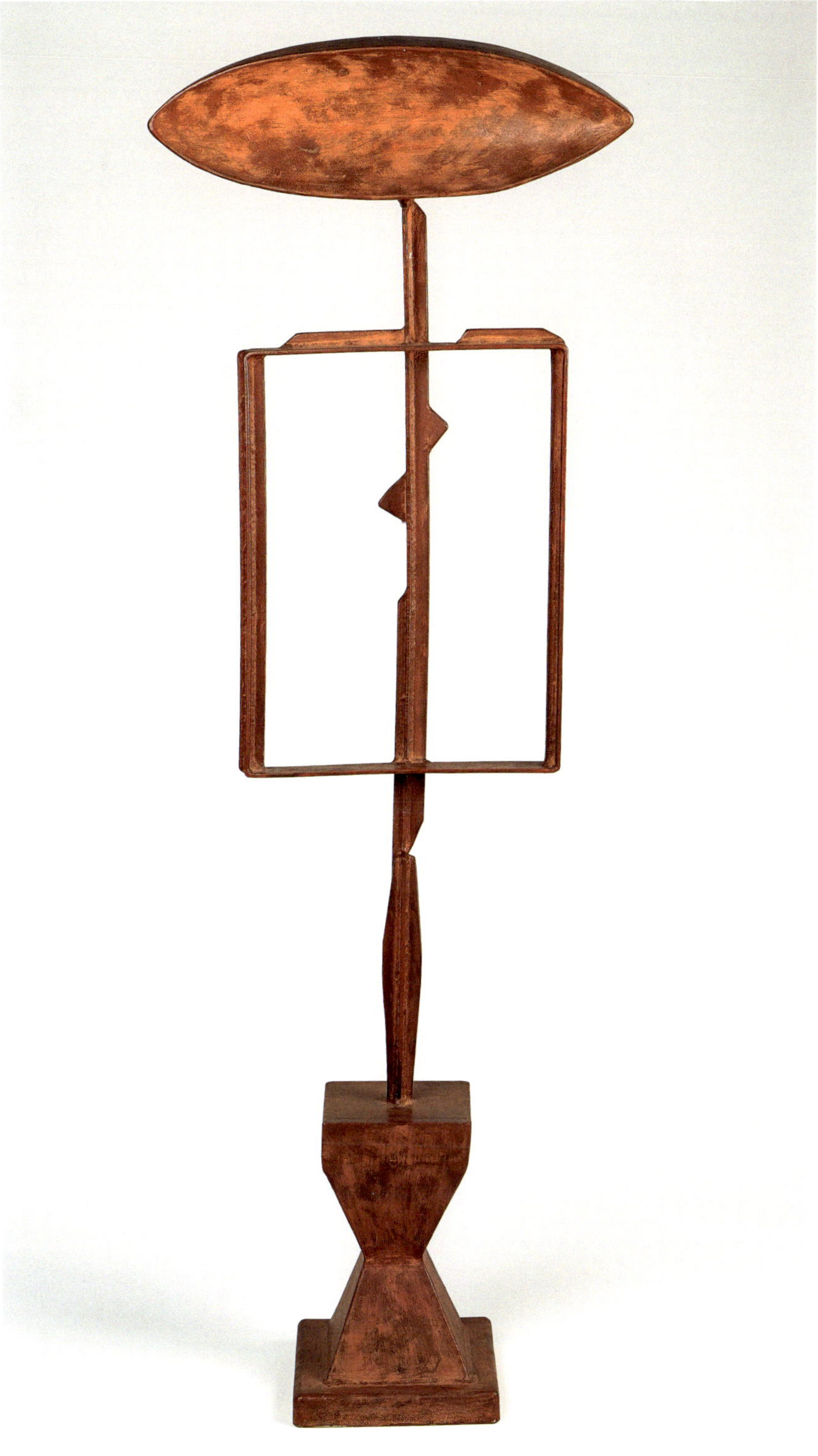

Fig. 27 | The Hero, 1951–52, Brooklyn Museum

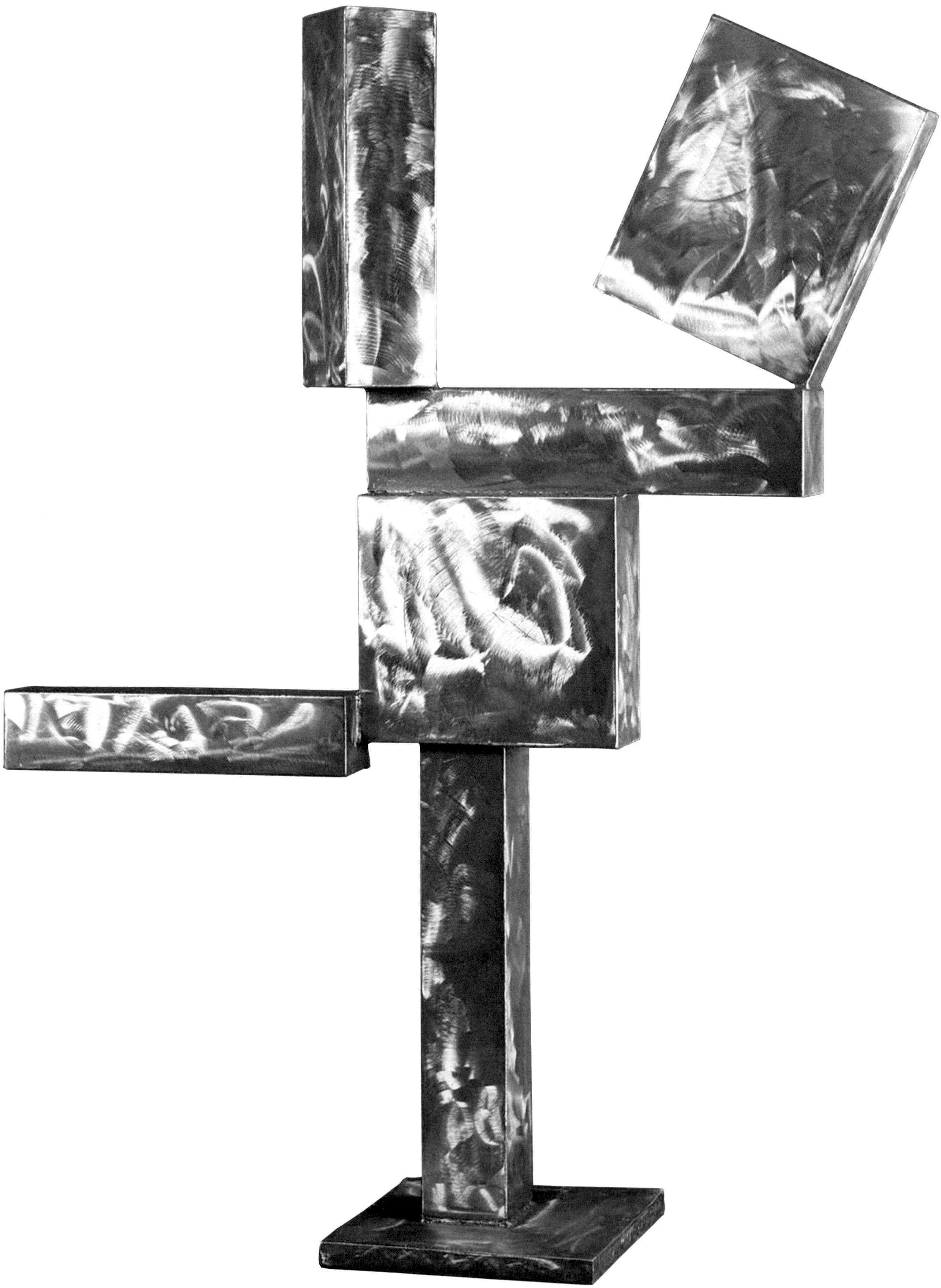

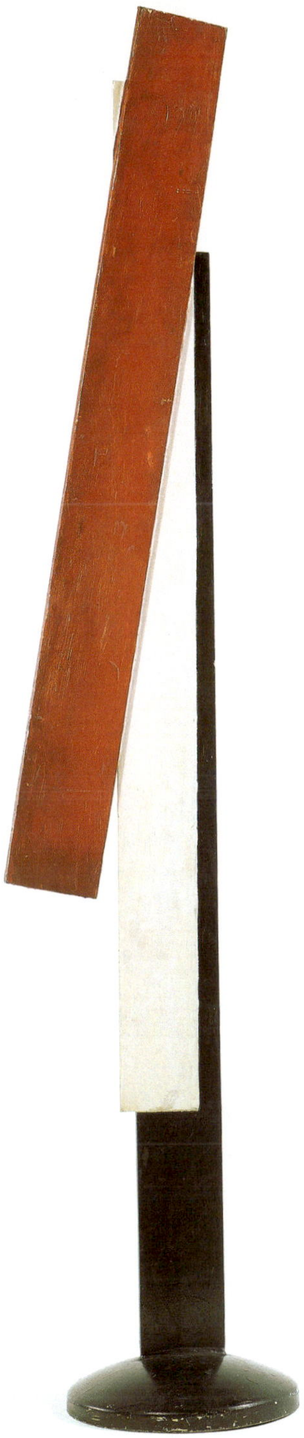

Left: **Fig. 28 | Cubi V**, 1963, Jon and Mary Shirley

Above: **Fig. 29 | Three Planes**, 1960–61, Museo Tamayo, Mexico City

Following spread: **Fig. 30 | Cubi XXIII**, 1964, Los Angeles County Museum of Art

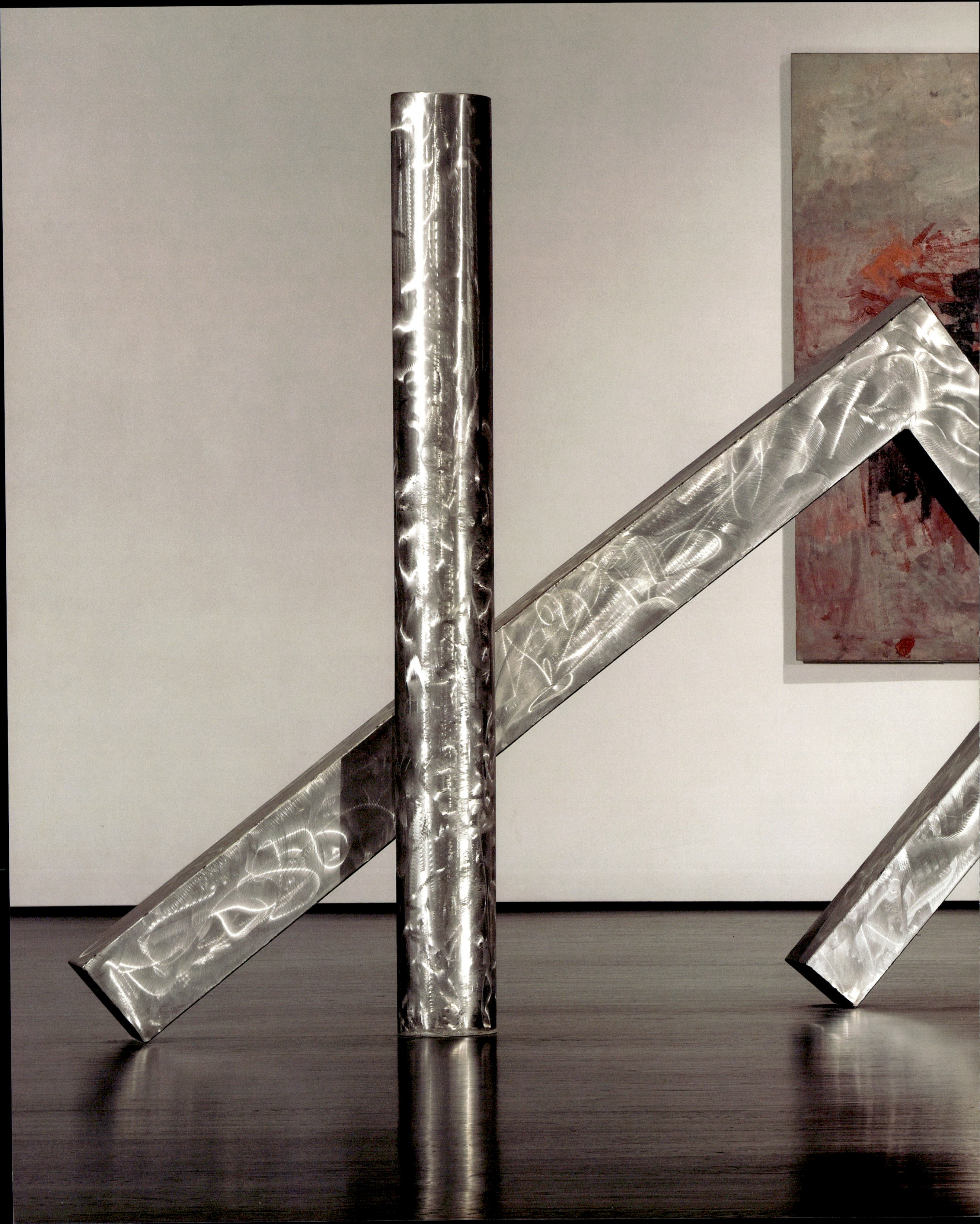

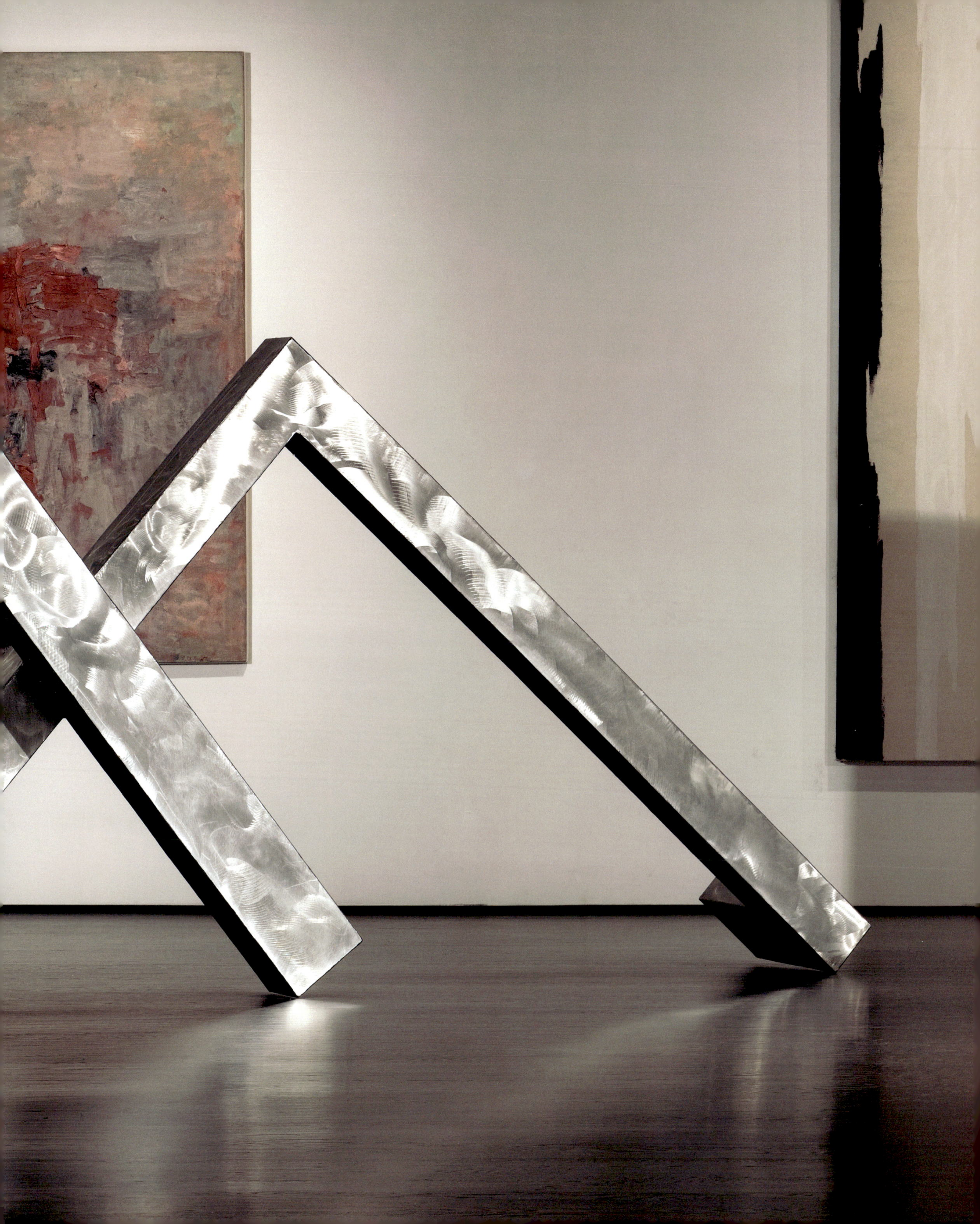

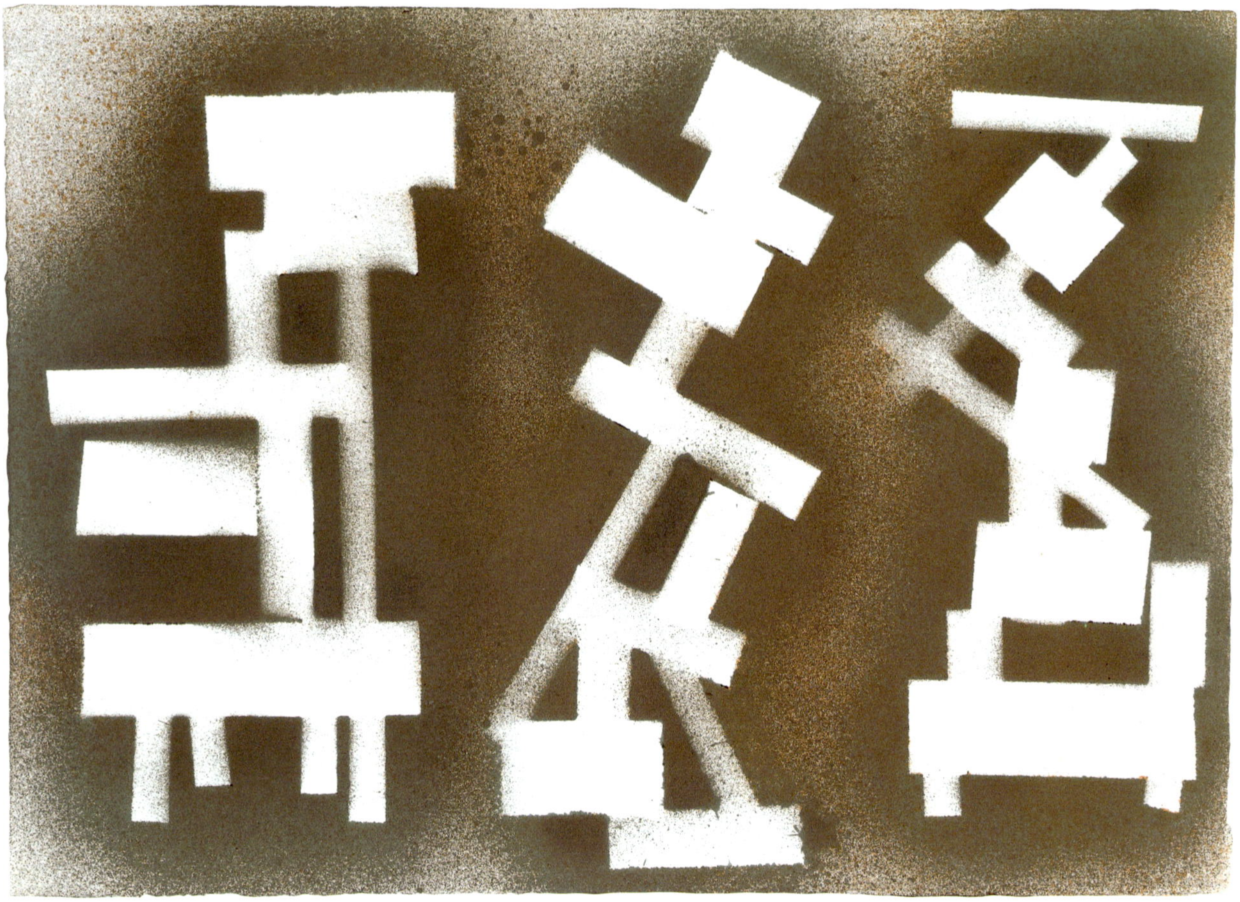

Fig. 31 | Untitled (Three Cubi Studies), 1962–63,
The Estate of David Smith

Similarly, Mondrian's primary colors appear in Smith's work in both obvious and subtle ways. In *Bec-Dida Day* (1963, fig. 39), titled in honor of Smith's beloved daughters, Rebecca and Candida, Smith makes joyous use of the primary colors associated with Mondrian in a cartoonlike figure that strides forward with energy and purpose. In a much more discreet allusion to Mondrian, Smith initially painted the carefully selected and welded geometric units of *Zig III* (1961, see fig. 8) red, yellow, and blue—Mondrian's main colors—and then painted over them in a scumbled black, allowing the colors beneath to show through but just barely (fig. 40; see also p. 10). Mondrian's lozenge paintings have also been cited as a precedent for the diamond shape of Smith's *Zig IV* (1961, see fig. 13).[68] In a 1961 interview with the British art critic and curator David Sylvester, Smith spontaneously compared himself to Mondrian, suggesting a close connection between the two artists in the sculptor's own view:

> Sylvester: You do it all yourself, don't you? I mean you could now afford studio assistants . . .
> Smith: I can't use studio assistants any more than Mondrian could have used assistants to paint in solid areas.[69]

The influence of Vasily Kandinsky on Smith's work is less clear, though certainly both artists shared an interest in geometric forms, especially the circle (figs. 39–49). In 1962, Smith expressed his understanding of the circle in the sweeping context of human history and culture: "Circles have long been a preoccupation, more primary than squares. Wheels are circles with mobility, from the first wheel of man to wheels on Indian stone temples, to a target on a pyramid I painted in 1934, to all the suns and poetic imagery of movement."[70] Three decades earlier, Kandinsky had intoned his own paean to the circle, writing that it is "the most modest form, but asserts itself unconditionally."[71] He also considered the circle "a connection to the cosmos."[72]

Although existing scholarship rarely discusses Smith and Kandinsky in relation to each other, Smith himself pointed out in 1960 that well into the 1940s, Kandinsky and Mondrian were considered part of the same artistic lineage as Picasso, González, and the Russian avant-garde: "The lines had not [yet] been drawn by the pedants—in cubist talk, Mondrian and Kandinsky were included."[73] Other statements by Smith over the years—including a 1952 lecture in which Smith referred to artists "who have contributed to my aesthetic heritage like

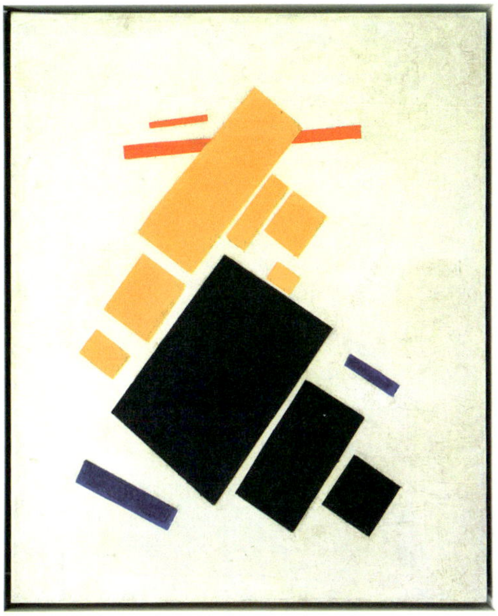

Fig. 32 | Kazimir Malevich, **Suprematist Composition: Airplane Flying**, 1915, oil on canvas, 22 7/8 x 19 in. (58.1 x 48.3 cm), The Museum of Modern Art, New York, purchase, acquisition confirmed in 1999 by agreement with the Estate of Kazimir Malevich and made possible with funds from the Mrs. John Hay Whitney Bequest (by exchange)

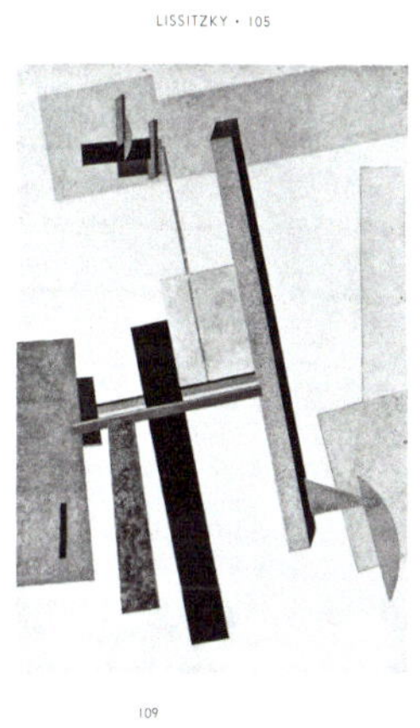

Fig. 33 | El Lissitzky, **Proun 2 (Construction)**, 1920, oil, paper, and metal on panel, 23 7/16 x 15 11/16 in. (59.5 x 39.8 cm), Philadelphia Museum of Art, A. E. Gallatin Collection, 1952, as reproduced in Philadelphia Museum of Art, *A. E. Gallatin Collection*, exh. cat., 1954. This work entered the Gallatin Collection (at that point housed in New York) in 1939 and was bequeathed to the Philadelphia Museum in 1952.

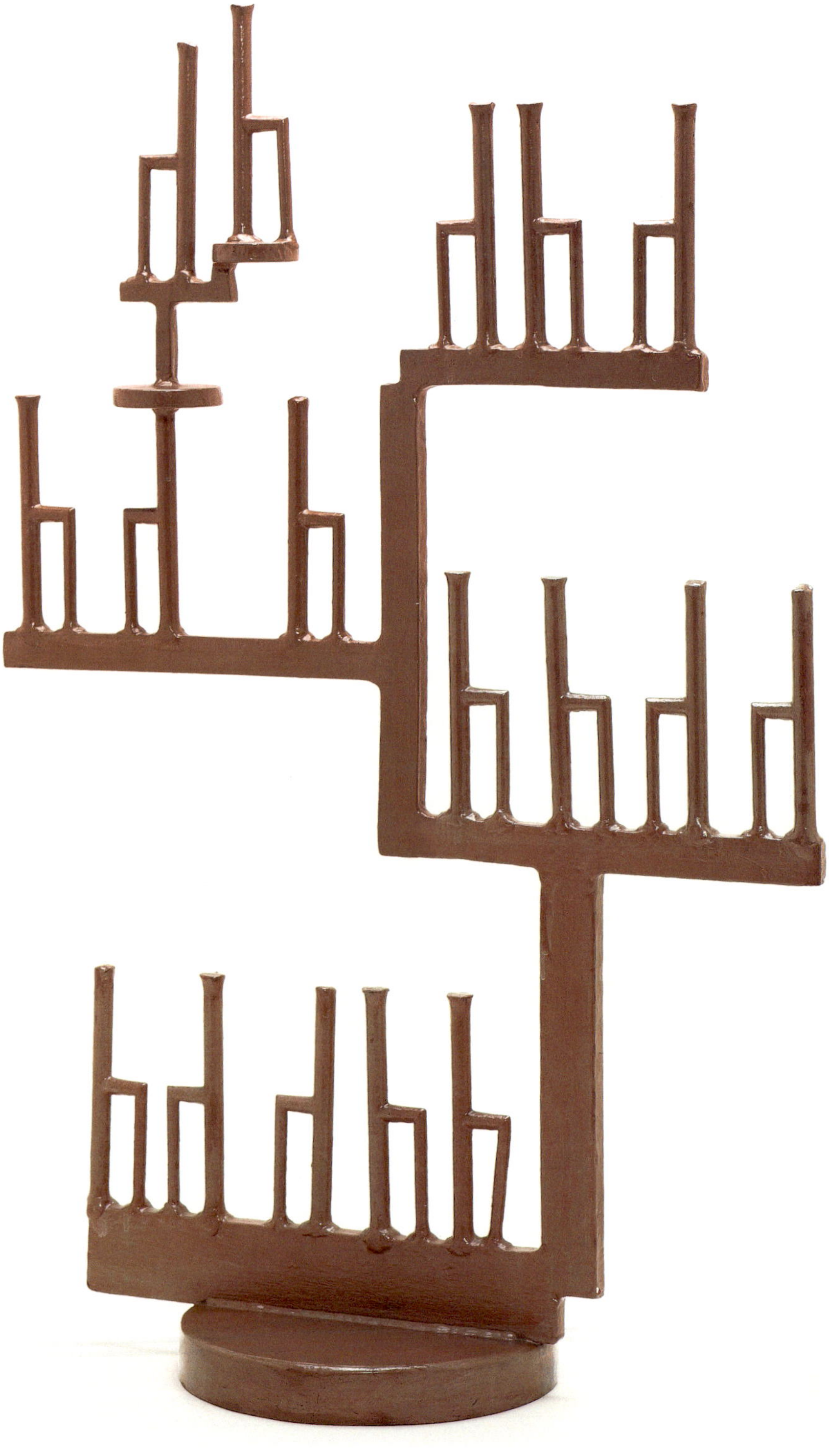

Fig. 34 | 17 h's, 1950, The Estate of David Smith

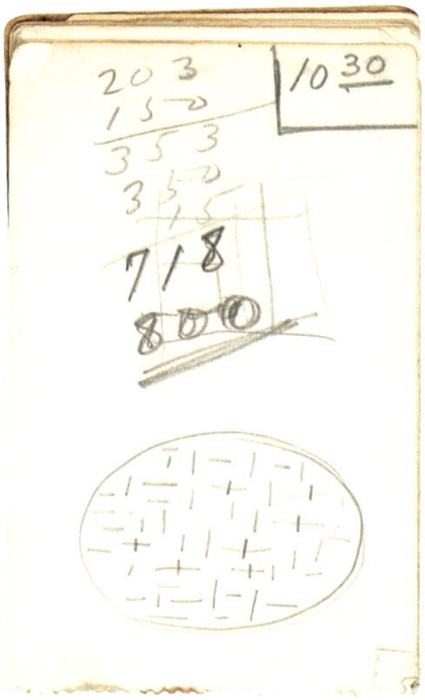

Fig. 35 | Page from Sketchbook #39, 1952–54, The Estate of David Smith

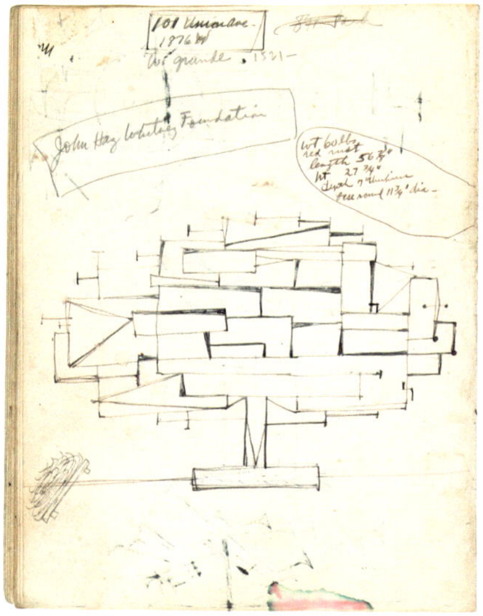

Fig. 36 | Page, c. 1952–54, from Sketchbook #40, 1950–54, The Estate of David Smith

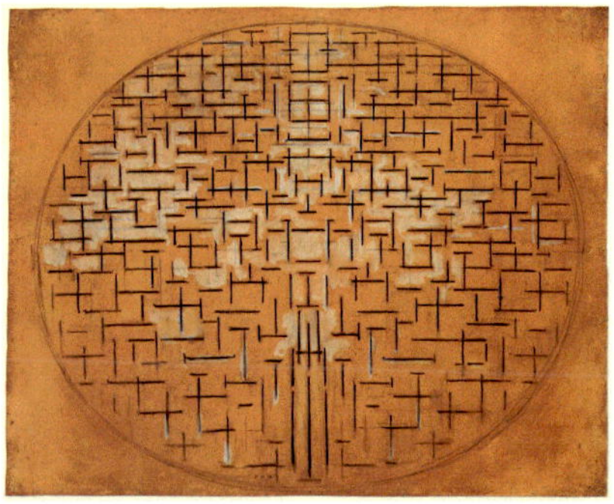

Fig. 37 | Piet Mondrian, **Pier and Ocean 5; "Zee en Sterrenlucht" (Sea and Starry Sky)**, 1915, charcoal and watercolor on paper, $34\frac{5}{8}$ x 44 in. (87.9 x 111.7 cm), The Museum of Modern Art, New York, Mrs. Simon Guggenheim Fund. This and many other *Pier and Ocean* works were exhibited in New York in the early and mid-1940s.

Cézanne, Kandinsky, and Mondrian"[74]—also demonstrate that Kandinsky was indeed part of Smith's artistic pantheon and a formative influence on the younger artist. The blue circle, red rectangle, and yellow triangular form in *Bec-Dida Day* (see fig. 39) indicate that Smith clearly understood the specific correlations Kandinsky made between geometric forms and primary colors in the Preliminary Course he taught at the Bauhaus.[75]

Kandinsky in the late 1920s and early 1930s made numerous spray drawings that foreshadow Smith's sprays of the late 1950s and 1960s (figs. 46–49).[76] Many of these Kandinsky sprays were exhibited in New York in the 1930s and 1940s, both in commercial galleries and at the Museum of Non-Objective Painting (renamed the Solomon R. Guggenheim Museum in 1952). Smith likely would have seen Kandinsky drawings of this type, particularly given that the commercial venues included the J. B. Neumann Gallery (which was owned by the business partner, from 1938 to about 1945, of Smith's dealer Marian Willard; in fact, Smith's second New York solo show, in 1940, was at the Neumann-Willard Gallery).[77]

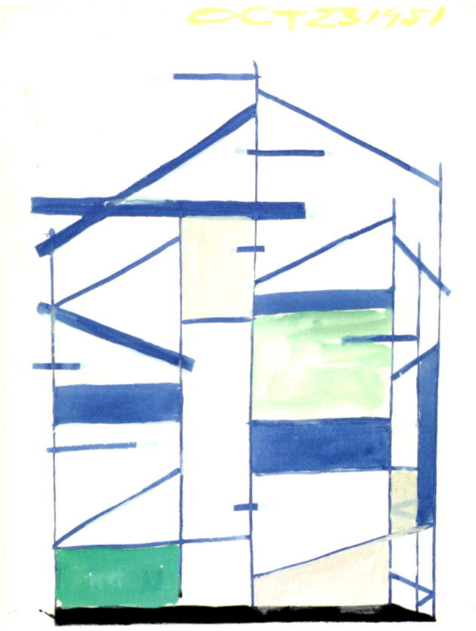

Fig. 38 | Untitled, 1951, The Estate of David Smith, courtesy Galerie Gmurzynska, Zurich

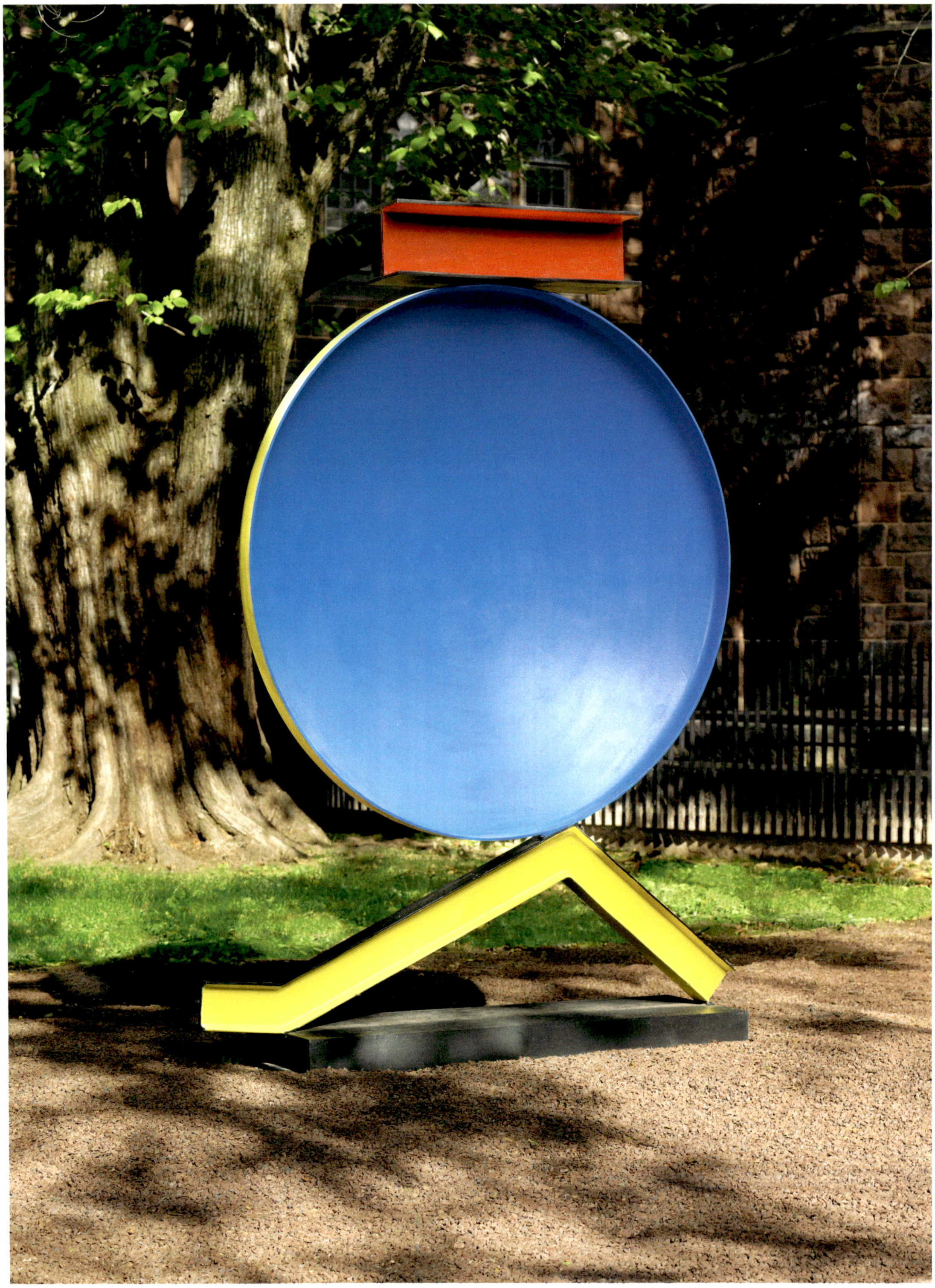

Fig. 39 | Bec-Dida Day, 1963, Yale University Art Gallery

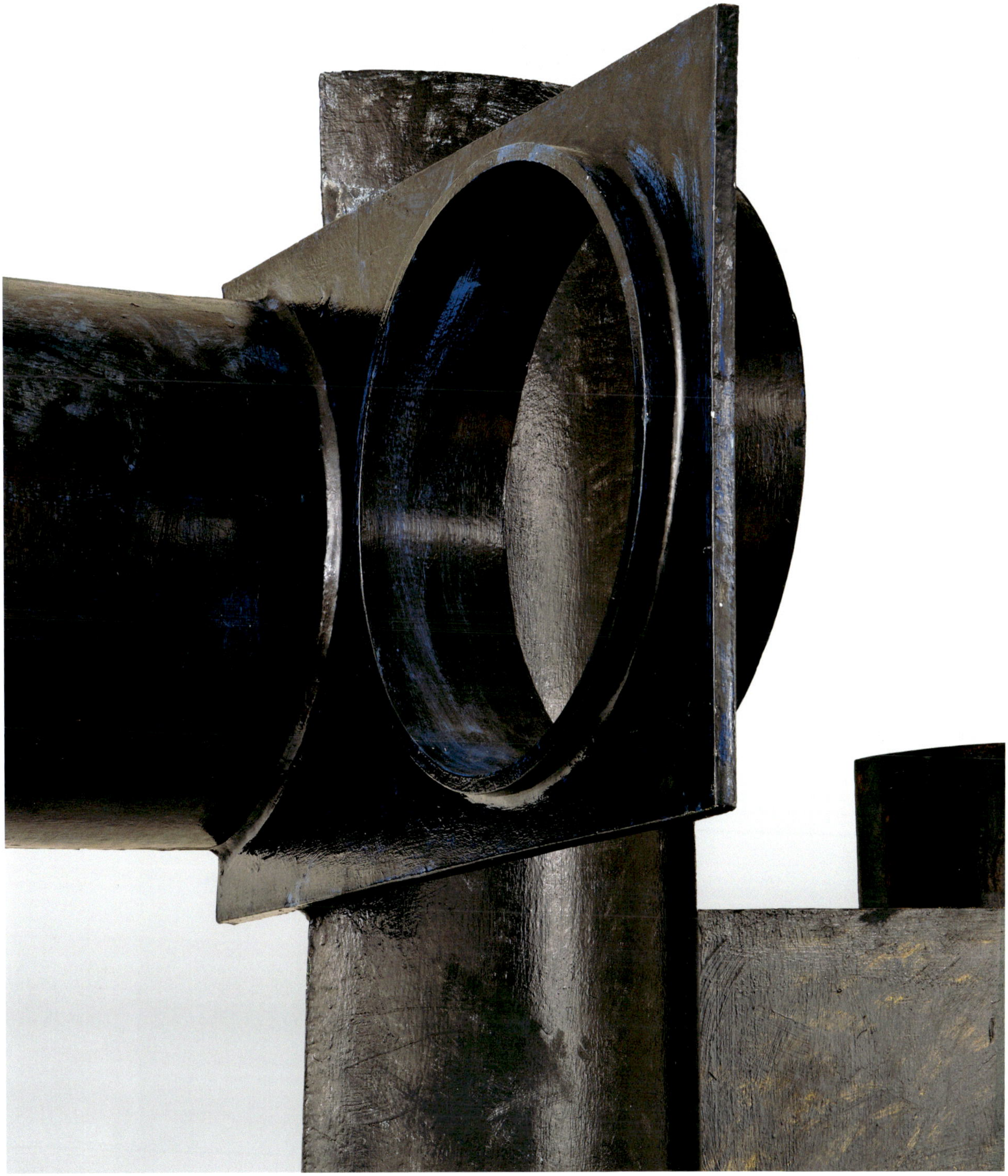

Fig. 40 | Zig III (detail), 1961, The Estate of David Smith, courtesy Gagosian Gallery

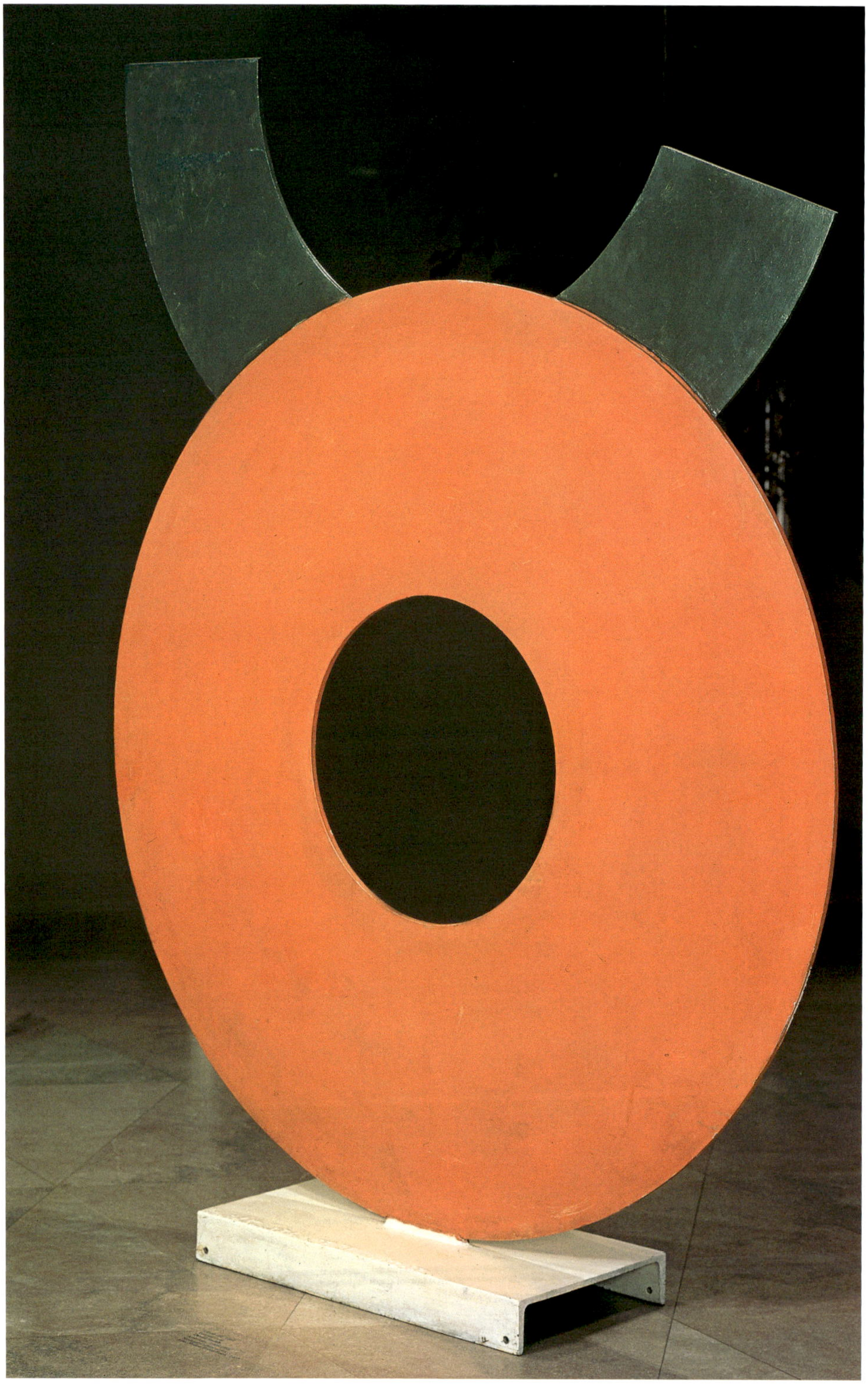

Fig. 41 | Circle III, 1962, National Gallery of Art, Washington

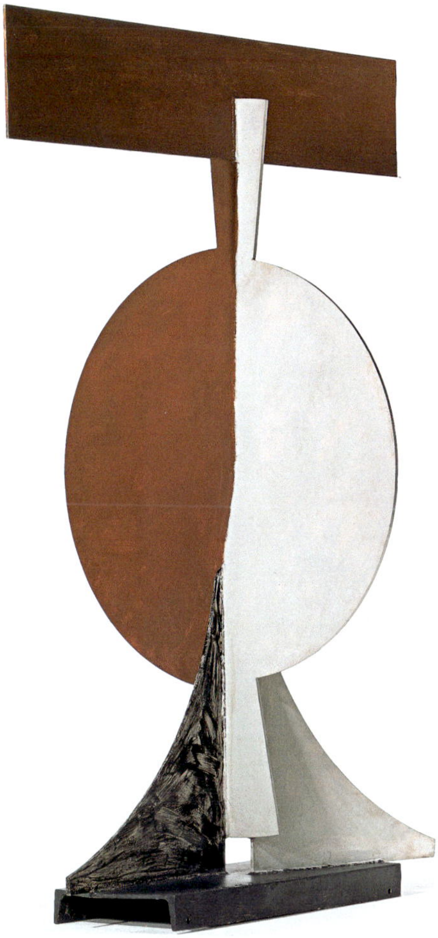

Fig. 42 | Circle IV, 1962, The Estate of David Smith, courtesy Gagosian Gallery

Smith acknowledged the primacy of geometric forms in his last works, which he described as never varying "from just . . . squares, rectangles, and cylinder forms." Where his interest in geometry might have taken him had he not died in a car accident at age fifty-nine on May 23, 1965, is, of course, a fascinating question. Donald Judd's one published review of Smith's work (a late 1964 show that included a number of *Cubis* and other recent sculptures), in which the younger artist wrote that "David Smith's sculpture is some of the best in the world," suggests intriguing possibilities.[78] Ultimately, however, the question is unanswerable. We can only look back; we cannot see the

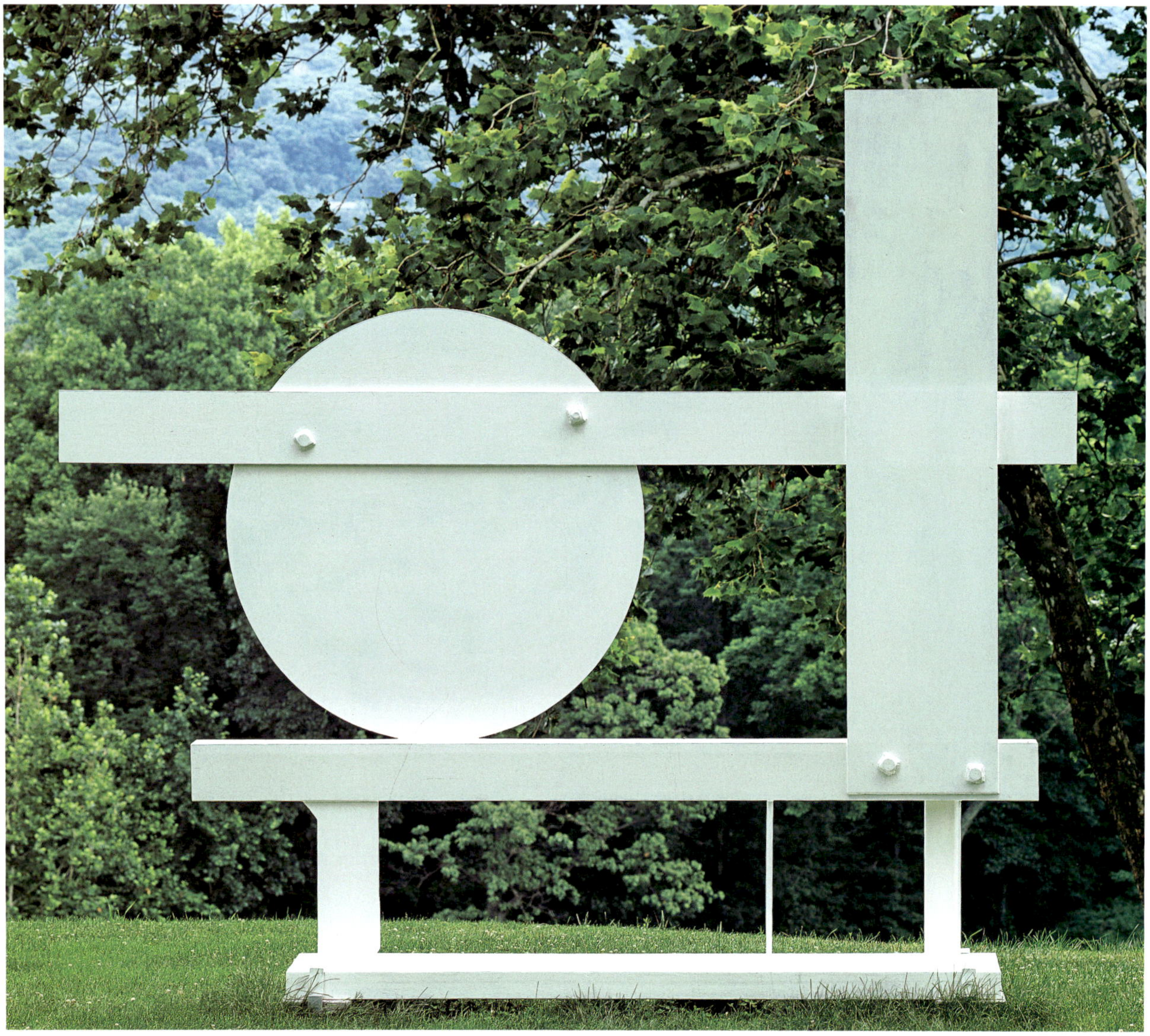

Fig. 43 | Primo Piano III, 1962, The Estate of David Smith, courtesy Gagosian Gallery

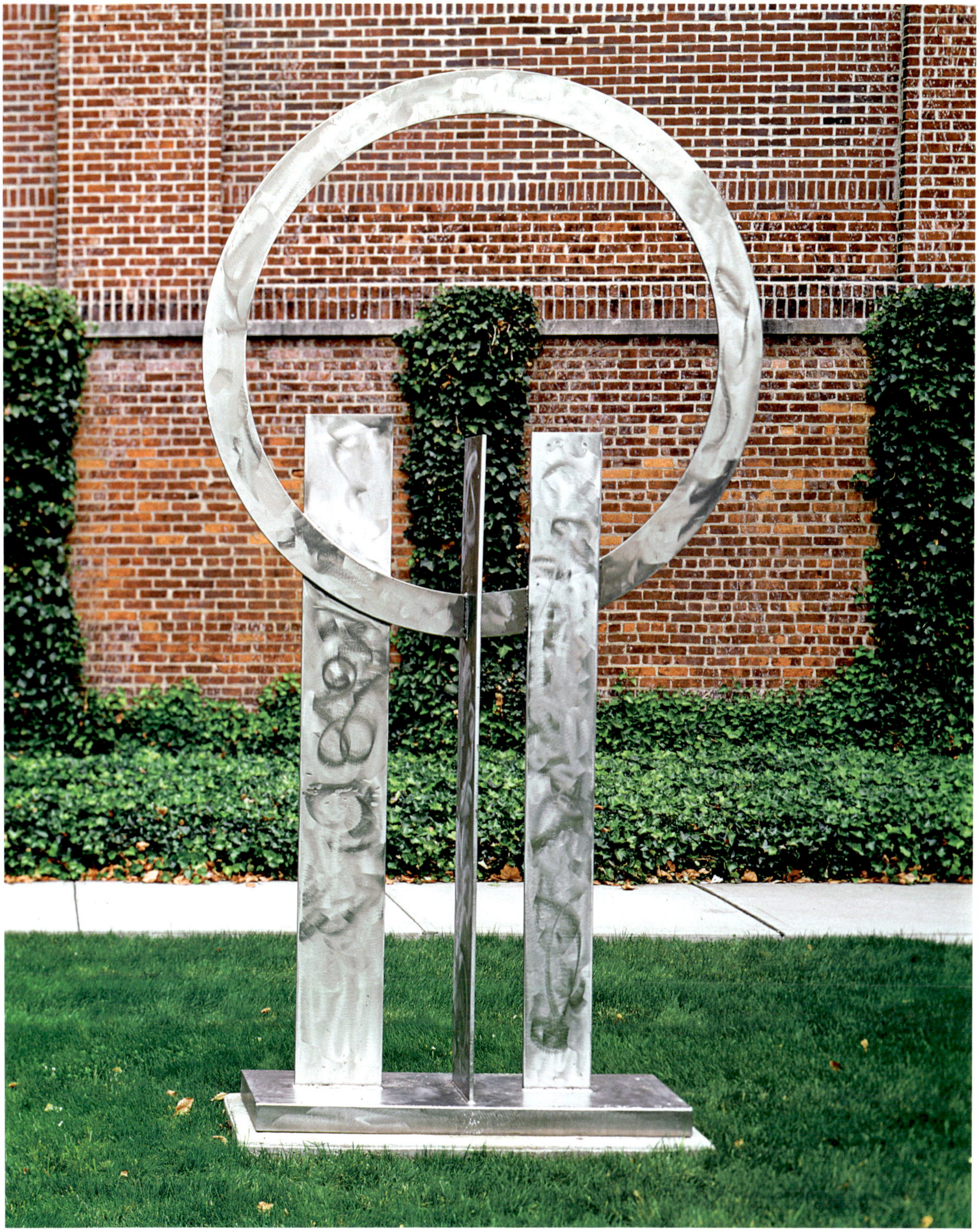

Fig. 44 | Untitled, 1964, Newark Museum

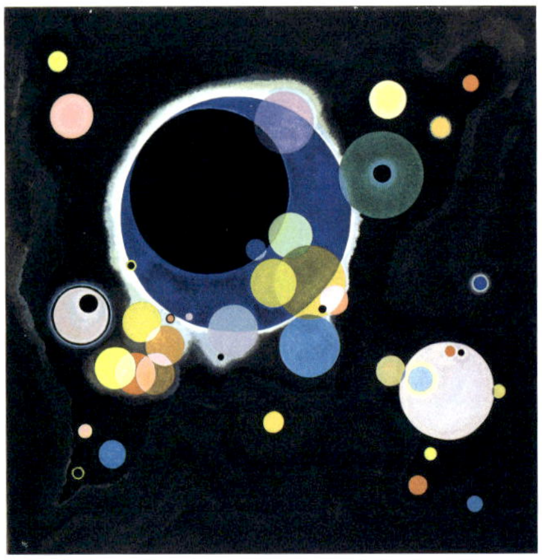

Fig. 45 | Vasily Kandinsky, **Several Circles**, 1926, oil on canvas, 55 1/4 x 55 3/8 in. (140.3 x 140.7 cm), Solomon R. Guggenheim Museum, New York, Solomon R. Guggenheim Founding Collection, by gift, 41.283

future, let alone a future that never came to pass. Smith himself wrote a decade earlier, just as Judd came onto the New York scene, "Art history is one thing to the art historian and another to the creative artist . . . His art is not made up of [an] historian's words of judgment. His choices are made the same way he makes the work of art—by the visual, irrational, creative. His history is a selection of his own preferences."[79]

David Smith's own lifelong interest in geometry evolved from his own "preferences" and essential nature, and then from looking at art that affirmed those beliefs and instincts. Smith's self-definition as a member of the working class, along with his fascination for the industrial and the mechanical, pointed him from the first years of his career toward the work of early twentieth-century avant-garde artists who expressed utopian optimism through geometric constructivism. He, in turn, adopted and adapted those pure geometries throughout his career, creating a body of work that remains among the richest and most powerful ever made.

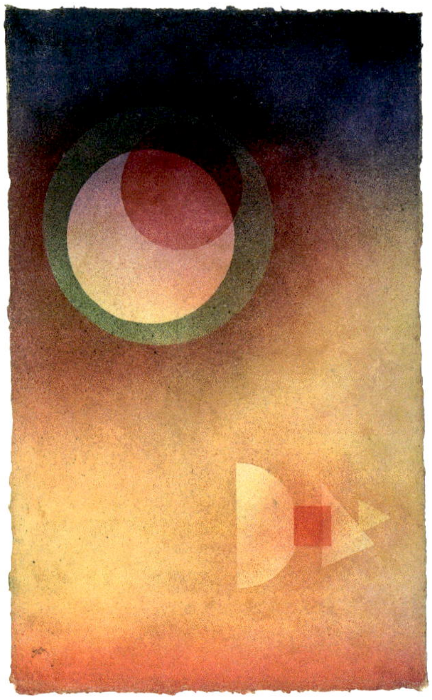

Fig. 46 | Vasily Kandinsky, **Evasive**, 1929, watercolor on paper, 22 1/4 x 14 in. (56.4 x 35.5 cm), The Hilla von Rebay Foundation, on extended loan to the Solomon R. Guggenheim Museum, New York, 1970.137

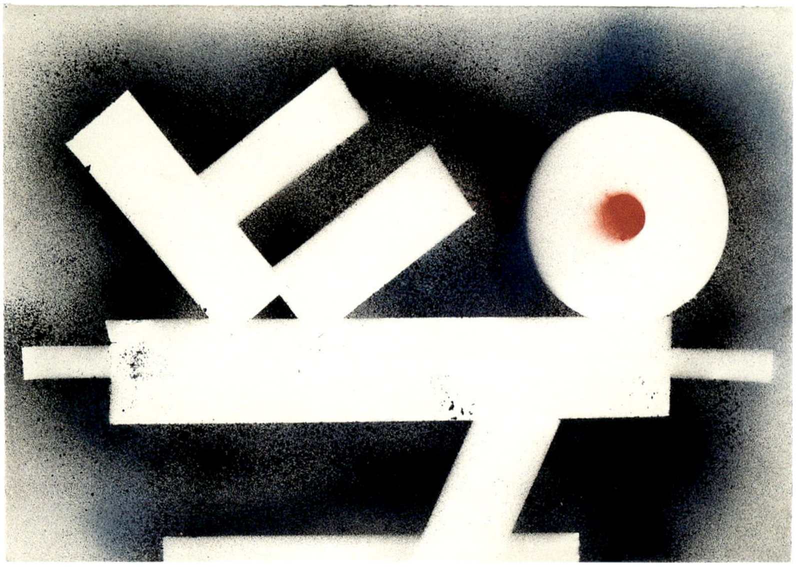

Fig. 47 | **Untitled**, 1962, Dallas Museum of Art

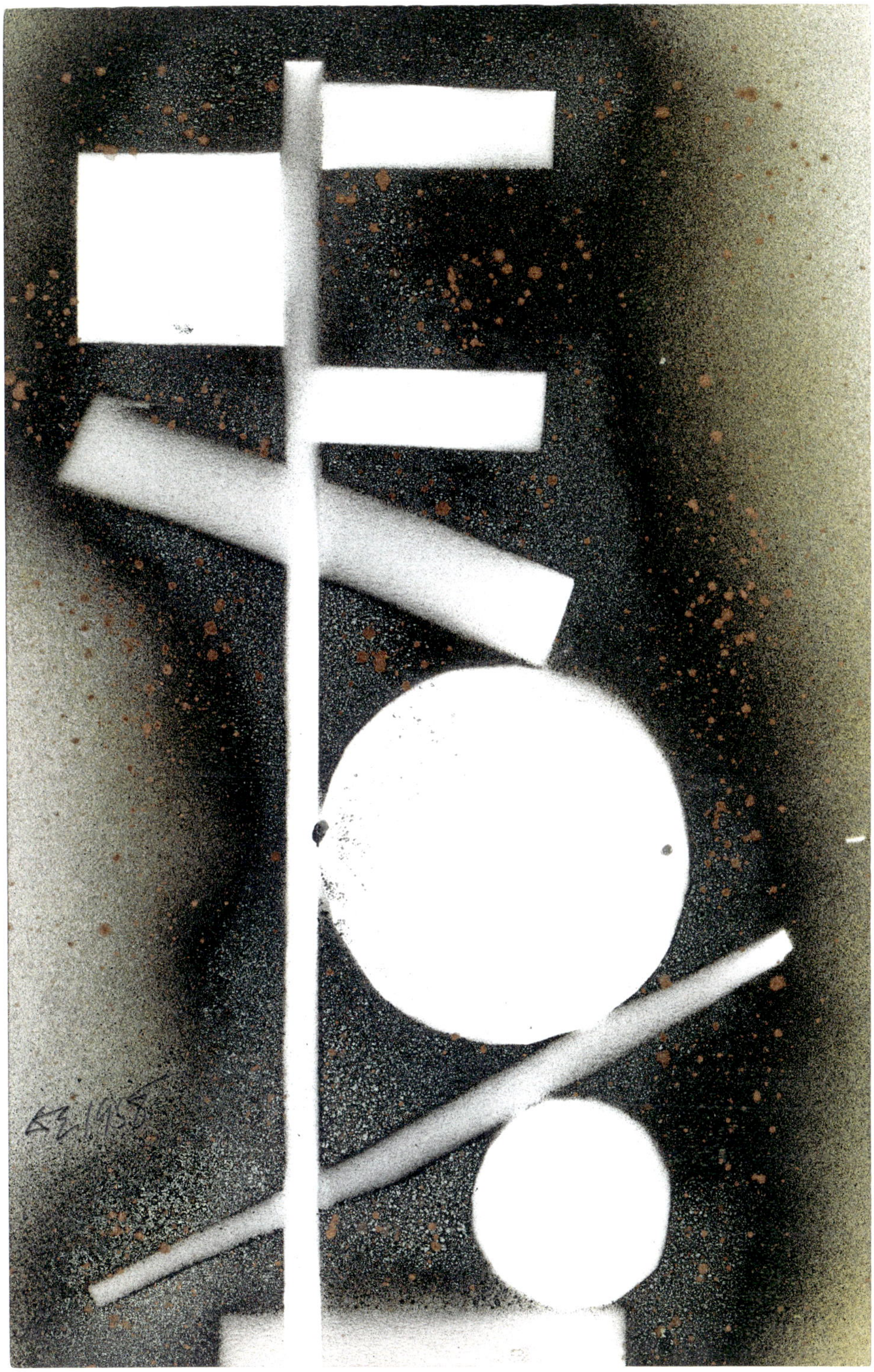

Fig. 48 | DS 1958, 1958, The Metropolitan Museum of Art, New York

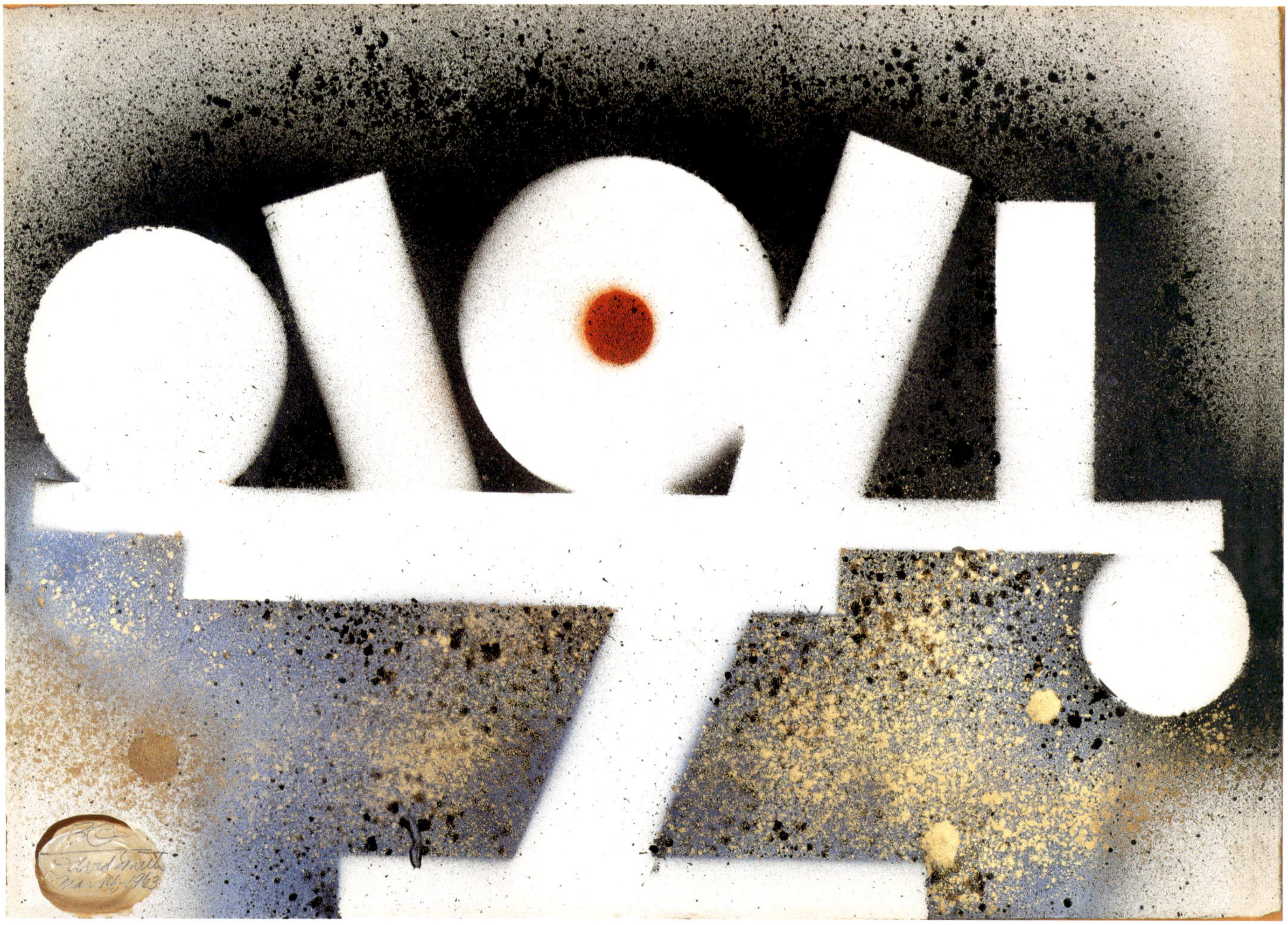

Fig. 49 | Untitled, 1963, Jon and Mary Shirley

1. Thomas B. Hess, "The Secret Letter: An Interview with David Smith, June 1964" (transcript with handwritten edits, The Estate of David Smith, Archives, box 12), n.p., published in *David Smith*, exh. cat. (New York: Marlborough-Gerson Gallery, 1964), n.p.; reprinted in *David Smith,* ed. Garnett McCoy (New York: Praeger, 1973), 175.

2. Gene Baro, "Some Late Words from David Smith," *Art International* 9, no. 7 (October 20, 1965): 49.

3. For a comprehensive chronology, see Bénédicte Ajac and Nat Trotman, "Chronology," in *David Smith: A Centennial*, exh. cat., ed. Carmen Giménez (New York: Guggenheim Museum, 2006), 387–416.

4. Hess, "The Secret Letter," reprinted in McCoy, *David Smith*, 183.

5. Ibid.

6. Ibid., 176.

7. See Paula Wisotzki, "Artist and Worker: The Labor of David Smith," *Oxford Art Journal* 28, no. 3 (2005): 365. As Wisotzki explains, the specifics of Smith's employment at Studebaker are not known, as the now-defunct company's records from that era are no longer extant. According to Smith, he worked in Department 346 and also in Department 348, Steel Frame Assembly. See Katharine Kuh, "David Smith," in *The Artist's Voice: Talks with Seventeen Artists* (New York: Harper and Row, 1962), 221.

8. Cleve Gray, ed., *David Smith by David Smith* (London: Thames and Hudson, 1968), 24.

9. Garnett McCoy, "The David Smith Papers," *Archives of American Art Journal* 8, no. 2 (April 1968): 7.

10. Wisotzki, "Artist and Worker," 365.

11. Gray, *David Smith by David Smith*, 24. This chronology, which covers the years from Smith's birth to 1947, is thought to date from around 1950.

12. Dore Ashton, "Reflections on Six American Sculptors," in *Crossroads of American Sculpture: David Smith, George Rickey, John Chamberlain, Robert Indiana, William T. Wiley, Bruce Nauman*, exh. cat., ed. Holliday T. Day (Indianapolis: Indianapolis Museum of Art, 2000), 17. Smith himself wrote that he "got anarchy and cones and cubes from John Sloan." See David Smith, "Notes on My Work," *Arts Magazine*, February 1960, reprinted in *David Smith, 1906–1965: A Retrospective Exhibition*, exh. cat. (Cambridge, MA: Fogg Art Museum, Harvard University, 1966), 103.

13. Smith not only saw Kandinsky and Mondrian's work in reproduction but also saw it in person at A. E. Gallatin's Gallery [later Museum] of Living Art in Greenwich Village, which opened in 1927. He saw Russian constructivism reproduced in German art magazines in the late 1920s and likely saw it in person at a 1929 exhibition in New York. See *Exhibition of Contemporary Art of Soviet Russia: Painting, Graphic, Sculpture*, exh. cat. (New York: Grand Central Palace, 1929).

14. Kuh, "David Smith," in *The Artist's Voice*, 221.

15. Ibid., 221–22.

16. See Smith's chronology entry for 1933 in Gray, *David Smith by David Smith*, 25. He refers to the iron constructions he saw reproduced in *Cahiers d'art* as "created jointly" by Picasso and González.

17. David Smith, "Portland, Oregon, March 23, 1953" (unpublished manuscript, The Estate of David Smith, Archives, box 11), n.p.

18. González learned to weld in 1918 at the Renault factory, outside Paris.

19. David Smith, letter to Herman Cherry, December 15, 1955, Herman Cherry Letters from David Smith, 1950–1964, roll 1037, frame 134, Archives of American Art, Smithsonian Institution, Washington, D.C. Used with permission from the Herman Cherry Estate.

20. David Smith, letter to Jean Xceron, December 7, 1955, Jean Xceron Letters from David Smith, 1940–1957, reel no. 3482, frame 854, Archives of American Art, Smithsonian Institution, Washington, D.C.

21. David Smith, "González: First Master of the Torch," *Art News*, February 1956, 34–37, 64–65. For a complete listing of Smith's published writings, see the bibliography compiled by Sarah B. Kianovsky in *David Smith: A Centennial*, exh. cat., ed. Carmen Giménez (New York: Guggenheim Museum, 2006), 433–47.

22. Smith, "González: First Master of the Torch," 36.

23. Ibid., 37. Piet Mondrian, Theo van Doesburg, and Georges Vantongerloo, among others, also attended the meetings in Torres-García's studio.

24. See Ajac and Trotman, "Chronology," in *David Smith: A Centennial*, 390.

25. See *David Smith, 1906–1965: A Retrospective Exhibition*, 6, 84.

26. See Ajac and Trotman, "Chronology," in *David Smith: A Centennial*, 392.

27. See Wisotzki, "Artist and Worker," 351, 351n5.

28. Hess, "The Secret Letter," reprinted in McCoy, *David Smith*, 178.

29. Dorothy Dehner, "SR3—Dehner Synch Interview—CR3&4" (interview transcript, Barbara Rose Papers, series 2, box 1, folder 17, Getty Research Institute, Los Angeles, n.d.), 5/2.

30. Ibid., 4/3. The American Artists Congress was founded in 1936 largely as an antifascist organization.

31. David Smith, letter to Herman Cherry, December 16, 1964, Herman Cherry Letters from David Smith, 1950–1964, roll 1037, frame 477, Archives of American Art, Smithsonian Institution, Washington, D.C. Used with permission from the Herman Cherry Estate.

32. Elaine de Kooning, "A Stroke of Genius," *Horizon*, May 1984, 41.

33. David Smith, "On Abstract Art" (lecture, United American Artists Forum on Abstract Art, New York, February 15, 1940), excerpted in David Smith, "Abstract Art," *The New York Artist*, April 1940, 15; clipping in the David Smith Files, Willard Gallery, New York. I am grateful to Miani Johnson for access to these files.

34. Jean C. Brooks, letter to Marian Willard, March 29, 1952, David Smith Files, Willard Gallery, New York.

35. Hess, "The Secret Letter," reprinted in McCoy, *David Smith*, 179. Emphasis added.

36. David Smith, letter to Emanuel Navaretta, November 1959, reprinted in *David Smith,* ed. Garnett McCoy (New York: Praeger, 1973), 208.

37. Wisotzki, "Artist and Worker," 368. Smith's use of the word "fraternity" connotes the idea of a brotherhood of workers. He likewise called the waterfront laborers "good friends" and "guys [who] were fine."

38. See Ajac and Trotman, "Chronology," in *David Smith: A Centennial*, 397.

39. "David Smith, 59, Metal Sculptor," obituary, *New York Times*, May 25, 1965.

40. Frank O'Hara, "Art New York: Sculpting Master of Bolton Landing" (script prepared for recording by Channel 13/ WNET on November 6, 1964, and airing on November 11 and 13, 1964, Frank O'Hara Papers, folder 24, Archives, The Museum of Modern Art, New York), 12.

41. Hilton Kramer, *The Age of the Avant-Garde: An Art Chronicle of 1956–1972* (New York: Farrar, Straus and Giroux, 1973), 323. The italics are Kramer's.

42. Smith often only eked out a living as an artist—his letters over the years are peppered with references to money concerns—and augmented his income in various ways, including lecturing and teaching, as well as this ALCO job.

43. See Wisotzki, "Artist and Worker," 366.

44. Ibid.

45. McCoy, "David Smith Papers," 7.

46. Elaine de Kooning, "David Smith Makes a Sculpture," *Art News*, September 1951, 39.

47. McCoy, "David Smith Papers," 7.

48. David Smith, untitled radio talk given on WNYC on October 30, 1952 (transcript, The Estate of David Smith, Archives, box 11), 2.

49. Smith, "Portland, Oregon, March 23, 1953," n.p.

50. David Sylvester, "Tape-Recorded Interview with David Smith, Sculptor, at the International Building, New York City, June 16, 1961; Interviewer: David Sylvester, of the British Broadcasting Corp." (transcript, The Estate of David Smith, Archives, box 12), n.p.; reprinted as "Interview" in *David Smith,* ed. Garnett McCoy (New York: Praeger, 1973), 172.

51. Ibid., 173.

52. See note 13.

53. As Smith famously described his own evolution, "My student period was only involved with painting. The painting developed into raised levels from the canvas. Gradually the canvas became the base, and the painting was a sculpture. I have never recognized any separation [between painting and sculpture] except one element of dimension." David Smith, "The New Sculpture" (paper, The Museum of Modern Art, New York, February 21, 1952, The Estate of David Smith, Archives, box 11), n.p., published in *David Smith,* ed. Garnett McCoy (New York: Praeger, 1973), 82. It is worth noting that González also started out as a painter.

54. David Smith, "The Language Is Image," *Arts and Architecture*, February 1952, 33.

55. Flora Iakovlevna Syrkina, "Tatlin's Theatre," trans. Mária Julian, in *Tatlin*, ed. Larissa Alekseevna Zhadova (New York: Rizzoli, 1988), 163.

56. See Stanley E. Marcus, *David Smith: The Sculptor and His Work* (Ithaca, NY: Cornell University Press, 1983), 52.

57. See www.pmphoto.to/worlds_fair/wf_tour/theme-1.htm.

58. Marcus, *David Smith: The Sculptor and His Work*, 53.

59. Similarly, Smith later used automotive paint on his sculptures and described "how he built up his paint layers in a way [comparable] to the methods used on automobiles." Albert Marshall, "A Study of the Surfaces of David Smith's Sculpture," in *Conservation Research 1995: Studies in the History of Art* 51, Monograph Series II (Washington, D.C.: National Gallery of Art, 1995), 103.

60. See, for example, Edith Balas, "The Sculpture of Brancusi in the Light of His Rumanian Heritage," *Art Journal* 35, no. 2 (Winter 1975–76): 94–104.

61. This notorious and highly publicized case, played out over several years, determined that the Romanian artist's *Bird in Space* of 1926 was in fact a work of art. On its entry into the U.S., it had incurred an import duty imposed on "articles or wares not specially provided for," as opposed to being considered art, which was defined as "original paintings in oil, mineral, water, or other colors . . . original sculptures or statuary," which entered the country duty-free. See Ann Temkin, "Brancusi and His American Collectors," in *Constantin Brancusi, 1876–1957*, exh. cat. by Friedrich Teja Bach, Margit Rowell, and Temkin (Philadelphia: Philadelphia Museum of Art, 1995), 61–62, 71n91.

62. At an interim point in the process, before the imposition of the import duty was finally overturned, the editor of *The Arts* wrote, "Mr. Brancusi, painful as it may be for him to pay a duty of $4,000, will receive in compensation about $10,000 worth of publicity." Ibid., 62.

63. *Brancusi*, exh. cat. by Roger Vitrac (New York: Brummer Gallery, 1933), n.p.

64. Smith, "The New Sculpture," published in McCoy, *David Smith*, 82.

65. The Estate of David Smith believes the base for *Growing Forms* is a found object, though there is no firm documentation for this. According to Susan Cooke, associate director of the estate, Charles Palmer (the original owner of the cast of *Growing Forms* that is in the LACMA exhibition) didn't like the base and asked Smith to change it. The artist refused. Cooke believes Smith may have found the base at Brummer Gallery in New York, where Brancusi (as well as Smith's friend John Graham) exhibited in the late 1920s and 1930s.
Cooke writes: "Is it possible Brummer fabricated some Brancusi-like wood pedestals for the Brancusi sculptures that were shipped from France? (Pedestals that might have been left over after the show?) Or perhaps Smith was inspired by Brancusi . . . to hew his own wood pedestal. Interestingly, [the estate does] have a photograph of *Growing Forms*, taken at Bolton, probably in the late 1930s, that shows the sculpture set up on a different wood base [but also rough-hewn with modular geometries], which seems to have disappeared." Susan Cooke, email to author, December 8, 2009.
In addition to the *Endless Column* shown in New York in 1926, three other versions were exhibited there in 1933.

66. In considering Brancusi's importance for Smith, it is also worth noting that Smith, like Brancusi, took hundreds of photographs of his own sculptures, both individually and collectively (see fig. 24 and pp. 94–115). Neither artist intended for these photos to be exhibited publicly, yet for both they served as what has been called "a commentary on essential form." See Friedrich Teja Bach, "Brancusi and Photography," in *Constantin Brancusi, 1876–1957*, exh. cat. by Bach et al. (Philadelphia: Philadelphia Museum of Art, 1995), 312.
Photography was also a way of contextualizing the artist's work and helping to show the sculptures in what each artist considered the appropriate light, both literally and figuratively.
It is hard to imagine that Smith was not aware of this parallel between his practice and Brancusi's. For more on Smith's and Brancusi's photographs, see Rosalind E. Krauss, "David Smith's 'New Vision,'" in *David Smith: Photographs, 1931–1965* (New York: Matthew Marks Gallery, 1998), 9–10. See also Christopher Bedford's essay in this volume.

67. David Smith,"Dream," in "Report from Voltri" (manuscript, The Estate of David Smith, Archives), 11, published as "Report on Voltri" in *David Smith*, ed. Garnett McCoy (New York: Praeger, 1973), 161.

68. See E. A. Carmean Jr., *David Smith*, exh. cat. (Washington, D.C.: National Gallery of Art, 1982), 120.

69. Sylvester, "Tape-Recorded Interview with David Smith," reprinted in McCoy, *David Smith*, 173.

70. Smith, "Report from Voltri," 13, published in McCoy, *David Smith*, 162.

71. Vasily Kandinsky, letter to Will Grohmann, October 12, 1930, quoted in *Kandinsky*, exh. cat. by Tracey Bashkoff et al. (New York: Guggenheim Museum, 2009), 240. Of course, Smith's *Circle* series is also specifically indebted to his friend the painter Kenneth Noland; see "The Circles," in Carmean, *David Smith*, 136–39.

72. Bashkoff et al., *Kandinsky*, 10.

73. David Smith, "Notes on My Work," *Arts Magazine*, February 1960, 44, quoted in Gail Levin, "Kandinsky and Abstract Expressionism," in *Theme and Improvisation: Kandinsky and the American Avant-Garde, 1912–1950*, exh. cat. by Levin and Marianne Lorenz for the Dayton Art Institute (Boston: Little, Brown, 1992), 200.

74. David Smith, "Problems of the Contemporary Sculptor" (lecture sponsored by the Metropolitan Art Association, delivered at the Detroit Institute of Arts, January 23, 1952, The Estate of David Smith, Archives), 1. I am grateful to Susan Cooke for this reference.

75. Kandinsky correlated blue with circles, red with squares, and yellow with triangles. See Annegret Hoberg, "Vasily Kandinsky: Abstract. Absolute. Concrete.," 38, 55n64, and also Karole Vail, object entry, 240, in *Kandinsky*, exh. cat., Bashkoff et al. (New York: Guggenheim Museum, 2009).

76. Kandinsky likely used an atomizer for his sprayed watercolors, while Smith used spray cans of automotive enamel for his sprays. See Candida Smith, "Foreword," in *David Smith: Sprays*, exh. cat. (New York: Gagosian Gallery, 2008), n.p.

77. Smith's first show with Marian Willard, shortly before she partnered with Neumann, was in 1938.

78. Donald Judd, "In the Galleries: David Smith," *Arts Magazine*, December 1964, 62. Judd's library at his death in 1994 included fourteen monographs and catalogues on Smith dating from 1959 to 1990; see http://library.juddfoundation.org/JUDDlibsearch/recordlist.php.

79. David Smith, "Second Thoughts on Sculpture," *College Art Journal* 13, no. 3 (Spring 1954): 205.

David Smith: Heavy Metal

Anne M. Wagner

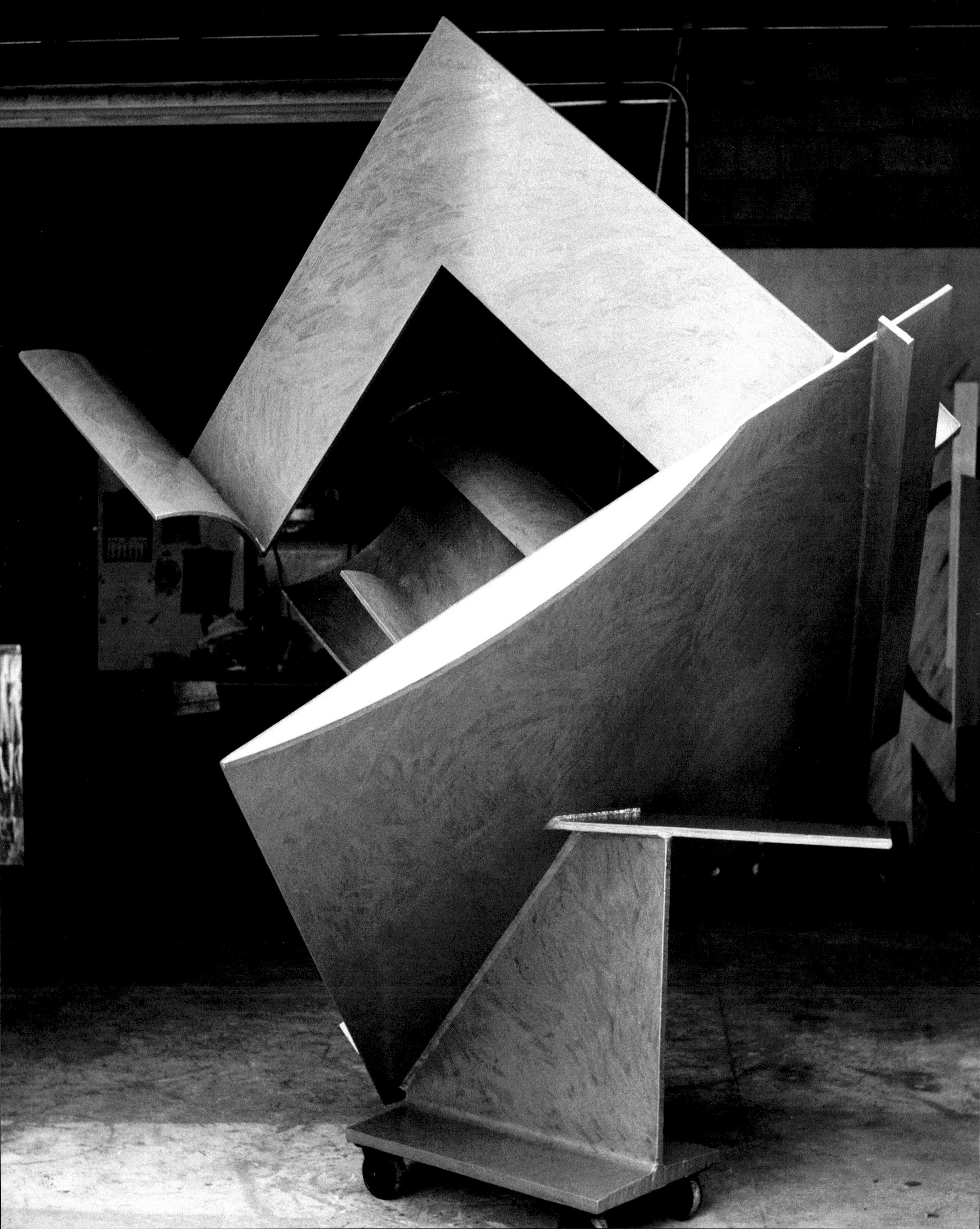

Late in the fall of 1965, the Los Angeles County Museum of Art mounted an exhibition meant to memorialize David Smith. In its planning stages, the aim of the show had been quite different: to present fourteen recent pieces, two *Zigs* (including *Zig IV*, figs. 1, 3) and twelve *Cubis*, all selected by the artist himself. In the end, though, these chosen sculptures were asked, despite the electric animation of their precariously stacked forms and high-speed polish, to eulogize their maker in the wake of his unexpected death. The catalogue too took up the task of mourning, its cover speaking (maybe too portentously) of tragic martyrdom, and its concluding photograph—the artist's welding helmet, still sitting where he had left it in the studio—offering a more subtle and immediate evocation of bodily loss (figs. 2, 4). Think of this valedictory image—taken by LACMA's young head photographer, who was sent east to document the artist's Bolton Landing complex—as Smith's final sculpture, one last construction, in which polished steel volume meets appropriated thing.[1] With its stacked components, this accidental artwork manages both to suggest and to update Constantin Brancusi, not least through the quasi-narrative, even autobiographical, connection between its juxtaposed parts.

This essay aims to clarify the two main plotlines implied by Smith's inadvertent construction: one concerns sculpture as making, while the other takes the maker as its theme. Both Smith's practice and identity as a welder are thus at issue. This seems inevitable; for Smith, identity and practice were one and the same. Moreover, Smith's use of metal and welding was polemical. It not only took a stance toward industrial production as a social and economic reality in the United States at midcentury but also insisted that art is deeply embedded in the technological relations of its time. Smith understood such embedding as necessary to, even definitive of, artistic practice. In this, of course, he was not alone. If Marcel Duchamp's readymades are usually seen as providing the definitive paradigm, a model that seeks to destroy the difference between art and commodity, leveling the terms of their production, then Smith's welded works present the counterargument. His key propositions concern art's relationship to manual labor and technical skill, as defined in twentieth-century industrial terms. For Smith, their complex intersection cannot—must not—be elided, distanced, or destroyed. Nor is the use of mere appropriation (assisted or not) to be understood as offering a sufficient, relevant accounting of how art and industrial production interact. On the contrary, their interaction must be actively embodied, with the physical—that is, bodily—terms of sculpture allowing it to figure art's fraught relation to capitalist management of workers and work. Smith's body of sculpture, we

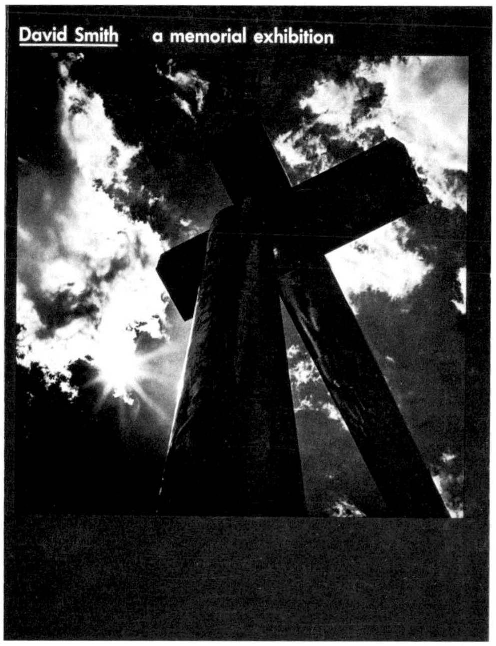

Fig. 2 | Cover of **David Smith: A Memorial Exhibition,** published by the Los Angeles County Museum of Art, 1965

Fig. 1 | **Untitled** (**Zig IV** in workshop doorway, Bolton Landing), c. 1961, The Estate of David Smith

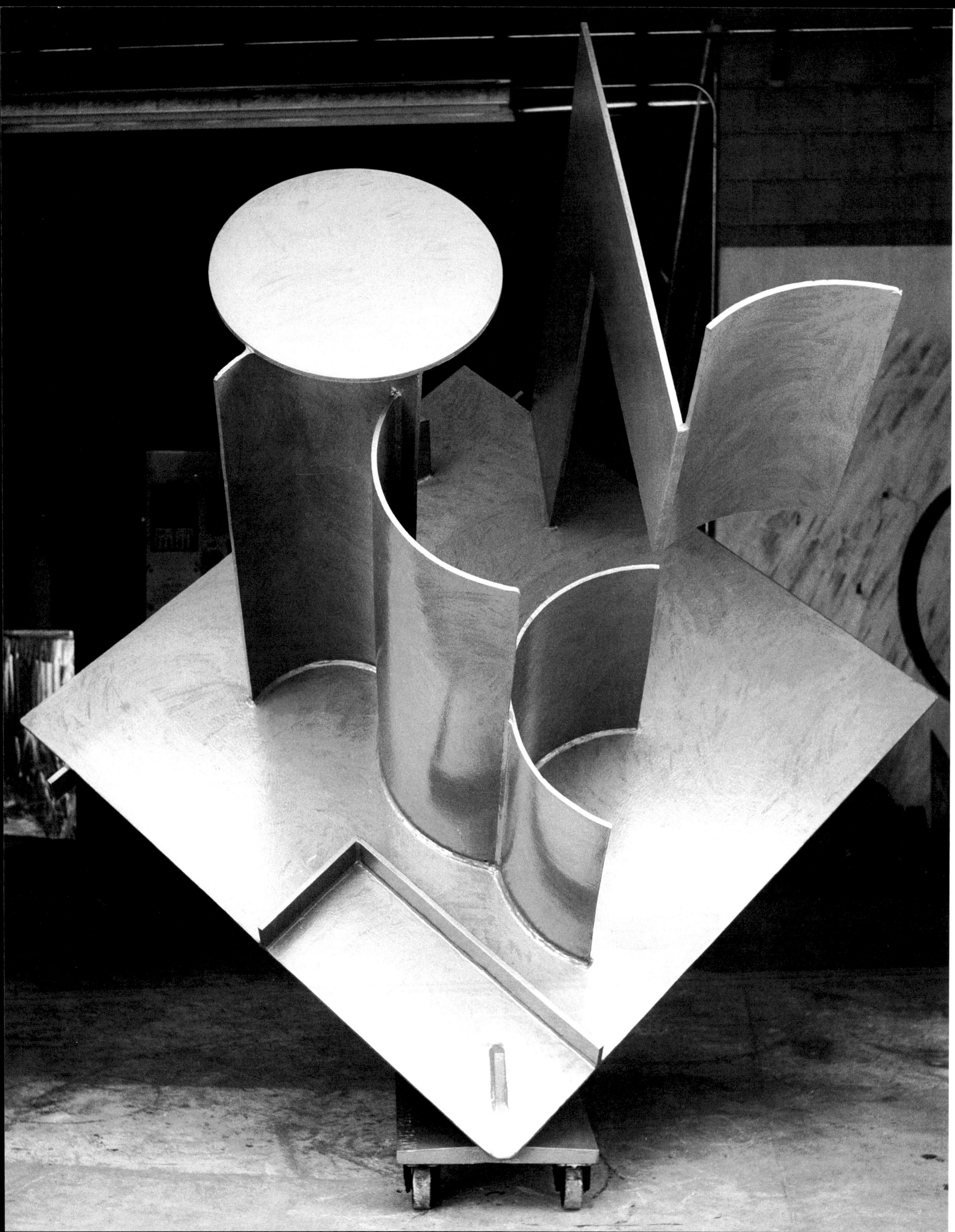

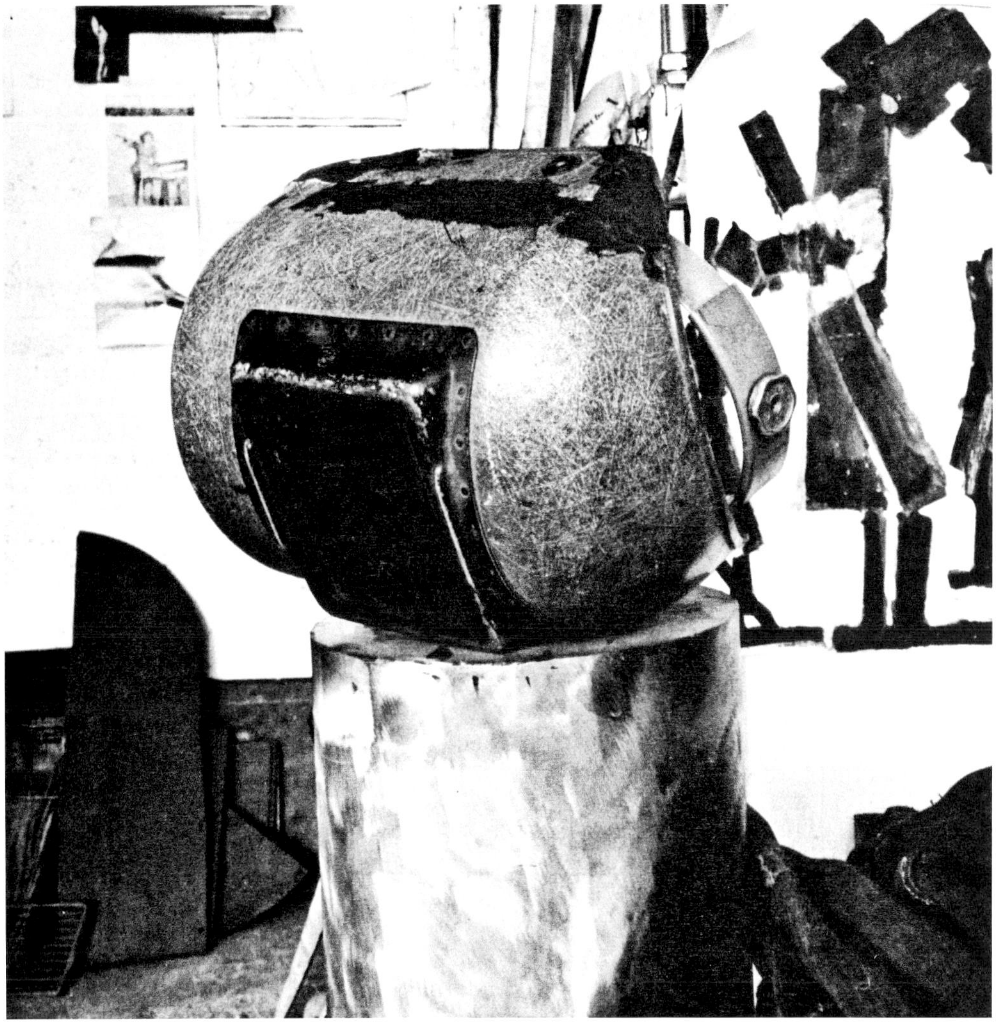

Left: **Fig. 3 | Untitled (Zig IV** in workshop doorway, Bolton Landing), c. 1961, The Estate of David Smith

Above: **Fig. 4 |** The last image in the catalogue for **David Smith: A Memorial Exhibition**, 1965

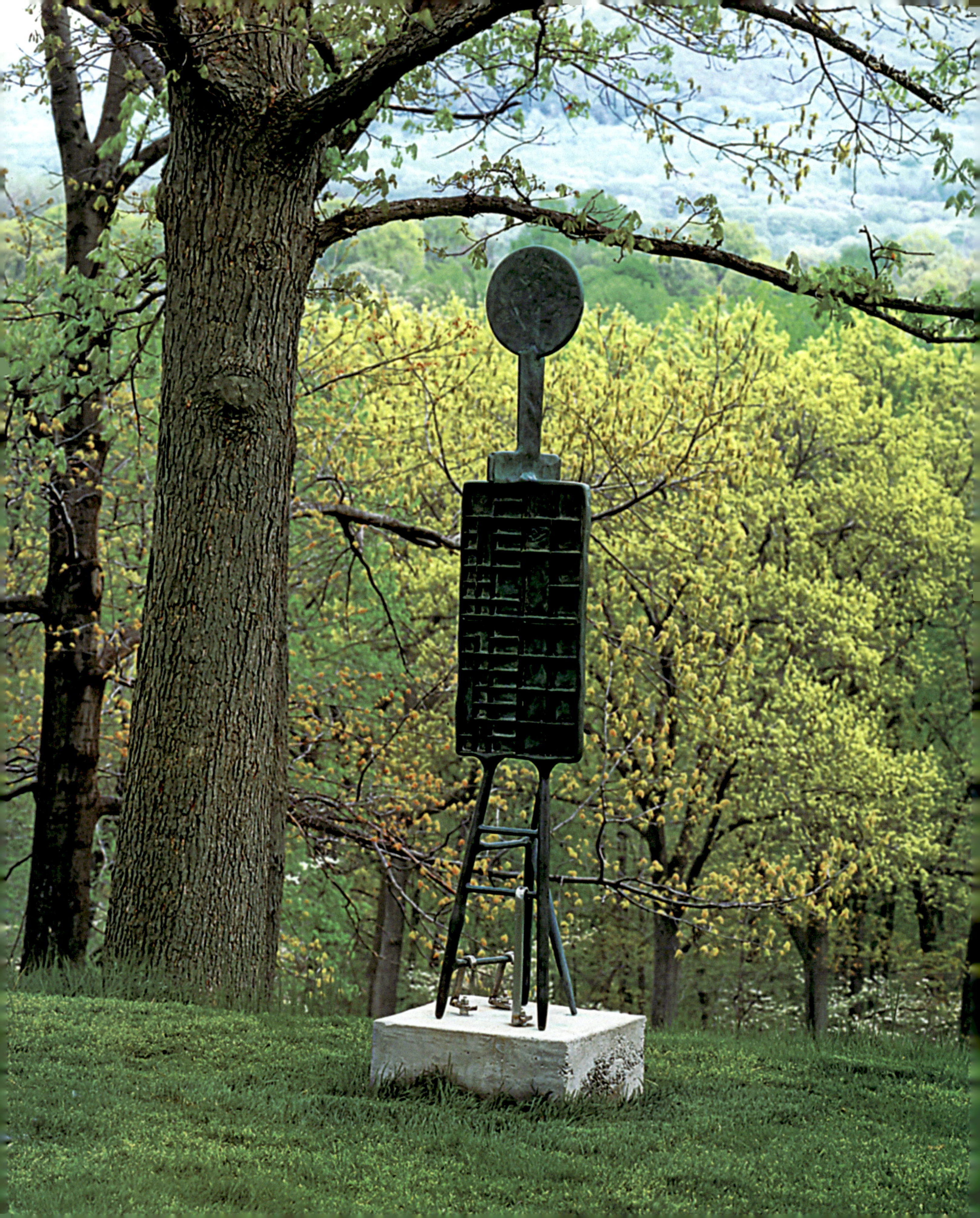

might say, offers a long meditation on everything concealed and revealed by the synecdoche "manual labor." That "everything" includes both class and gender, as well as the fabricating systems that Smith mobilized and to which his work refers.

By "fabricating systems," I have something quite particular in mind. The point I aim to develop here goes beyond the relatively straightforward matter of Smith's sculptural techniques, although I do have something to say about how he made his work and what that making means. If we consider sculpture as a category or medium, however, the stakes start to soar. This is not just because sculpture shares so much with other models of three-dimensional representation: dolls and coins and mannequins and medals and the rest. To mount that argument would be merely to offer a reworked version of the basic thesis presented so succinctly by Svetlana Alpers in *The Art of Describing*: the idea that paintings are firmly nested within picturing systems, by which is meant the full array of representational conventions that govern different image forms—maps, say, or optics, or the photograph.[2] Indeed, the specific techniques at the disposal of pictorial representation—color floated into wet plaster, pigment suspended in an egg or oil medium, ink or charcoal drawing, the acid-bitten lines of an etching—are primarily techniques for picturing. They evolved for this purpose. When painters enter into dialogue with these methods, they speak to their own specific practices, to the tradition of which they are already a part.

Not so with sculpture. To speak of sculpture's relationship to fabricating systems, by contrast, is to insist on its constant dialogue with other forms of manufacture, forms that extend to the whole complex history of making (fig. 5). Even the most basic techniques of three-dimensional forming—fired or unfired clay, cut stone, cast and chased metal, often carefully alloyed—were not developed merely to make sculptures. They are the central *technes* of civilization, the means of the production of a distinctively human world. All worthwhile sculpture resonates against other sculpture, yes, but even more against such landmarks as the brick, the wall, the barrel, the bowl, the column, the coffin, the hand ax, the howitzer, the missile, and the microchip. It involves a range of reference that covers and collapses the enormous material and temporal range of sculpted form.

The fabricating systems addressed by sculpture encompass hands and tools, machines and factories, gardens and buildings, craft and industry, munitions and warfare. They may envy and emulate movement yet are always artificial, although their artifice often involves

Fig. 5 | The Sitting Printer, 1954–55, Storm King Art Center, Mountainville, New York

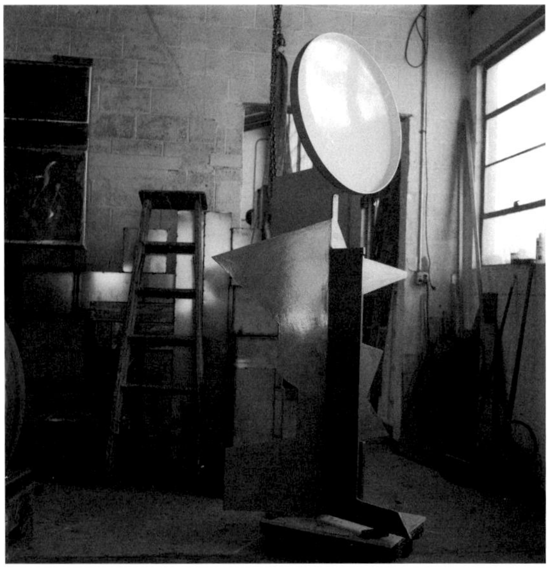

Fig. 6 | Untitled (4/28/61, Bolton Landing workshop), 1961, The Estate of David Smith

concealing their tricks. Finally, the social worlds such systems construct or imagine—particularly how they are addressed in twentieth-century sculpture—need not be found in contemporary capitalism, even if capitalism necessarily provides the main containing frame.

This essay seeks to show what Smith's commitment to welding metal meant on at least some of these fronts, as doing so helps to suggest what being a modern American artist could convey to those who, like Smith, self-consciously embraced that role. Let us begin with the most basic physical fact of sculpture, the sculptor's own body, because it is the catalyst of the operations that bring any sculpture to be. More than twenty years ago, in a book about the nineteenth-century French sculptor Jean-Baptiste Carpeaux, I dissected the various processes of education and acculturation that generated both workers and sculptors from the same social roots.[3] Their training was identical, up to a point, with the differences between them emerging in the making, so to speak. Success and failure first opened, then widened, the gap. But it was the industrialization of production initially accomplished in Carpeaux's studio (and then elaborated upon in Auguste Rodin's) that pulled worker and artist even further apart. In the later nineteenth century, sculpture embraced its inherent reproductive potential with a vengeance, whether as "ceramics" in the case of Carpeaux's workshop or in Rodin's by ringing mechanically enabled changes on materials and scale: this is why Rodin's employee Henri Lebossé was so valuable; he was a past master of the pointing machine.

In this newly commodified context, the obligatory physical work of the paid laborer allowed the artist to develop not just products but a brand. The new division of labor inevitably minimized the artist's bodily contribution. He merely supervised the development of monumental versions of smaller compositions or vice versa. Yet the same means of delegation and specialization paradoxically made the signature effects of artistry—its bravura treatment of touch and surface, whether in bronze or marble—more widely available in the whole gamut of reproductions in circulation as the artist's work. In other words, the artist's employees did what was necessary to duplicate both the master's compositions and the signature effects of his hand. It was only in the early years of the twentieth century that the widespread erasure of the physical labor of sculpture yielded to its active embrace—or better, its repossession—as assertively the artist's own. Under these new protocols of production, an artist (take Henri Gaudier-Brzeska, for one founding twentieth-century example) could celebrate modern technology as an avowed futurist, a blaster, yet still present himself as the hands-on carver of declaredly primitivizing works.

Enter David Smith.[4] In him such paradoxes apparently were resolved. Now fitted with everything necessary—torch, gloves, protective headgear—the sculptor assumed a new role. The transformation was total, so much so that his helmet became a part of him, like an attribute or an auxiliary organ. No wonder there are so many photos of Smith as a welder, though in them he inevitably seems to lack what Freud called the "true magnificence" that machine-age prostheses suggest yet too seldom provide.[5] When the torch was turned off, Smith returned to mere mortality, lifting his visor as automatically as we park our sunglasses on top of our heads. It was a long-standing habit; the goggles he wore in the 1930s and 1940s met the same treatment, the better to ensure their workaholic wearer a prompt return to his self-appointed task. If goggles and helmet are signs of the welder, their omnipresence reminds us that Smith's commitment to welding was complete.[6]

It isn't difficult to establish how much Smith invested in his technique, not monetarily, though he did insist (in a text composed in 1951) on "the best material [and] the finest tools and equipment."[7] "Every labor-saving machine, every safety device," he continued, was an absolute necessity, and his hoard of tools and materials was a matter of pride (fig. 6). In fact, he drew up a list—which he surely would have wanted quoted at length, preferably against the backdrop of studio photos like those shot by the young Ed Cornachio on the occasion of the 1965 LACMA show: "Stocks of bolts, nuts, taps, dies, paints, solvents, acids, protective coatings, oils, grinding wheels, polishing discs, dry pigments, waxes, chemicals, spare machine parts." All this was "kept stocked on steel shelving," he wrote, "more or less patterned after a factory stockroom." But there was more: "Stainless steel, bronze, copper, aluminum, are stocked in 1/8 inch by 4 foot by 8 foot sheets for fabricating. Cold and hot rolled 4 foot by 8 foot sheets are stacked outside the shop in thicknesses from 1/8 inch to 7/8 inch." And finally: "Lengths of strips, shapes, and bar stock are racked in the basement of the house or interlaced in the joists of the roof." To this Smith added, with more than a little self-knowledge, "Maybe I brag a bit about my stock." Maybe so.

Smith's list is the closest we will ever come to that art-historical treasure trove, a written inventory of his studio contents, and as such it preceded his death by fourteen years.[8] By then much had undoubtedly changed. We know that the stocks that survived him were promptly dispersed by Clement Greenberg, executor of the estate, with the artists Anthony Caro and Kenneth Noland both beneficiaries of Greenberg's misplaced largesse.[9] Yet this sorry fate doesn't exhaust the interest of Smith's materials. Understanding them is essential to grasping the fabricating systems to which Smith's work belongs.

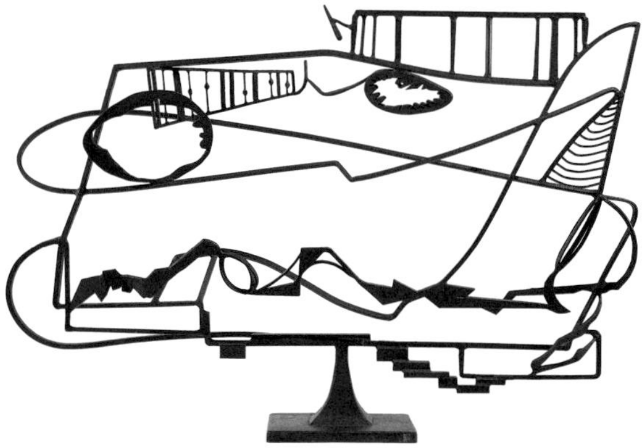

Fig. 7 | Hudson River Landscape, 1951, painted steel and stainless steel, 49 15/16 x 73 3/4 x 16 9/16 in. (126.8 x 187.3 x 42.1 cm), Whitney Museum of American Art, New York, purchase

To speak of those systems in the context of twentieth-century sculpture is, as already suggested, to address its unsteady relationship to the commodity and its origins in capitalism. This is a relationship of which Smith was well aware. Indeed, he chose his materials with those implications in mind. He used iron and steel almost exclusively, sometimes equating them ("the material called iron or steel"), though elsewhere dwelling on steel in particular because it is simultaneously versatile, resilient, and strong—and much more besides. Consider another Smith list: "Steel can be stainless, painted, lacquered, waxed, processed, and electroplated with molybdenum. It can be cast . . . it can bend cold . . . it can be drawn, cupped, spun, and forged . . . it can be cut and patterned, chiseled, ground, filed, and polished. It can be welded, the seams ground down leaving no evidence."[10] But steel and its parent iron really attracted him because, as he put it, "What associations it possesses are those of this century: power, structure, movement, progress, suspension, destruction, brutality."[11] This chain of connotations was forged in an essay of 1952. It would be hard to assemble a more historically apposite list, or one that applies so well to Smith's own work.

There can be no denying that, as Smith used them, welding and metal were synonymous with modernity, and with his modernism. "Being called a modernist, an abstractionist, and admitting to an advanced conception in aesthetics," he wrote, he was "forced" to find a method to meet his needs.[12] Welding was that method, because its flexible and pragmatic utility lent itself to abstraction almost eagerly. Its main limitations are conceptual rather than structural: parts can be joined in any logic that works. The body need not impose the template to which the sculptural object must conform. Space becomes visible as mass disappears. *Hudson River Landscape* (fig. 7) is the perennial paradigm of this achievement, and deservedly so. Its effects of speed and movement (the product, as Karen Wilkin puts it, of Smith's "compressing, dissecting vision") have little to do with nature, despite their landscape theme.[13] Instead, they speak of a world seen at a distance from the windows of a train, not once but journey after journey, each time moving fast enough for details to give way to sensations whose sculpted counterparts evoke something more volatile than place. "When I make sculpture," Smith wrote, "all the speeds, projections, gyrations, light changes are involved in my vision, as such things I know in movement associate with all the possibilities possible in other relationships."[14] The "possibilities possible" in *Hudson River Landscape* (which, like his declaration, dates from 1951) are a frictionlessness, an efficiency, that override its moments of circularity and stasis, as if to erase the artist's concentrated labor in favor of a dream of what labor can do. "Power, structure, movement, progress, suspension"—all these remain. Given the sheer energy of this sculpture, it seems important to remember that Smith also said that welding served him so well as a process because its demands were well matched to his muscles and height. In other words, welded works can invoke, even celebrate, the body of the maker (his strength, his endurance), even though they needn't represent a body at all. And power and movement were qualities that Smith wanted his body to have.

We are right to conclude that Smith's body conducted its own dialogue with the fabricating systems on which his work relied. This is one reason why it is worth recalling how Smith acquired his skills. Learning to weld gave him access to industrial production in more than a merely instrumental way. Welding actively shaped the man Smith came to be.

The process was slow. It started in 1925, with a summer spent riveting, soldering, and spot welding at the Studebaker auto plant in South Bend, Indiana. Smith was nineteen, an aspiring painter, and still lived at home. He took the job, he said, strictly for the money, which would allow him to move to New York. Nine years later, he found studio space in Brooklyn, a rental that famously gave him access to a foundry, Terminal Iron Works. The studio came with the added benefit of a "men-only" saloon down the street, which for him served as both a watering hole and a classroom: the regulars were a gold mine when it came to techniques and methods, he said (fig. 8). During the six years he kept a studio in Brooklyn, he was able to mount his first solo show (a presentation of abstract and figural constructions that failed to sell).[15]

The last stage in what I am casting as Smith's bodily transformation began in 1942, a few months after the U.S. entered World War II. To avoid being drafted, Smith took a job at the American Locomotive Company in Schenectady, New York, assembling locomotives, M7 tanks, and tank destroyers. Unlike anything he had yet attempted, this was real labor, at the full-on pace required by mobilization for war. He had

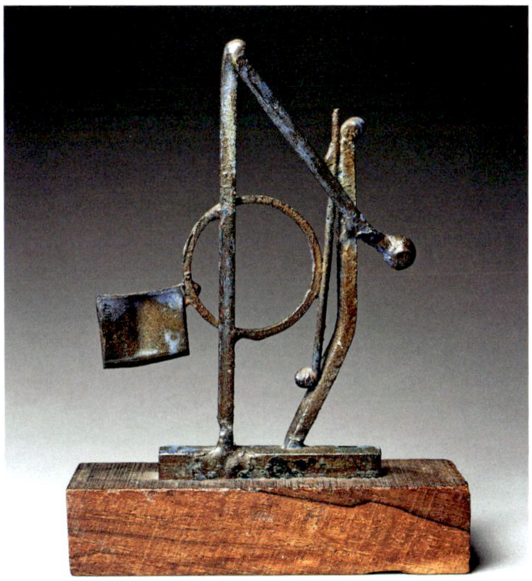

Fig. 8 | Untitled, 1938, private collection

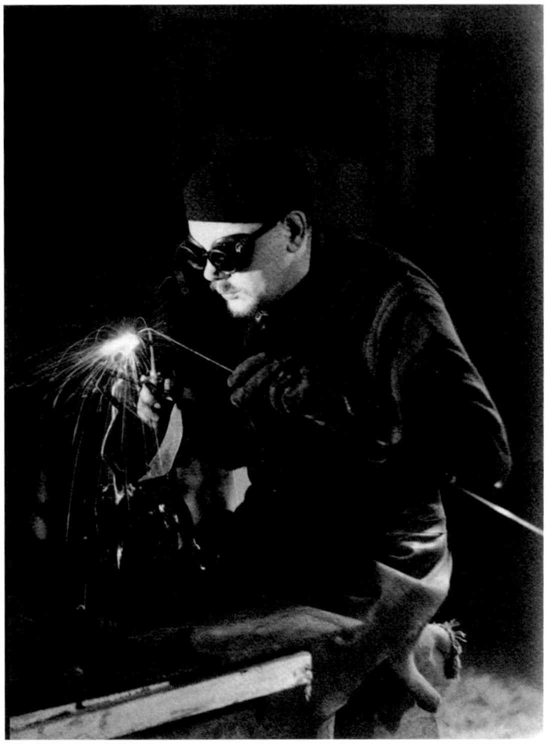

Fig. 9 | Smith welding, 1940

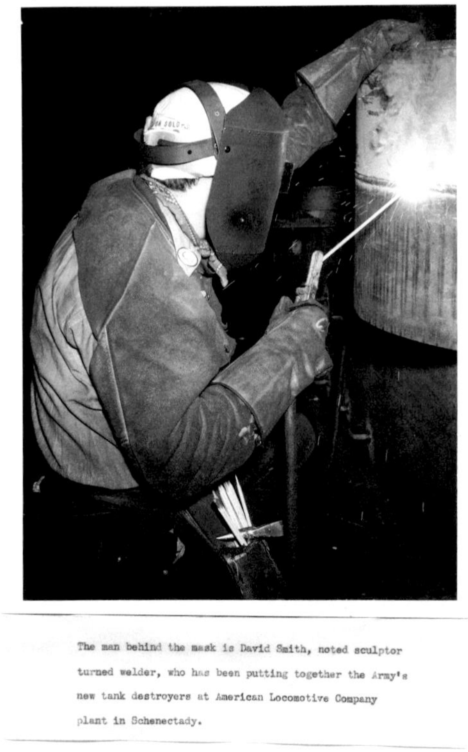

Fig. 10 | Smith welding at the American Locomotive Company, 1942

a lot to learn and fast, including how to look and act the part. It didn't help that the propaganda machine (in this case the World Wide Photo Agency) followed him into the factory, producing images that seemed bent on underscoring the notion that (in the words of the caption that accompanied them) the "noted sculptor turned welder" was different from everyone else. As indeed he was, until his coworkers waylaid him and forcibly shaved off the raffish goatee he had sported for the last eighteen years.[16]

A man's man—a worker—was born. The before-and-after pictures show the difference: look at 1942 versus 1940 (figs. 9, 10).[17] No more scraggly beard, no more welding, as sometimes happened, while wearing a sweater and tie. The incident was more than a hazing, though. It enforced a masculinity in keeping with the norms of the factory system. The transformation again reminds us of Smith as a version of the twentieth-century prosthetic god. Fully dressed in his regalia, he is protected from the myriad risks of a hostile environment, especially the ones posed to his bodily self (risks that the young Richard Serra would later so aggressively flaunt).

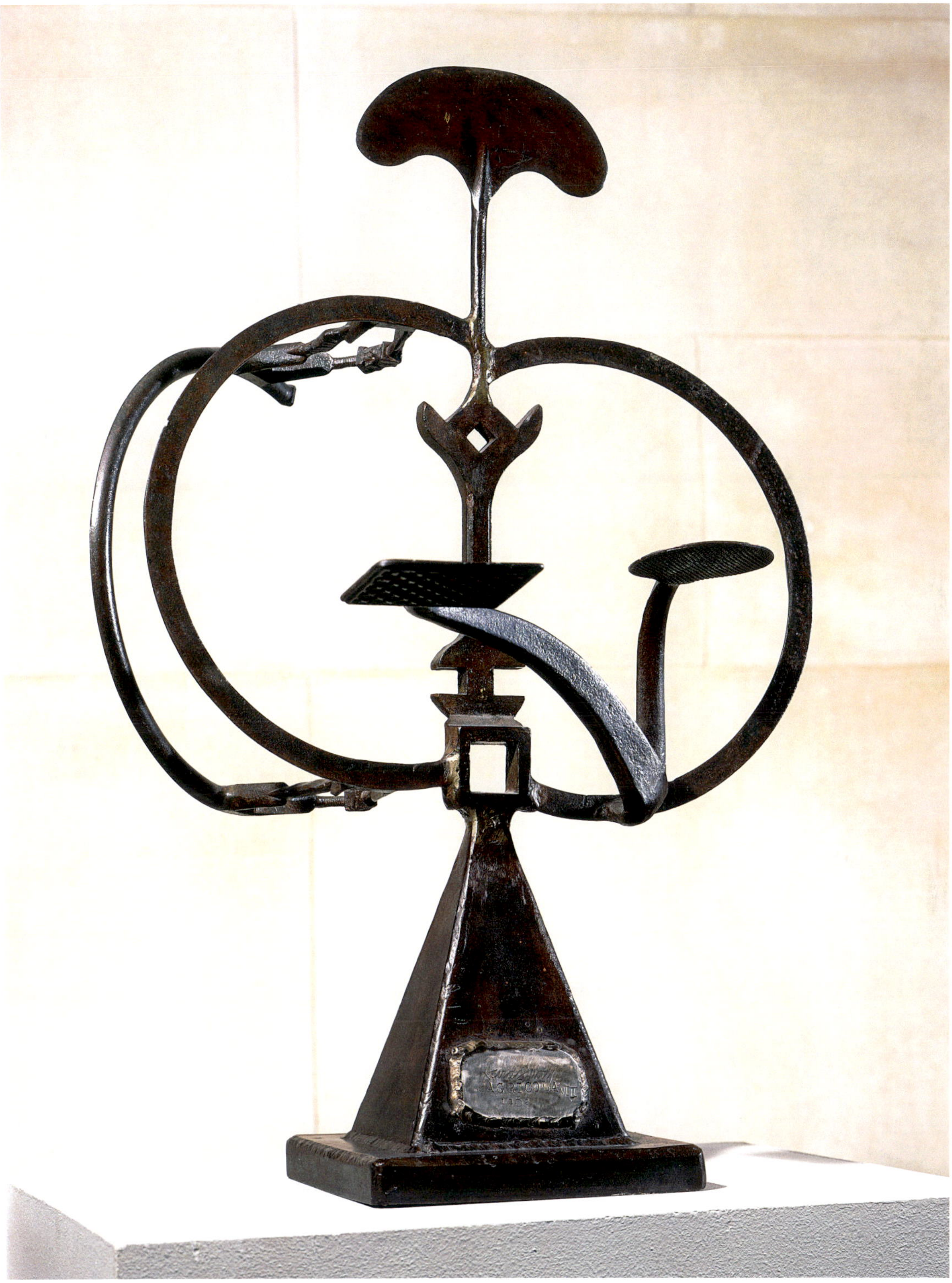

Fig. 11 | Agricola VIII, 1952, steel and bronze, painted,
31 3/4 x 21 1/4 x 18 3/4 in. (80.6 x 53.9 x 47.6 cm),
The Estate of David Smith, courtesy Tate, London

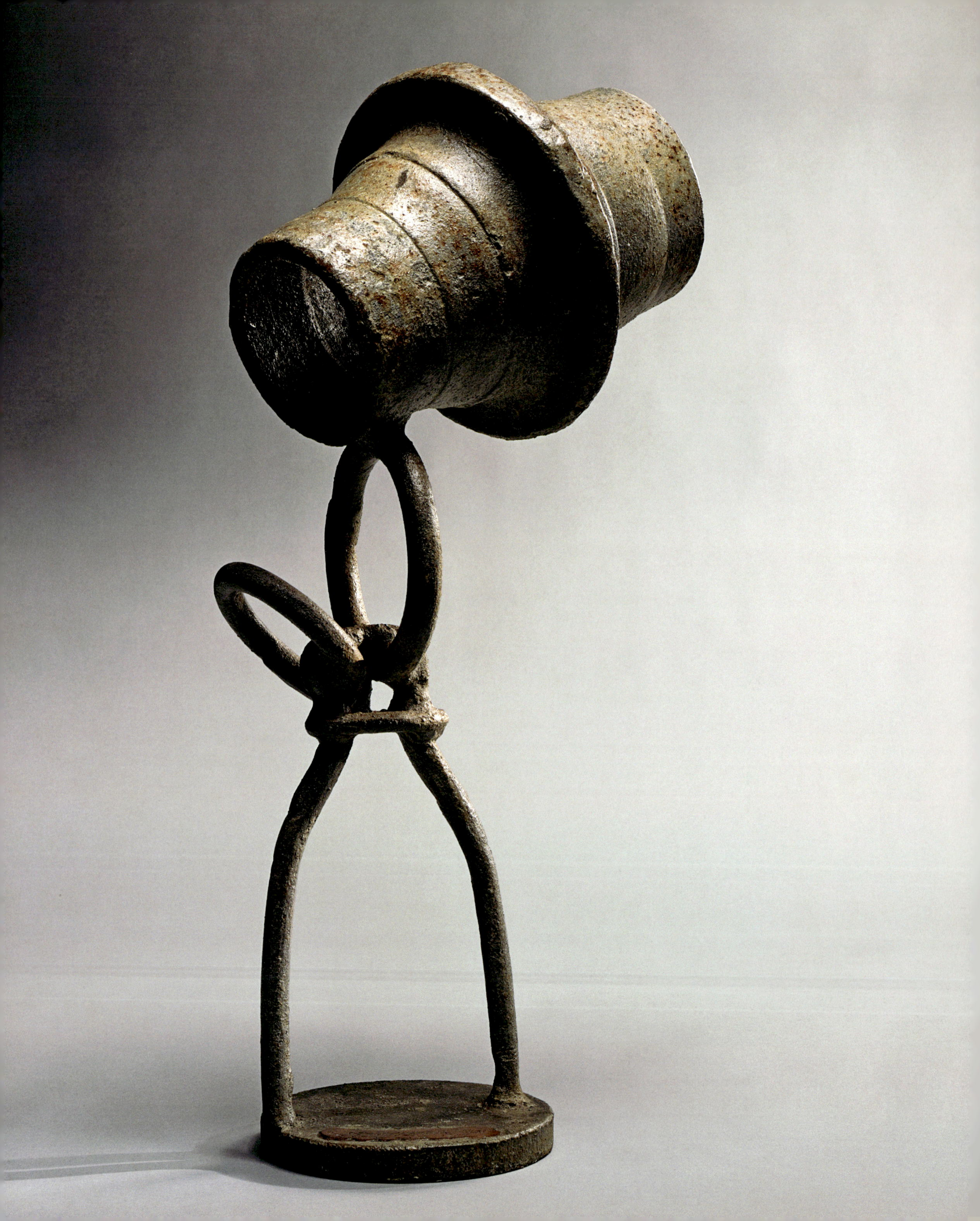

It was in the wake of Smith's contributions to the war effort that a self-conscious dedication to a program and its necessary procedures began to emerge. From this point forward, and not before, he began to insist on his sculpture's intersections with both industrial and preindustrial fabrication, and to assert them as his crucial themes. The question that remains is how. For purposes of argument—an argument that insists Smith's work ought to be seen as offering a counterproposal to the readymade—it seems right to limit the discussion to sculptures that visibly integrate prefabricated elements, such as a piece or pieces of cast-off metal. In the case of *Agricola VIII* (1952, fig. 11), these range from the wrench that serves as the sculpture's stem or center to the square gasket from which spring its arcing pieces, and on to the two pedals or plates that reach out toward the viewer. Most notably, there is also the elegant, crestlike blade—perhaps a weeder or chopper—atop the whole. Or look at *Agricola IX* (1952, p. 131), whose most dramatic elements are the eight arms or branches (they may be made from connecting rods plundered from old farm machinery) that bristle or gesture above their zigzagging support. Ultimately, perhaps what they do is play: in a notebook jotting, Smith termed them "eight notes."[18] In any event, they have an aggressive aliveness belied by the work's title. But might both the works and their titles be less pastoral than we think? Plowshares and swords go together: as told by the historian Tacitus, Agricola was one of Rome's great generals. It was he who finally subdued the warlike Britons, leaving, as Tacitus wrote, a desert in his wake. They made a desert and called it peace. To look at the cannonlike "head" of *Agricola XVII* (1957, fig. 12) is to be offered a narrative of how subjugation can be brought about, and to hear Smith saying again of steel, "It is also brutal, the rapist, the murderer, and death-dealing giants are also its offspring."[19] A similar race of giants seems to be remembered in this group of works.

All of these sculptures are part of a series that Smith began in 1951, a series that transformed an appropriative practice begun in the early 1930s with works like *Saw Head* (see p. 22), and then sustained and expanded it through the later 1950s and beyond. Here, *Tanktotem VII* and *Tanktotem IX* (figs. 13, 14) are key cases in point. The works deploy bits and pieces of outdated machines and implements; Smith was an avid collector of such castoffs—fragments of a bygone America—and not only as potential materials piled outdoors in an ever-growing heap. Displayed on the walls of both his house and studio, they hovered uncertainly between a possible future as part of an artwork and a life being savored as forms in themselves. Meanwhile, clippings

Fig. 12 | Agricola XVII, 1957, steel, 24 1/4 x 8 1/2 x 11 1/4 in. (61.6 x 21.6 x 28.6 cm), The Estate of David Smith

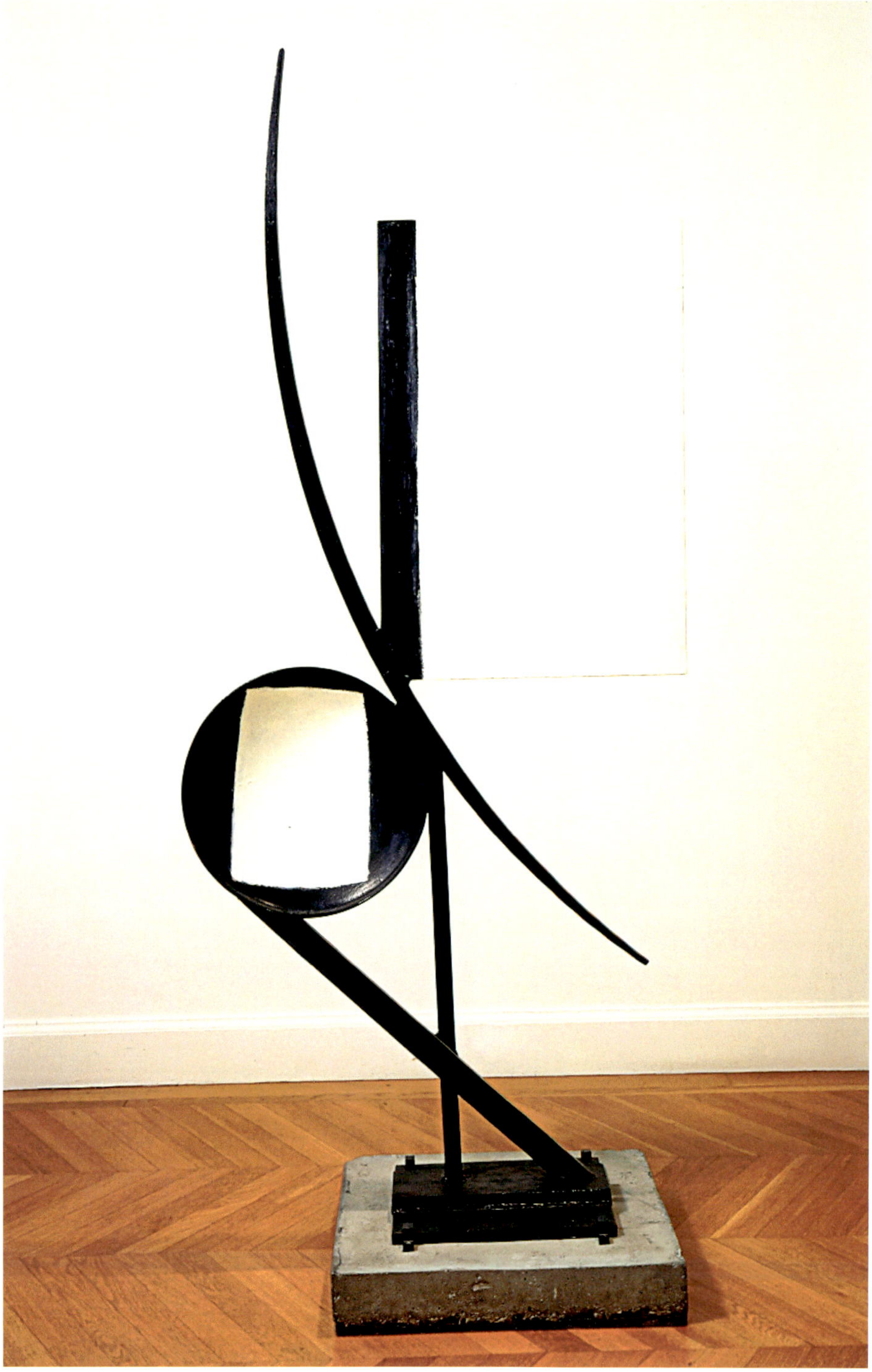

Fig. 13 | Tanktotem VII, 1960, Storm King Art Center, Mountainville, New York

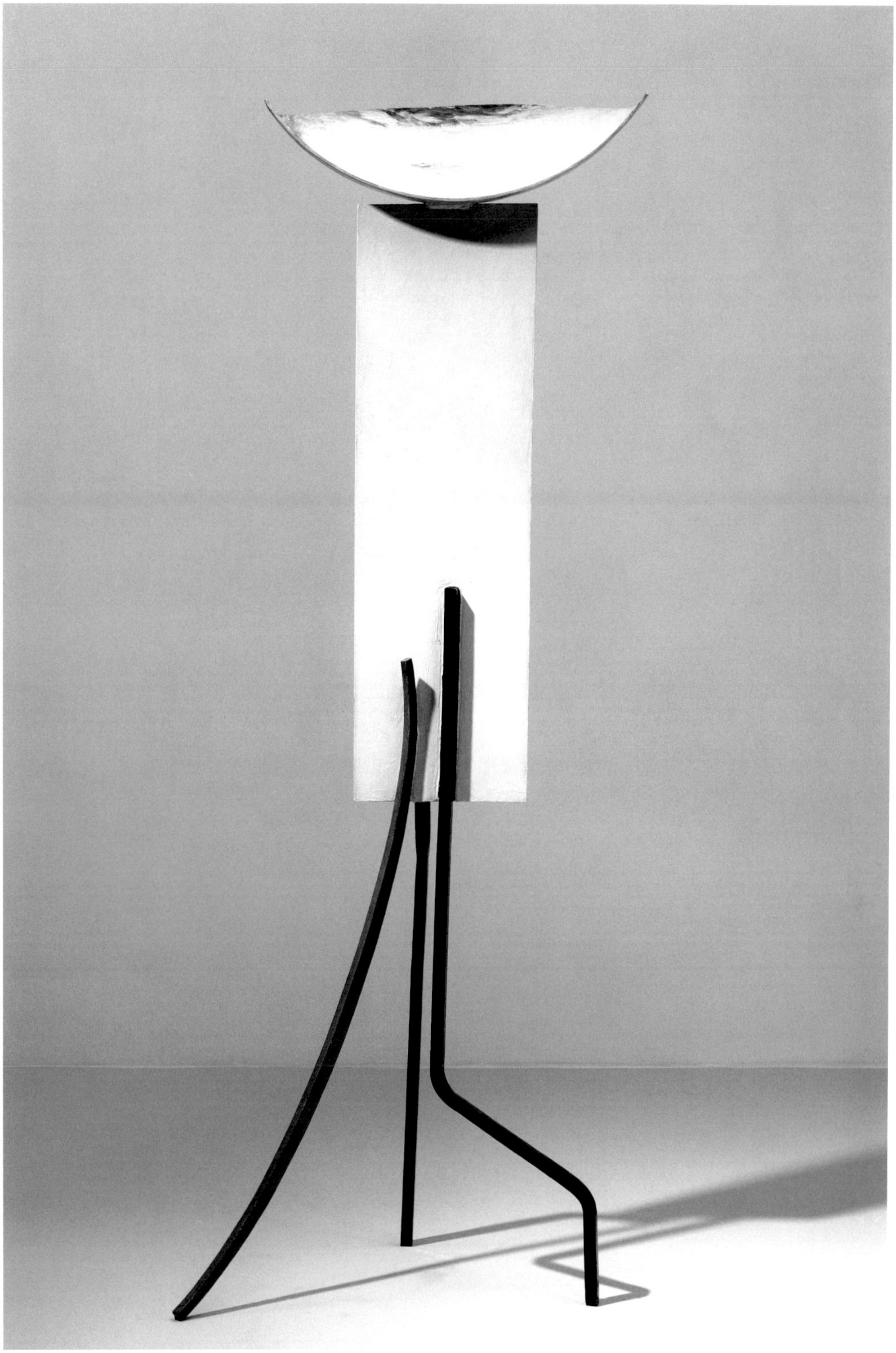

Fig. 14 | Tanktotem IX, 1960, The Estate of David Smith

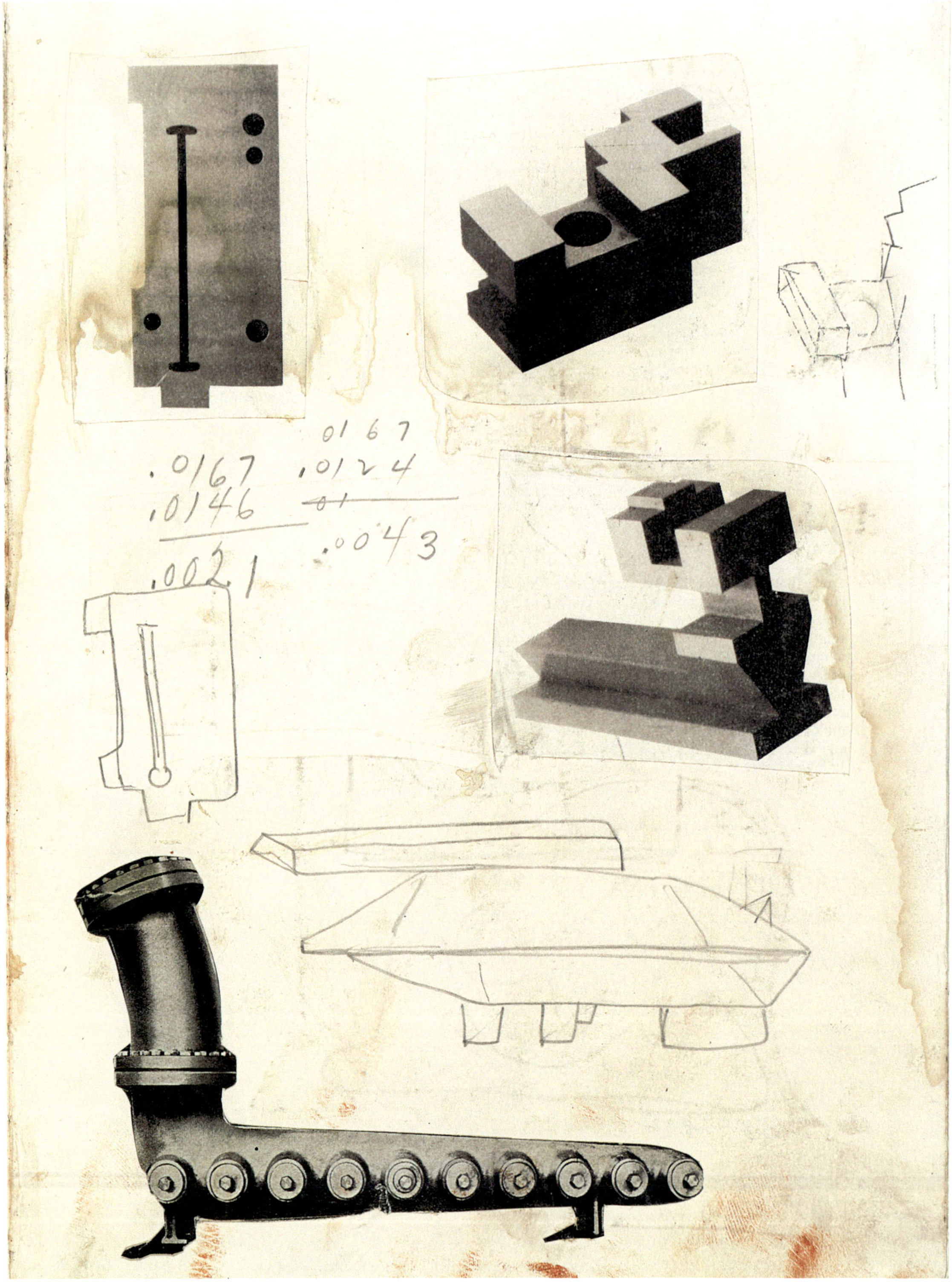

Fig. 15 | Page from Sketchbook #23, 1933–45, pencil and collage on paper, 10 1/2 x 8 in. (26.7 x 20.3 cm), The Estate of David Smith

pasted into a sketchbook assemble the machines of the present in a bestiary of behemoths, mutant offspring generated by an impossible union of present and past (fig. 15).

Smith's interest in utilitarian elements, both old and new, reflected his strong appreciation for the labor of others. He knew what had gone into the making of most metal objects because he could make them himself. By 1947, a process that began in 1942 with his struggle to meet the pressure of factory labor (his technical skills then had been so spotty that he enrolled in thirty-two hours of after-work classes on the "design and properties of welds and welded structures")[20] ended with him coming to understand the great fact of production under capitalism and the eventual fate of the skills he and other workers had acquired at such cost. The machinery the welder assembled—machinery, he said, "which rolls our present-day industrial culture"—inevitably will be discarded, the victim of wear or obsolescence or both. With it would go the evidence of the welder's role in production, the labor that represents mastery of its own set of skills. This is where sculpture, particularly welded sculpture, comes in. When the age of tanks and locomotives ended, sculpture would preserve what welding once achieved. Smith knew that obsolescence was inevitable, but he thought of welded sculpture as both a quintessential product of its moment and a means to preserve and display not a product or commodity but the skilled labor that brought it to be.[21] In so doing, welded sculpture testifies to skills, to livelihoods and life-worlds that, as Smith recognized, capitalism makes use of so as to leave behind. Under these conditions, artwork and archive are one. The studio thus becomes a site of both production and conservation, a place of safety for skills once so valuable to the laborers of the past.

Smith's ambitions for welding also extended to the *Tanktotems* and *Cubis*, which so brilliantly assimilate and exploit their prefabricated parts in increasingly seamless and integrated invocations of bodily structures, or in the case of the *Cubis*, as structured bodies in themselves. Standardization becomes difference in his hands. Looking at Smith's rows and piles of waiting materials,[22] who would not be reminded of the notorious claim put forward twenty-five years ago by the Belgian art historian and theorist Thierry de Duve? Namely, that with the advent of the paint tube—the industrially standardized production and consumption of pigments hitherto artisanally prepared—the status of painting as original is irrevocably changed.[23] For the first time in history, the artwork is created from standard colors for which the name of the manufacturer, not the artist, stands as guarantee.

There is no question that Smith would have grasped this new condition as a decisive historical circumstance. "In this industrial age," he wrote in 1947, "it is only natural that art utilize the advance of industry."[24] We should be careful how we interpret this statement. If your hackles start rising when you hear the word *natural*, or you imagine Smith means *progress* when he says *advance*, think again. His welding goggles were not tinted rose. And though his sympathies lay with the worker, he certainly recognized his own privileged difference as both the creator and producer of the objects he made. This, for him, was the chief benefit the artist enjoyed. None of this stopped him from championing an understanding of labor as skill, however. Unlike Duchamp, he was not prepared to relate to fabricating systems as the consumer does. He understood the logic of the commodity, he just refused to let it govern his work.

These beliefs address the readymade, and it is worth tuning in to what they say. For Smith, sculpture was a site, maybe even a theater, in which the havoc wrought by industrialization under capitalism could be repaired. If the deskilling demanded by the production line involves a stripping away of subjectivity in favor of automatized behavior, then Smith's weldings resupply subjectivity in spades. Skill—something he both depicts and demonstrates—involves mind, eye, and hand. It is idiosyncratic and individualized yet utterly alert to both the most basic laws of physics and the subtlest principles of interrelationship and form. Above all, it is skill materialized in the making, with the result that words can never match or capture precisely what welding has done, how we read or respond to its assembly of parts.

In such a system, the appropriated elements seem both present and absent. They are both physical facts and a means of *poesis,* along the lines of those connecting rods, which evoke a world of gauges and measurement now misaligned. This is what Smith has to say to the readymade. He speaks of an artwork that is both the living embodiment of skilled labor and the site where such labor can be remembered. To grasp that his welded constructions, each one physically unique and nonreproducible, remake the routinized rhythms of industrial production as sculpture is to see the terms of his modernism laid bare. Face-to-face with the possibilities that stem from reparation and remembering, doesn't the so-often-repeated formula of the readymade look, well, ready made?

To ask this question is to address a set of familiar critical allegiances, which is certainly part of my point. No one can deny the force of the challenge issued by Duchamp's *In Advance of the Broken Arm* (1915, fig. 16). Smith accomplishes something that Duchamp does not attempt, however. He forces us to imagine his efforts as having parallels in the world of work, and in so doing makes the world of objects seem new. There's a family resemblance between the two kinds of labor, between the worlds of artistic and utilitarian production, and, as Smith's viewers, we are obliged to consider the connotations of the various models of manufacture his objects put on view. A readymade is something else again: a changeling, an impostor, a cuckoo hatched in art's borrowed nest. Henceforth, it promises, artists need never work again. Art becomes a service, not a skill. For many twentieth-century artists, this seemed an impossible—and unpalatable—sacrifice. To surrender art as a physical making, a bodily doing, was just too great a loss. And no work of art, no matter how withdrawn or understated, can avoid being seen as a making, a doing, and measured as such. Except the readymade, that is, or so it hopes. Yet in so unquestioningly subscribing to the logic, or magic, of the commodity, its seamless mimicry manages to erase utterly the labor that produced the appropriated object it makes use of, while overvaluing the interest, to say nothing of the political relevance, of the artist's exercise of consumerist choice.

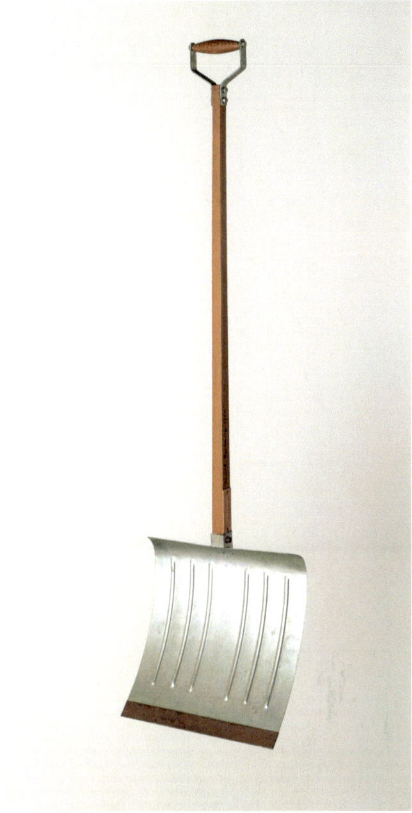

Fig. 16 | Marcel Duchamp, **In Advance of the Broken Arm**, 1964 (after lost 1915 original), wood and galvanized-iron snow shovel, 52 in. (132 cm) high, The Museum of Modern Art, New York, gift of the Jerry and Emily Spiegel Family Foundation

I am not suggesting that Smith's relation to fabricating systems is the only model or protocol to which an artist can productively adhere. His work may well be open to the charge that it revels a bit too enthusiastically in the complexity and idiosyncrasy allowed by his mastery of industrial technique. If the readymade magically conjures away labor, does Smith's own sleight of hand not overlook or erase the standardization of skills and movements to which the factory worker was forced to conform? The *Cubis* in particular raise this question, precisely because they so clearly set themselves the task of working with standard units, only to obscure the overlap among them by high-wire and high-energy performances of balance—or imbalance; it's hard to say which.[25]

As the standard story tells it, minimalism did away with all that. Its cubes are earthbound, even flattened, clinging like Carl Andre's metal pavements to the gallery floor. Or they are replaced by Dan Flavin's fluorescent fixtures, the Duchamp aesthetic having once more saved the day. Yet whether stacked or supine, minimalism's chosen components (though I really should say its chosen or expressly manufactured components) direct attention to themselves *as made*. This is

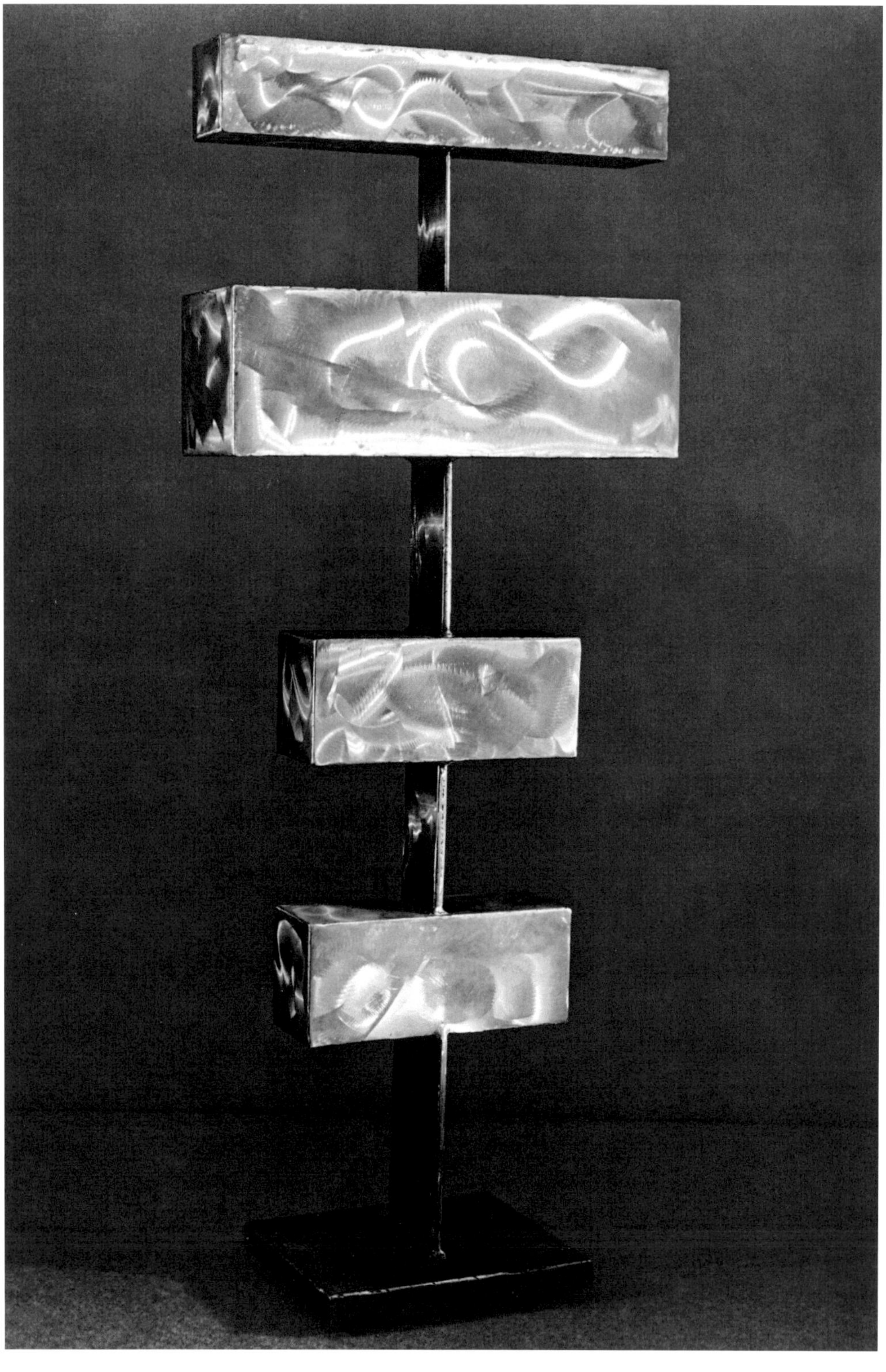

Fig. 17 | Four Units Unequal, 1960, Frederick R. Weisman Art Foundation, Los Angeles

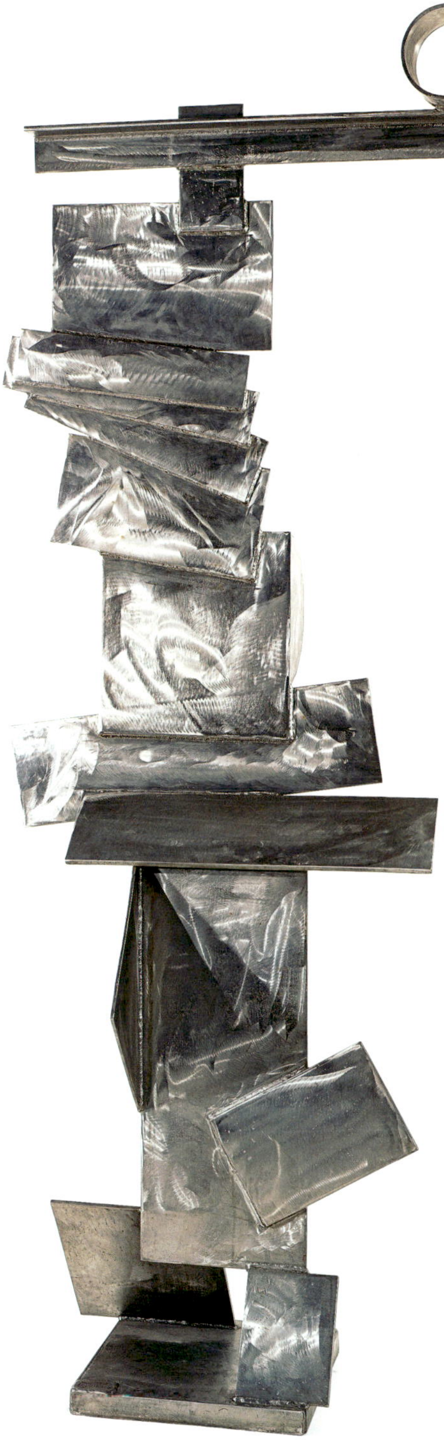

Fig. 18 | Lectern Sentinel, 1961, Whitney Museum of American Art, New York

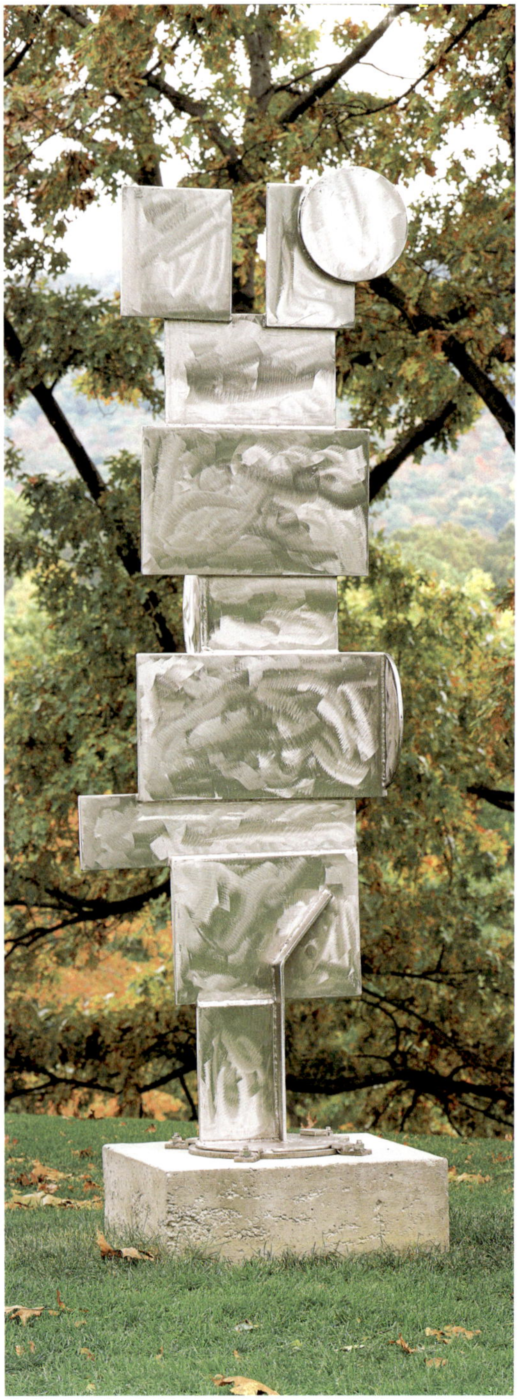

Fig. 19 | XI Books III Apples, 1959, Storm King Art Center, Mountainville, New York

one reason why, despite all the minimalist objects that soon enough succeeded it, Robert Morris's 1961 *Box with the Sound of Its Own Making* remains a crucial work. If Smith had made the box, though, the "making" of the title would have stood not for making alone, for literal process, but for skill itself. For minimalism, skill does not matter, though labor certainly does. Minimalism does not pretend the commodity doesn't exist, but it also does not turn its back on industrial production, and in this it shares more with Smith than at first we might think. It too is another effort to find a way around the commodity via modes of production that require and remember the simplest of structures and structural components, basic units and volumes, the wall and the floor (figs. 17–19). Next to Smith, minimalism always will seem primitive, but even its primitivizing was as astute and relevant a response to its historical moment as Smith's love for labor was to his. What Smith accomplished in his studio signals how much the artist's means of production offer a way to negotiate some sort of relationship, whether wishful or insistent, with the values he understood to have governed a wider social world.

1. The photographer was Ed Cornachio. His parents, coincidentally, were from the Bolton Landing area of New York and were acquaintances of Smith. Born in 1930, Cornachio was appointed head of the photography department at LACMA in 1964 and continued to work there until his retirement in 1980. (See www.saatchi-gallery.co.uk/yourgallery/artist_profile//5092.html.) His contact sheets from this shoot remain in the photography department at LACMA.

2. Svetlana Alpers, *The Art of Describing: Dutch Art in the Seventeenth Century* (Chicago: University of Chicago Press, 1983).

3. Anne M. Wagner, *Jean-Baptiste Carpeaux: Sculptor of the Second Empire* (New Haven, CT: Yale University Press, 1986).

4. The two texts that have paid the most attention to David Smith's social origins and class allegiances are E. A. Carmean Jr., *David Smith*, exh. cat. (Washington, D.C.: National Gallery of Art, 1982), and Paula Wisotzki, "Artist and Worker: The Labor of David Smith," *Oxford Art Journal* 28, no. 3 (2005): 347–70.

5. See Sigmund Freud, *Civilization and Its Discontents* (1930), in *The Pelican Freud Library*, vol. 12, *Civilization, Society, and Religion* (London: Penguin, n.d.), 280.

6. The goggles and helmet that appear in photographs of Smith at work reflect his adoption in the early 1950s of the technique of arc welding, which replaced the acetylene-torch method he had used in sculpture up to that point. See Carmean, *David Smith*, 41–44. Carmean's description of welding reflects his personal experience, as he was convinced that a real understanding of Smith's sculpture depended upon his learning how to weld. Carmean did so under the guidance of the New York sculptor James Wolfe.

7. David Smith, "Notes for *David Smith Makes a Sculpture*," 1951, published in *David Smith*, ed. Garnett McCoy (New York: Praeger, 1973), 74. The other citations in this paragraph are from the same source.

8. Note, however, that immediately after Smith's death, The Estate of David Smith commissioned Ugo Mulas to photograph the inside of Smith's house and workshop and to document all the sculptures on site. These photographs are available for viewing on microfilm (two reels) at the Smithsonian Institution's Archives of American Art in Washington, D.C.; see www.aaa.si.edu/collections/collection/mulaugo.htm. E. A. Carmean Jr. discusses the issues involved in a precise reconstruction of the studio and its contents in his *David Smith*, 58–59.

9. This information was provided by Peter Stevens, executive director of The Estate of David Smith, in a discussion with the author, January 2009.

10. David Smith, untitled text, n.d., quoted in *David Smith by David Smith*, ed. Cleve Gray, paperback ed. (London: Thames and Hudson, 1989), 53.

11. David Smith, "The New Sculpture" (paper, The Museum of Modern Art, New York, February 21, 1952), published in *David Smith*, ed. Garnett McCoy (New York: Praeger, 1973), 84.

12. David Smith, "Design for Progress—*Cockfight*," c. 1947, published in *David Smith*, ed. Garnett McCoy (New York: Praeger, 1973), 61.

13. Karen Wilkin, *David Smith* (New York: Abbeville Press, 1984), 92, quoted in *David Smith: A Centennial,* exh. cat., ed. Carmen Giménez (New York: Guggenheim Museum, 2006), 316.

14. Smith, "Notes for *David Smith Makes a Sculpture*," published in McCoy, *David Smith*, 75.

15. David Smith, letter to Emanuel Navaretta, November 1959, reprinted in *David Smith,* ed. Garnett McCoy (New York: Praeger, 1973), 208.

16. Bill Berkson, "Draft of a Chronology of the Life of David Smith" (unpublished manuscript, Archives and Special Collections, Homer Babbidge Library, University of Connecticut, Storrs, n.d.), 66. This chronology, which relies on interviews conducted by Berkson just after the artist's death, was intended for use in relation to a show on Smith planned but abandoned by The Museum of Modern Art, New York.

17. Susan Cooke, associate director of The Estate of David Smith, has offered the following notes on these photographs: "The image of Smith welding at American Locomotive Company, Schenectady, was taken in 1942, probably by a photographer from World Wide Photo. The image of Smith welding *Torso* may be a self-portrait; the original negative is in the archives with tape residue at the top and bottom, perhaps indicating Smith's crop marks (the image here is the cropped version). It was published in Maude Riley's article/interview, 'Sewer Pipe Sculpture: Fabricated Steel Makes Sculpture for a Forward-Looking Modern Artist,' *Cue* 9, no. 12 (March 16, 1940): 17–18." Susan Cooke, email to the author, February 13, 2009.

18. David Smith, Sketchbook #40, 1950–54, The Estate of David Smith.

19. Smith, "Notes for *David Smith Makes a Sculpture*," published in McCoy, *David Smith*, 75.

20. Berkson, "Draft of a Chronology of the Life of David Smith," 67. Berkson quotes the text of the certificate Smith received on January 21, 1943, on completion of a course at Union College in Schenectady.

21. See Smith, "Design for Progress—*Cockfight*," published in McCoy, *David Smith*, 60. The crucial sentences read: "While arc welding builds the machinery which rolls our present-day industrial culture, the machines will be discarded from wear or obsolescence to be remelted for new developments. But future generations will always be able to see arc-welded, signed, and dated sculpture still retained in museum collections."

22. For a photograph of the prefabricated components of the *Cubis* awaiting use, see Carmean, *David Smith*, 200, fig. 2.

23. Thierry de Duve, "The Readymade and the Tube of Paint," *Artforum*, May 1986, 110–21.

24. Smith, "Design for Progress—*Cockfight*," published in McCoy, *David Smith*, 61.

25. The rhetorical implications of the *Cubis*' deployment of standard units are only underscored by the fact that rather than the found result of industrial production, each component actually was fabricated on the basis of cardboard mock-ups made from liquor and cigar cartons by Smith himself. These were then translated by Smith and his assistant Leon Pratt into stainless steel. See Carmean, *David Smith*, 37–41, 201.

New Unities

Christopher Bedford

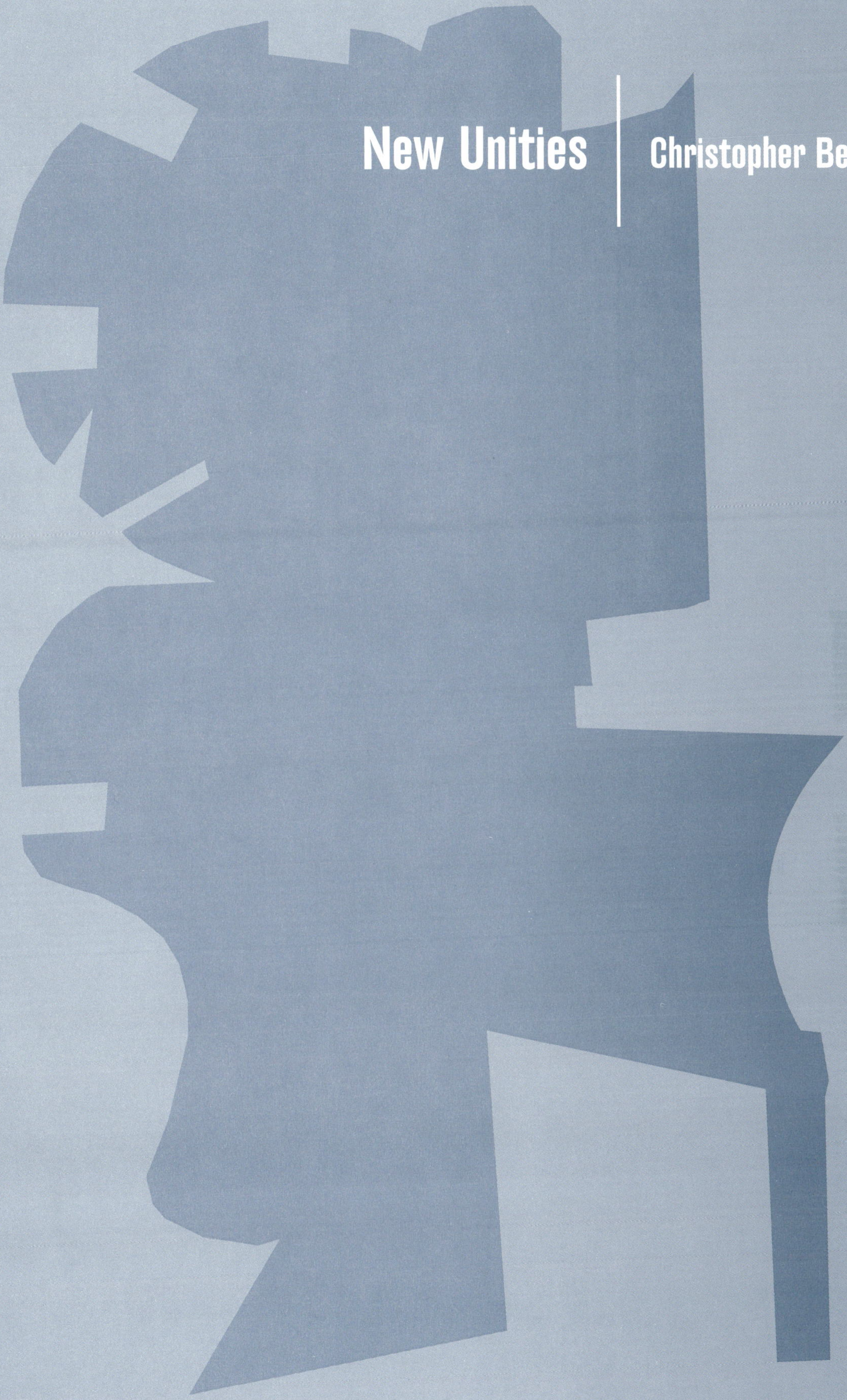

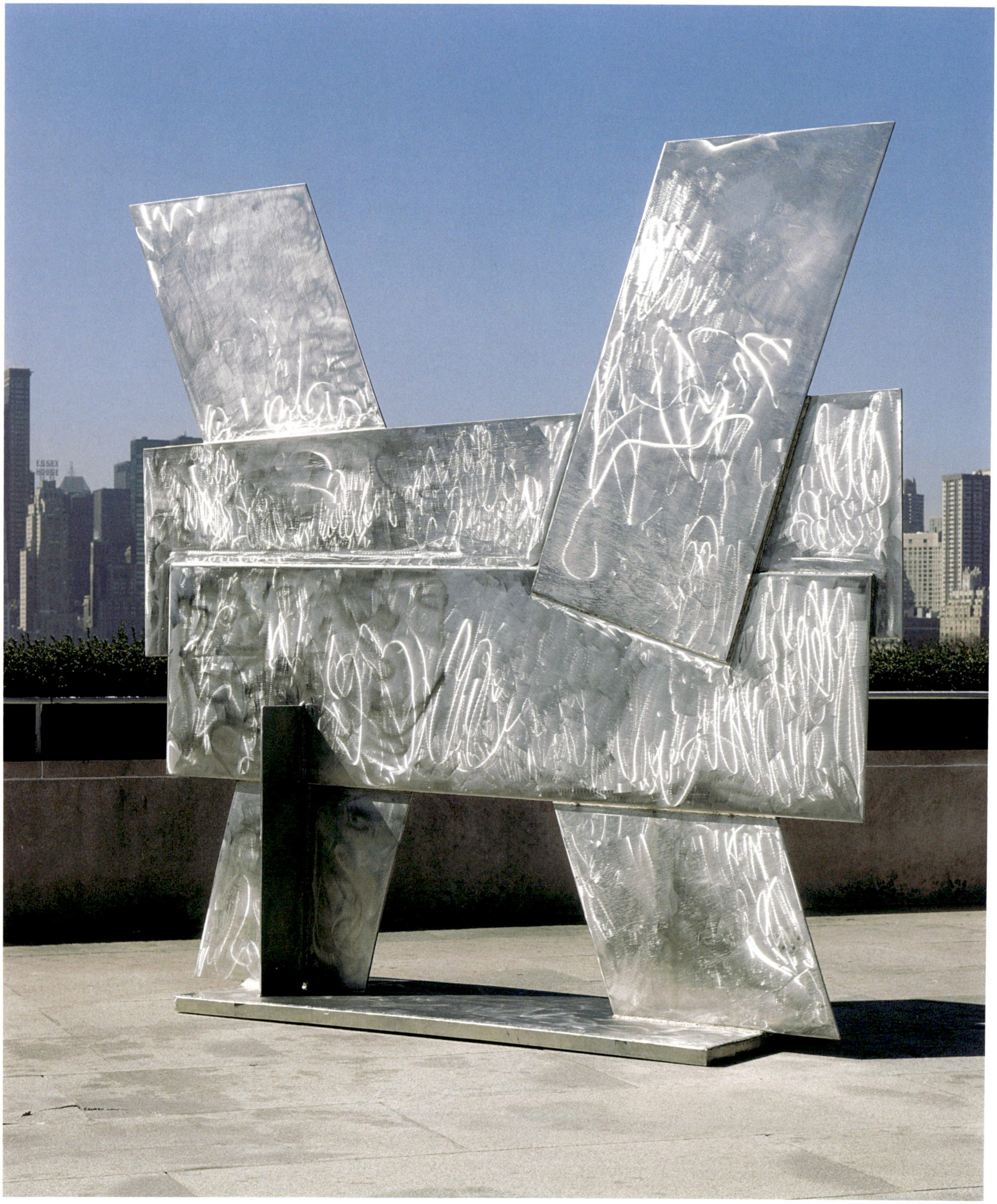

Fig. 1 | Becca, 1965, The Metropolitan Museum of Art, New York

> The more I work
> the more it flows.
> —**David Smith**

Even in their finished state, David Smith's sculptures are remarkable for their restlessness. This is not to suggest that they appear *un*finished, but agitated, implying a desire to grow into something further, something new, the next thing. A case in point is one of the artist's last works, *Becca* (1965, fig. 1), named for one of his daughters and completed shortly before his death. Standing over nine feet tall and spanning over ten feet, the stainless-steel sculpture is imposing but far from monumental. As with all of Smith's work, a close physical encounter with the sculpture does not discourage the conviction that this thing could have been made by hand. Traces of fabrication—of intensive labor—are everywhere, from the welded passages that join one section to the next to the burnishings that play across the surface. This sense of constructedness, of having been worked upon by hand, is made particularly explicit in the surface of this sculpture. Unlike much of Smith's later work (especially his *Cubis* [see pp. 16, 18], notable for their emphasis on volume), *Becca*, like its pendant, *Untitled* (*Candida*) (1965, fig. 2), is notably flat. Thin sheets of stainless steel are welded together to form an X with two overlapping horizontal bars running through its center. While the form of the sculpture is quite straightforward, solid, and static, the surface is alive with swirling gestures that offer a counterpoint to the rigid geometries of the work as a whole.

As if to emphasize the flatness of the sculpture's planes, Smith treated each surface as a pictorial field that he burnished, distressed, and polished to create a highly animate series of painterly gestures, each a clear index of the artist's hand as he applied his tool across the steel. As the viewer moves laterally from one side of *Becca* to the other, these whorls catch the light and glisten before growing dull and eventually disappearing, only to be replaced by new, equally spirited forms. So restless is the surface of this work, and so total is its embrace of irresolution as a formal idea, that one never has the experience of seeing the same surface in exactly the same way twice. The possibility of experiencing the work in its entirety thus is withheld. In other words, the sculpture seems to revise and reinvent itself again and again, never settling into a stable, unchanging state. The compositional dynamism many sculptors, Smith included, have achieved by exploiting the diversity of viewpoints offered by three dimensions, Smith accomplishes here in only two.

The manic restlessness and steadfast refusal of stasis evident in the surface of *Becca* make the sculpture an apt metaphor for Smith's legendary work ethic and prodigious output. Such emphasis on

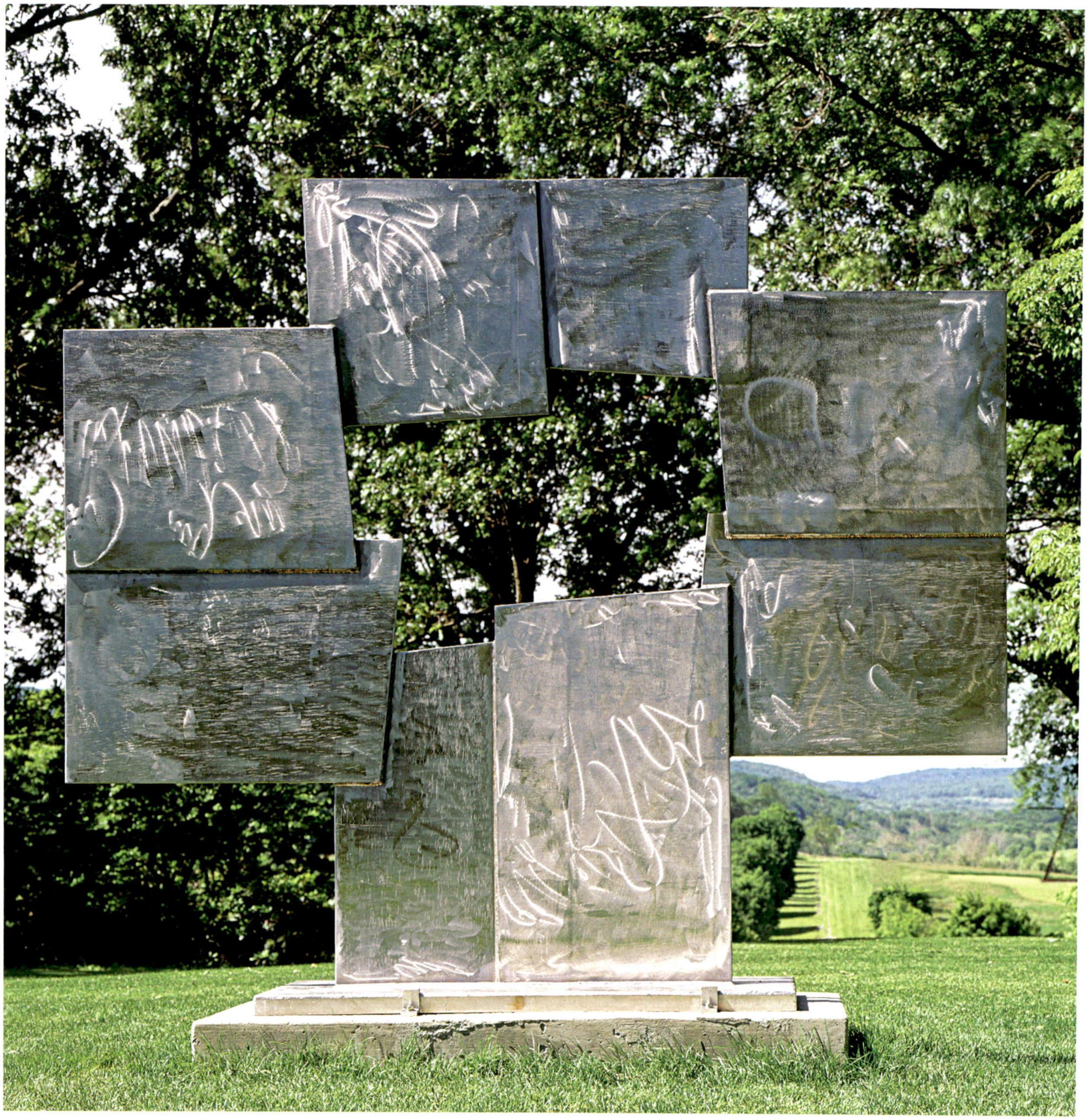

Fig. 2 | Untitled (Candida), 1965, The Estate of David Smith

change and irresolution was one of Smith's central convictions as an artist and a strategy that both produced dynamic individual works and propelled him forward from one work to the next, sustaining a clear correlation between his activities as an artist and his well-documented belief in labor as a social principle. Smith saw his work as an artist—specifically his work with metal—as labor in the most traditional sense. Accordingly, he remained a union member in good standing long after his time at the American Locomotive Company had ended, establishing a concrete relationship to nonartists who worked with their hands as he did. For Smith, each artwork was strongly connected both to his own other sculptures and to the labor of other welders. As he said, "When I begin a sculpture I am not always sure how it is going to end. In a way it has a relationship to the work before, it is in continuity with the previous work—it often holds a promise or a gesture toward the one to follow . . . If the end of the work seems too complete and final, posing no question, I am apt to work back from the end, [then] in its finality it poses a question and not a solution."[1] Nowhere is this commitment to perpetually deferred resolution—and to the propulsive, self-sustaining power of questions posed and answered through work—made clearer or more literal than in a distinctive group of photographs Smith produced of his own sculptures in the 1960s.

It is well known that Smith objected to what he pejoratively termed the "professional" documentation of his sculptures by commissioned photographers.[2] He believed with equal fervor, however, in the power of reproduction, noting with a mercenary's pragmatism that "reproductions stick in library files—and make contact in people's minds, so when they do get to New York they already know the work in part."[3] Recognizing the pivotal role images played in the broad dissemination of his work, after World War II Smith assumed sole responsibility for photographing his sculptures. Some of these photographs suggest that Smith believed ardently in photography as an independent, generative medium that could transform and interpret its subject, that could exceed the limits of mere documentation and produce a new object. Smith understood the evidentiary value of photographs and their currency as marketing devices, but he also knew that, like any other tool, the camera offered a way to make new work, to labor. Of his primary practice as a sculptor, Smith said, "If you ask me why I make sculpture, I must answer that it is my way of life, my balance, my justification for being."[4] Given the existential urges that quite clearly spurred Smith's relentless output, it should come as no surprise that any process related to this primary act could become comparably creative and productive.

The scholar with the most sustained interest in Smith and the most intimate physical understanding of his work is undoubtedly Rosalind Krauss. As part of her PhD dissertation begun in 1966, a year after the artist's death, Krauss started work on a catalogue raisonné of Smith's sculpture; the resultant publication remains the definitive reference. She completed the bulk of her research at Bolton Landing, Smith's isolated studio in rural upstate New York. In addition to the many large sculptures that populated the fields, Krauss also had to document "several hundred" sculptures "crammed together in the basement of the house."[5] Krauss would carry each sculpture to a platform outside the basement door, install the work in a very provisional fashion, take a photograph, and then return the sculpture.

To guide her documentary efforts, Krauss looked to Smith's own photographs of his work (many of which are published in *David Smith by David Smith*, edited by Cleve Gray). Writing retrospectively about this process, Krauss recalled two primary facets of these photographs: "I was sure Smith's photos would be a key to understanding how Smith himself viewed his work. The two aspects of [them] that immediately drew my attention were the anthropomorphizing presentation (several were photographed in the doorway to the studio, as though they were greeting the viewer) and the incompatible double views of a single work."[6] Krauss's latter observation suggests the central concern of this essay: Smith's tendency to use photography not simply to frame and direct the viewer's understanding of his sculpture—a fairly conventional strategy among sculptors, traceable to Auguste Rodin—but also to reanimate extant work, investigate new formal ideas, and, ultimately, to produce new compositions entirely.

Smith did not merely offer "double views" of certain sculptures but new views of new sculptural works. Protean producer that he was, Smith pushed his photographic practice to do more than provide a passive record of finished work or advance an ideal view of a given sculpture (though it should be noted that he was very diligent in providing his dealers with seductive, if sometimes unconventional, images of his work).[7] Instead, particularly late in his career, he used the medium as an exploratory compositional tool—roughly analogous to the cranes and winches he employed in his studio to move slabs of metal—to test new formal arrangements. Though the enduring physical manifestations of this extension of his "sculptural" work were only ever photographic, photography became a way for Smith to pose new questions and investigate compositional possibilities using existent work. In essence, photography was a tool to ensure that his sculptures remained in a generative state, despite having found their final physical form.

Some of Smith's photographs, it should be noted, do little more than record his sculpture's physical details, dramatized, perhaps, by careful siting in a striking landscape or against an expanse of sky. These relatively banal images only emphasize what is so different and arresting about other photographs he produced, however. The relatively small subset of Smith's photographs produced in the 1960s that is the focus here underscores more forcefully than other images the artist's investment in photography as a discrete medium with its own distinct properties independent of sculpture and capable of generating unique meaning. In this group, Smith exaggerated and exploited the pictorial quality of his later, strongly geometric sculptures through photographic representation, using his camera to manipulate the three-dimensional objects in relation to each other and to their environments, producing what might best be described as collages in space. These images clearly foreground Smith's use of photography as a tool for discovering new formal ideas in existent works, but as a group they also testify to the restless creative impulse that is the hallmark of Smith's life as an artist. In them, the viewer's experience of Smith's sculptures and the space they occupy is carefully complicated to produce a disorienting effect more like that of a two-dimensional geometric painting than a photograph of a fully

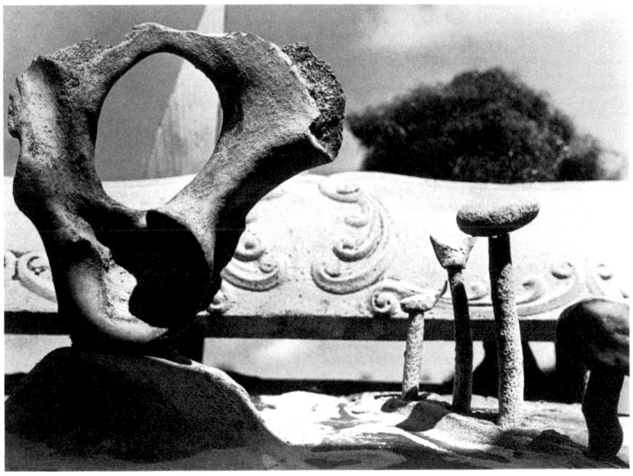

Fig. 3 | Untitled (Virgin Island assemblage), c. 1931–32, gelatin silver print, 3 1/8 x 4 1/8 in. (7.9 x 11.1 cm), The Estate of David Smith

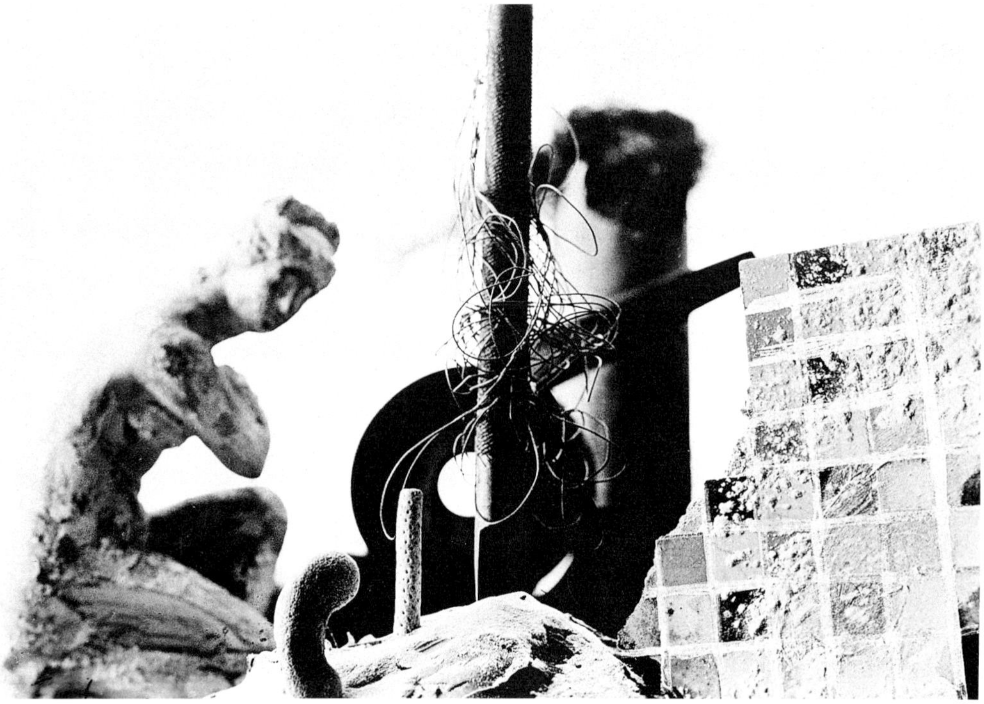

Fig. 4 | Untitled (tableau), 1933, gelatin silver print, 3 5/8 x 4 3/4 in. (9.2 x 12.1 cm), private collection

three-dimensional sculpture (or sculptures) occupying real space. Most important, what these photographs present is not a record or a document but something *new.*

Smith began working in photography as early as October 1931, when he and the artist Dorothy Dehner, his then wife, were living in the Virgin Islands. Among the works he produced there were photographs of sculptural tableaux composed from carefully arranged fragments of coral and bones (fig. 3). Upon his return to Bolton Landing in the spring of 1933, he continued to construct and record these tableaux, adding wood, wire, stone, and aluminum rod to his repertoire of materials (fig. 4). Joan Pachner, the scholar who has most comprehensively researched Smith's photography, claims that these images served as mere documents of completed sculptures, yet even these very early photographic experiments reveal the beginnings of Smith's desire to use three-dimensional objects as collage elements in pictorial compositions, to do what photographs do best, namely, reduce a three-dimensional view to a bounded two-dimensional composition. By the late 1930s, Smith's work as a sculptor would assume primacy,

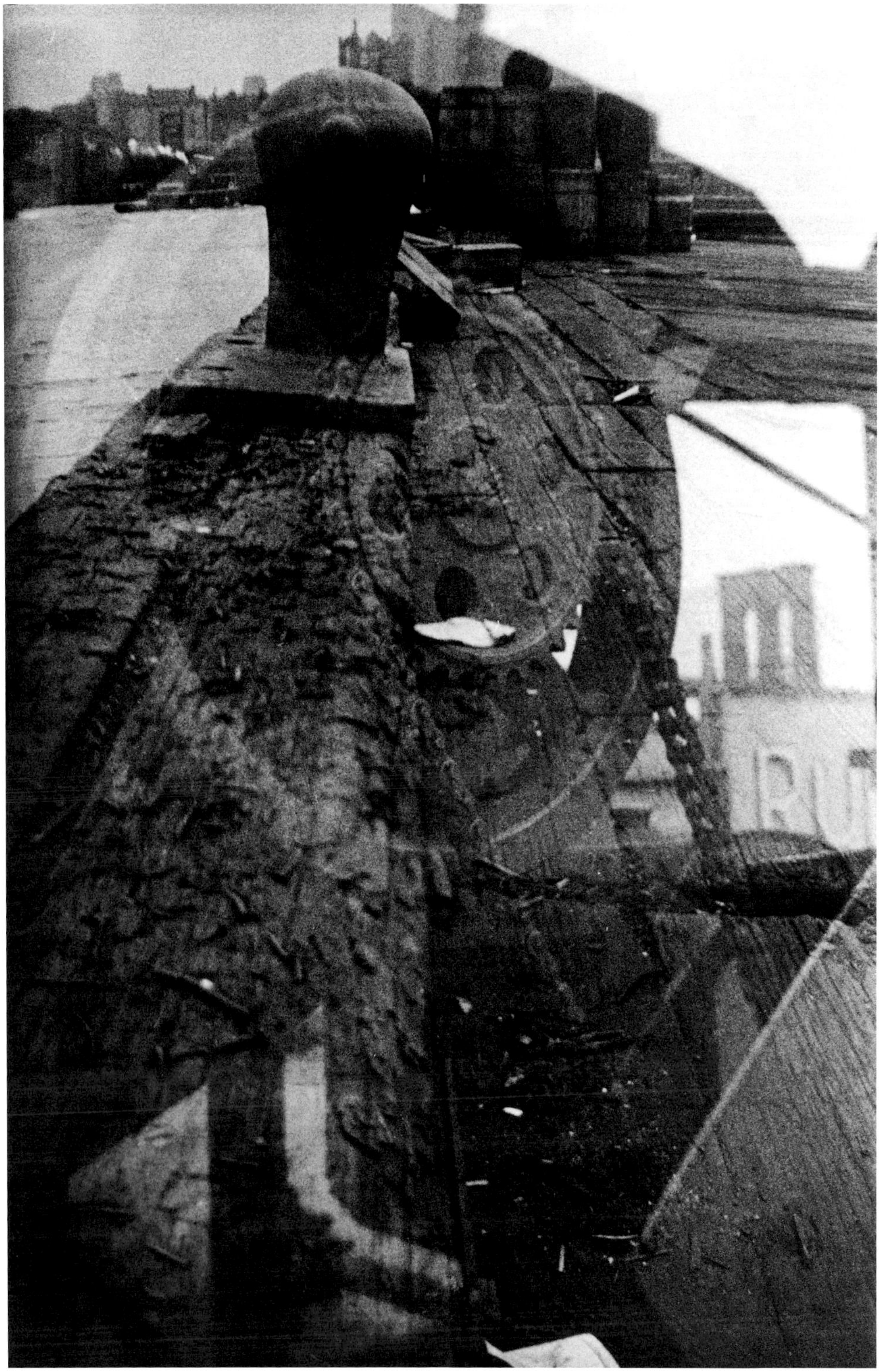

Fig. 5 | Untitled (dock montage), c. 1930, The Estate of David Smith

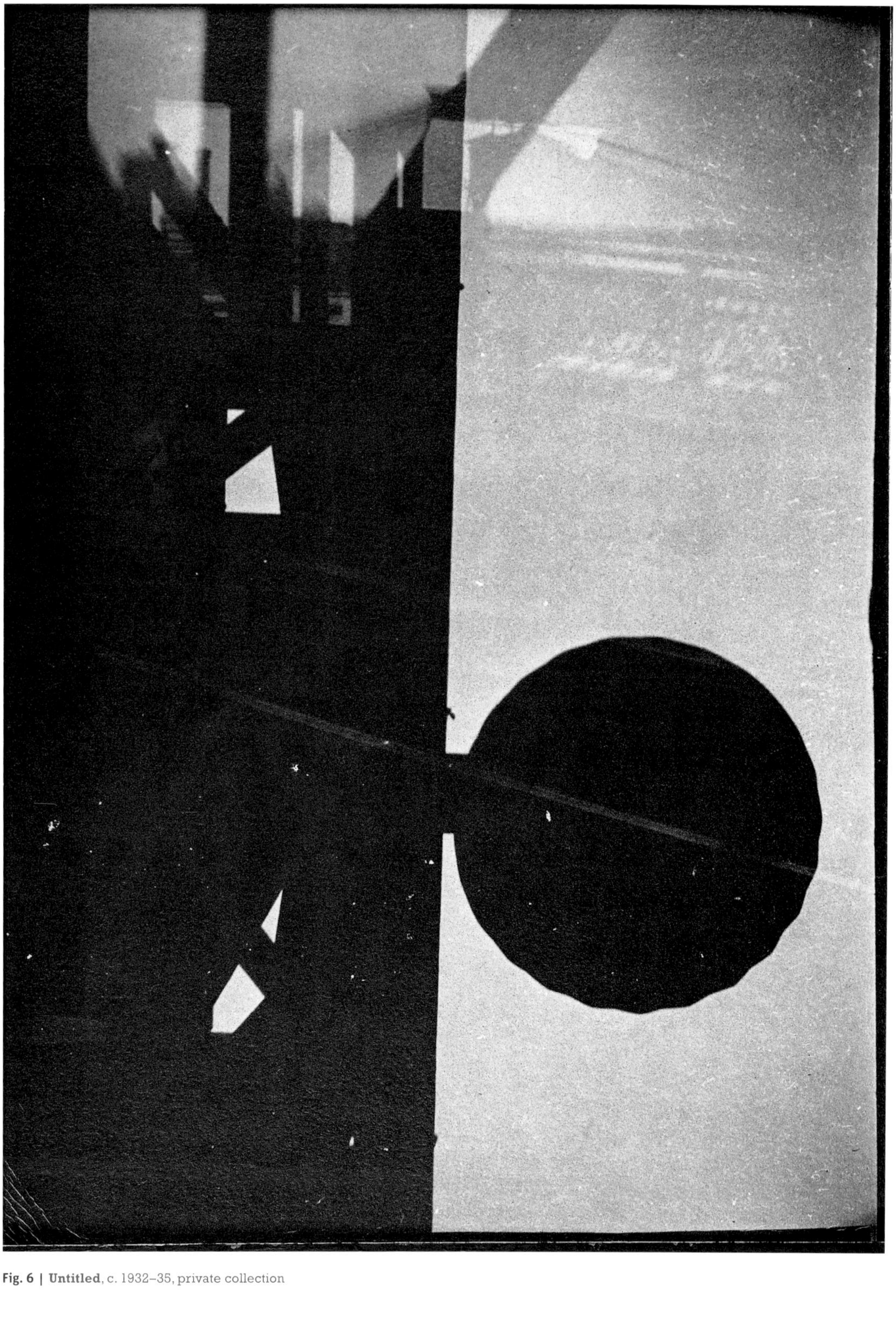

Fig. 6 | Untitled, c. 1932–35, private collection

but in the intervening years he continued to explore cameraless photographic techniques in artworks that often incorporated drawing, multinegative prints, photomontages, and abstract photocollages, the latter made by cutting up negatives and pasting them back together (figs. 5, 6).[8]

In fact, the genesis for the collages in space he produced in the 1960s using large-scale finished sculptures can be traced to photographs, often considered documentary, that he took in Brooklyn between 1932 and 1935 (figs. 7, 8). *Untitled* (on ship), for example, is, as the title suggests, a view of the deck of a ship. Two looming black funnels dominate the composition. Crisscrossing the image are ropes tethered to a central vertical structure. In the background, three smaller white funnels reiterate the photograph's prominent circular forms. Tightly framed so that the graphic shapes push forward and command the pictorial field, this found and constructed abstraction reveals an early crystallization of Smith's interest in the relationship among labor, industrial materials, and abstract aesthetics—a thread that runs through his work in sculpture and is the defining characteristic of the photographs Smith would take of his own geometric forms in the early 1960s.

Much the same can be said of *Untitled* (Brooklyn), which presents a more unruly rendering of a ship's deck: the geometries are earthier, less composed, and more obviously rooted in a working environment. Here again, though, the image is tightly framed, with the brute forms of the ship defining the composition. The tight focus emphasizes Smith's interest in form but never so much so that those forms do not seem embedded in, and defined by, their applications in the world of labor and commerce. The geometric forms serve a purpose in the world, and Smith does not disentangle them from that context, although he does permit them an equivalent formal power in the composition.

Such dualism aligns neatly with Smith's own hearty defense of abstraction as a socially resonant, radical form of art making in the years after World War I. In "On Abstract Art," a paper delivered at the United American Artists forum in New York in 1940, for instance, he offered his view of abstraction as a materialist practice, one rooted in the forms and functions of the social world and unrelated to the mystical, existentialist rhetoric surrounding abstract painting of the period. These aesthetic commitments lend credence to what Alex Potts has called Smith's "overt anticapitalism with a definite Marxist edge."[9] Smith's creative restlessness, his ardent belief in self-justification through labor, the persistent constructedness of his sculptures, and their invariably man-made scale all can be seen as articulations of the

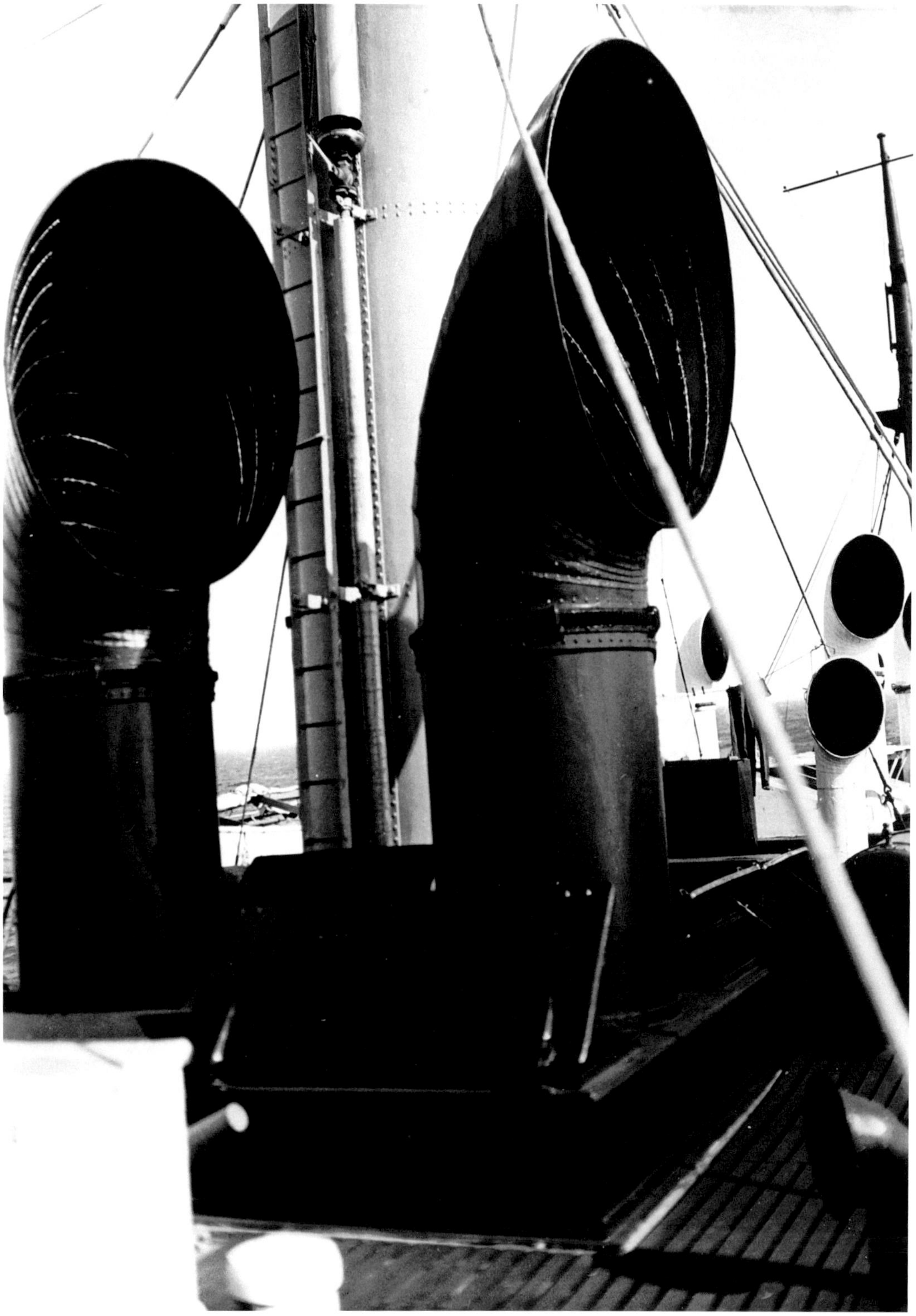

Fig. 7 | Untitled (on ship), c. 1932–35, The Estate of David Smith

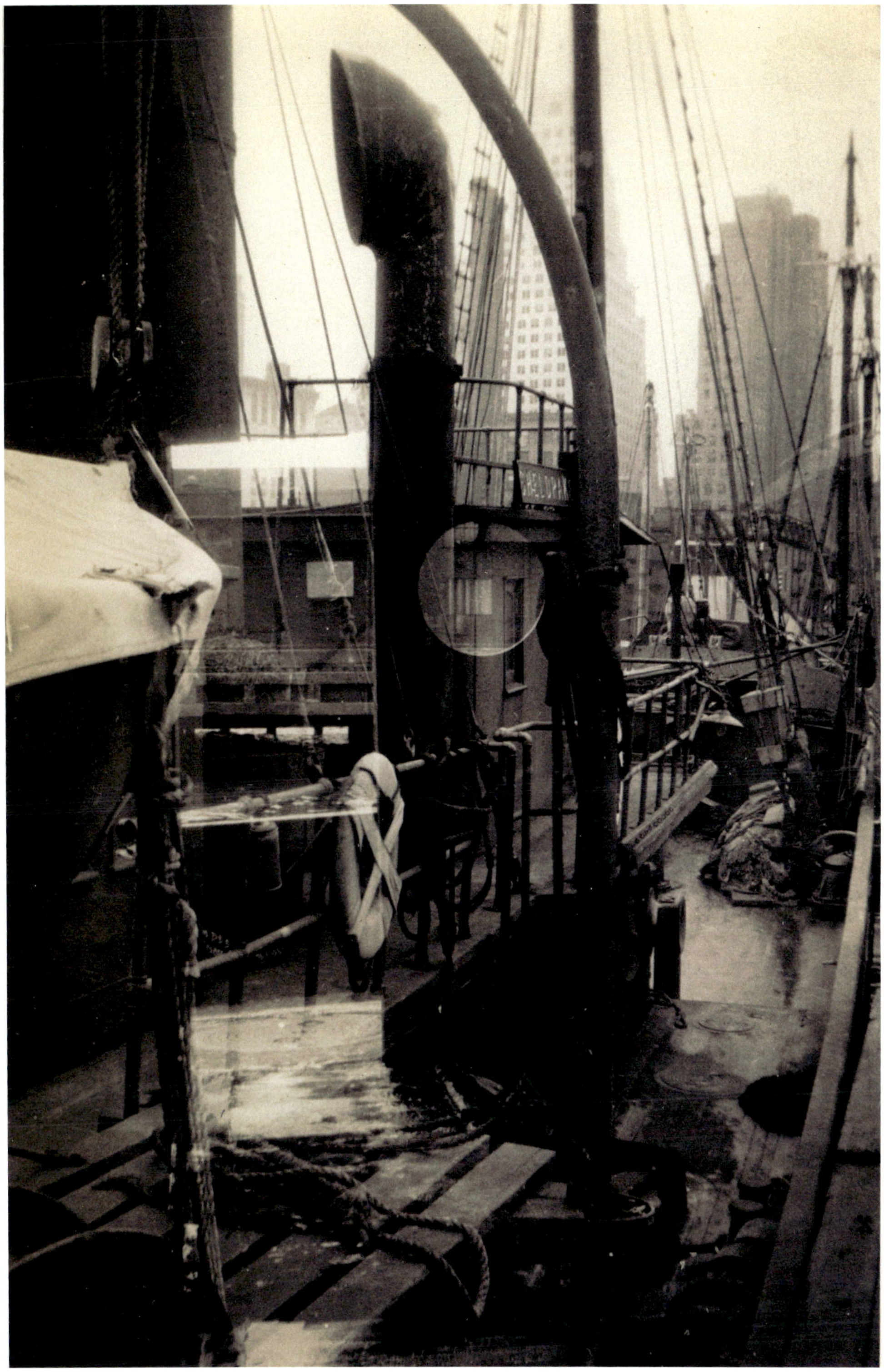

Fig. 8 | Untitled (Brooklyn), 1933–35, The Estate of David Smith

primary importance he placed on the relationship among labor, materials, and abstraction in his art. Expounding specifically on these concerns in 1948, Smith wrote: "By choice I identify myself with working men and still belong to Local 2054 United Steelworkers of America. I belong by craft—yet the subject of aesthetics introduces a breach. I suppose it is because I believe in the future [in] a working man's society and in that society I hope to find a place. In this society I find little place for identify[ing] myself economically."[10] In light of Smith's belief in labor as an inherently valuable act, his interest in making new work with any medium at his disposal, including photography, appears all the more consistent and logical.

Pachner contends with some certainty that Smith "largely abandoned his pursuit of photography as 'art' by the mid-1930s," focusing instead on dramatic documentary images of his sculptures for dealers to use in their marketing efforts.[11] Photographs he produced of single sculptures and sculptural groupings in the early 1960s undermine the validity of her claim, however. In these images, the emphasis on framing, vantage point, and shallow perspectival depth evident in his Brooklyn photographs reemerges decisively. In this case, though, the subject was not labor as a social condition but the products of his own labor, the conditions of which Smith made quite public: "My work day begins at 10 or 11 a.m. after a leisurely breakfast and an hour of reading. The shop is 800 feet from the house. I carry my 2 p.m. lunch and return to the house at 7 for dinner. The work day ends from 1 to 2 a.m. with time out for coffee at 11:30."[12]

The products of Smith's regimented labor were not only his metal sculptures but also the virtual sculptures he created with photography. Smith staged three-dimensional collages both in his Bolton Landing workshop and in the dramatic landscape that surrounded it.[13] Whether shot indoors or outside, these compositions blur the lines between objects, thus announcing themselves immediately as something other—something more—than documentary images. Photographs such as *Untitled* (*Hirebecca, Hi Candida, Untitled* [1959], and *Noland's Blues* [circular segments from] in Bolton Landing workshop) (1961, fig. 9) offer no clear account of any individual work. Instead, Smith shifts the sculptures in space (as well as his own vantage point) to yield a seamless collage in two dimensions and, thus, an entirely new composition. Working against the traditional impulse to sustain the illusion of three dimensions in photographic representation, and against the conventional documentary imperative to capture sculpture in the round, Smith instead used his eye and his camera's viewfinder to

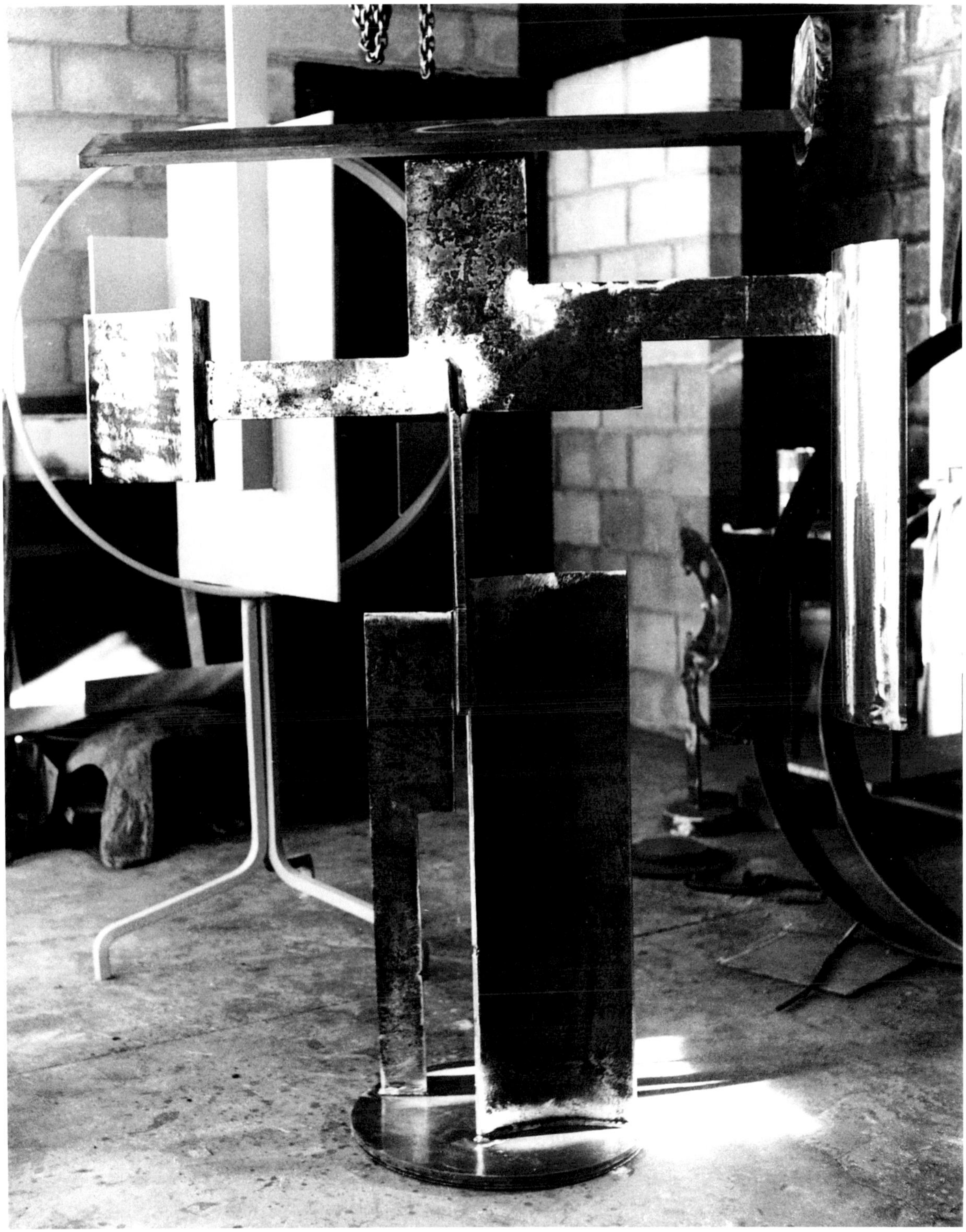

Fig. 9 | Untitled (Hirebecca, Hi Candida, Untitled [1959], and **Noland's Blues** [circular segments from] in Bolton Landing workshop), 1961, The Estate of David Smith

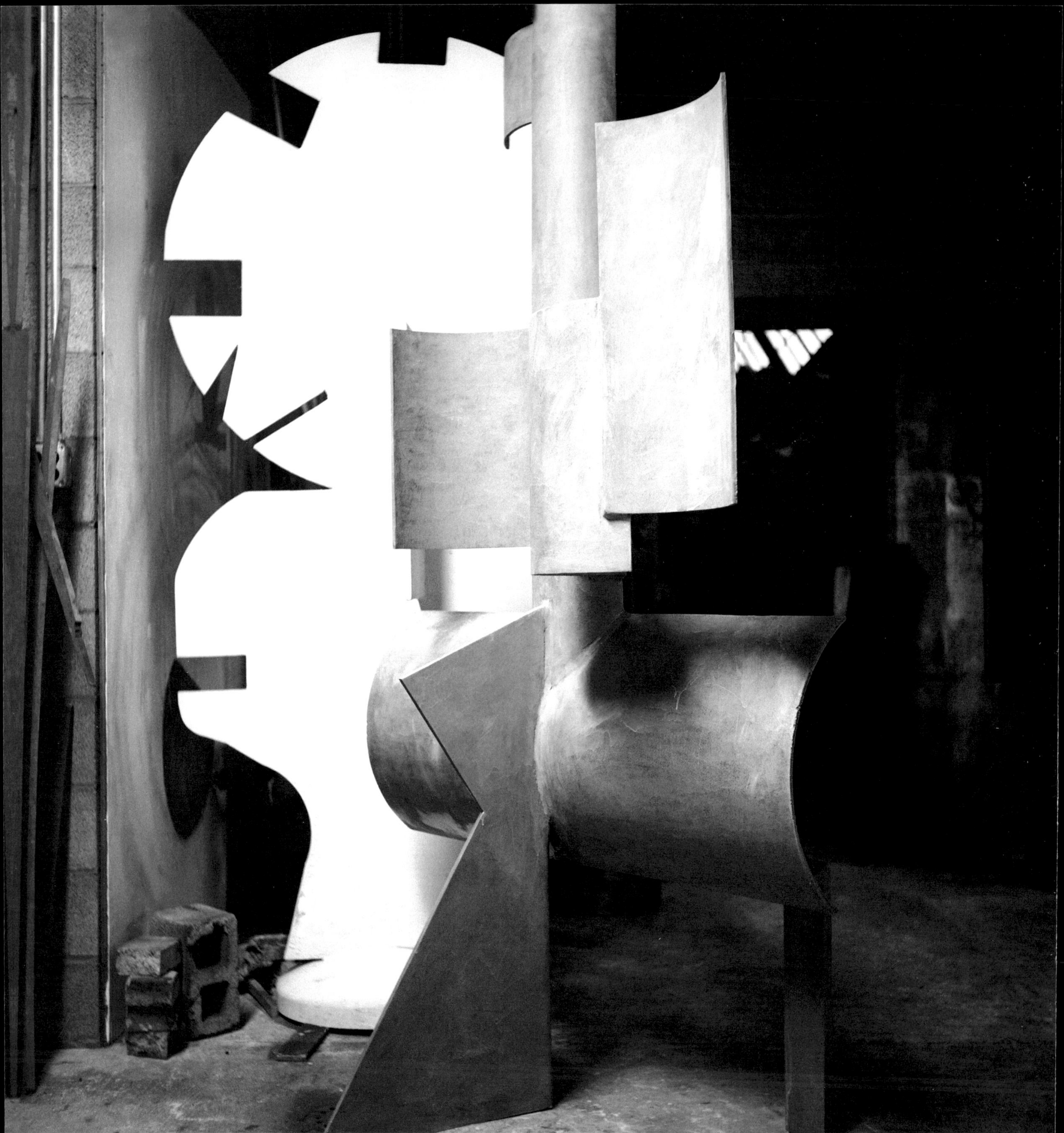

Fig. 10 | Untitled (**Dida's Circle on a Fungus** with **Zig I**, Bolton Landing workshop), c. 1961, The Estate of David Smith

manipulate the four sculptures in this image into an arrangement conducive to two-dimensional depiction, collapsing sculptural space and embracing the flatness of the photograph as a physical medium. The photograph need not embody three dimensions because the objects in the composition already have adapted to the conditions of two.

Smith often assembled such compositions in his workshop, using the architectural geometries of the building to further flatten the pictorial field, suggesting in some cases a seamless continuity between his collages and the spaces they occupied. There are numerous examples of this strategy, including *Untitled* (*Dida's Circle on a Fungus* with *Zig I*, Bolton Landing workshop) (c. 1961, fig. 10); *Untitled* (*Zig III* with *Black White Backward*[?], *Ninety Father*, *Ninety Son*, and *Black White Forward*, Bolton Landing workshop) (c. 1961, fig. 11); and *Untitled* (*Zig V* and *Zig IV* in Bolton Landing workshop) (c. 1961, fig. 12). Equally common are photographs shot outside that use the landscape or built structures to similar ends. *Untitled* (*Zig II* [unpainted] outside Bolton Landing workshop) (c. 1961, fig. 13), unlike many of the photographs in this informal group under consideration, features only one sculpture. Here, Smith picks up on the geometric affinities between *Zig II* and the fragments of wood and steel leaning against the wall outside his studio, creating an elegant, abstract composition that appears at first glance to be absolutely flat. But this specific assembly of elements is most remarkable for the fact that it flawlessly blends a fully realized sculpture with assorted detritus to yield a continuous field of abstract forms. More typical is *Untitled* (*March Sentinel* [stainless-steel plates], *Two Box Structure*, *Two Circle Sentinel*, and *Zig II* [unpainted] next to Bolton Landing workshop) (c. 1961, fig. 14), in which Smith integrates so many sculptural elements into his composition (including the exterior corner of his studio building) that it is hard to determine where one structure ends and another begins.

One of the most elegant of these outdoor photographs is *Untitled* (*Zig VII* and *Zig VIII*, Bolton Landing) (c. 1964, fig. 15). This composition rests on the same basic idea of a three-dimensional assembly carefully arranged to read as a collage, but this image does not present a flat pictorial composition that monopolizes the frame as we saw in the early Brooklyn photographs and in many of the sculptural collages from the 1960s described above. Rather, this collage exists as a grand, composite, fully three-dimensional sculpture in the landscape. The collaging of the two sculptures in this instance does not produce a pictorial effect but the illusion of a single, unified sculpture. The interlocking geometric elements that make up *Zig VII* and *Zig VIII*

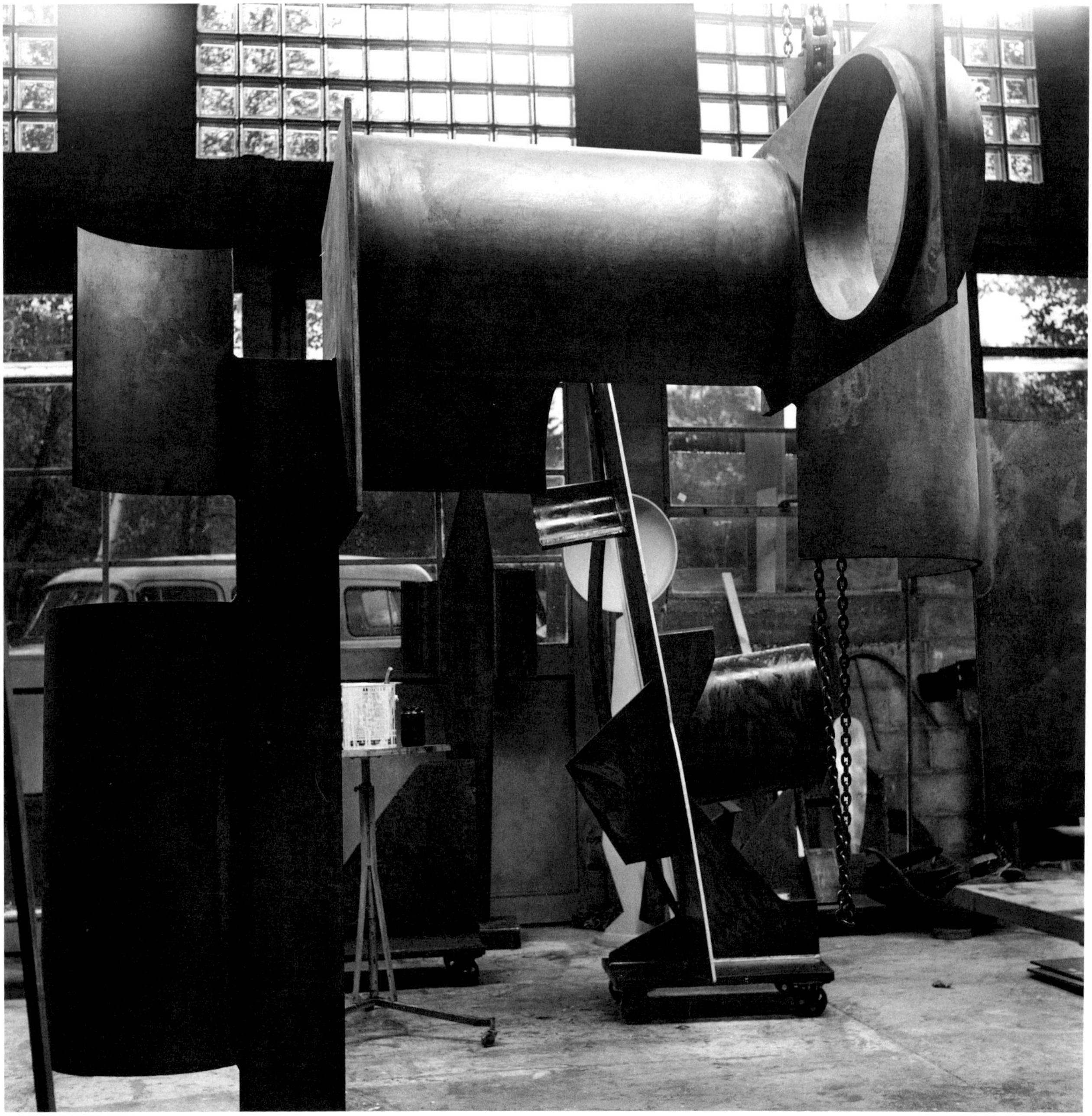

Fig. 11 | Untitled (**Zig III** with **Black White Backward**[?], **Ninety Father**, **Ninety Son**, and **Black White Forward**, Bolton Landing workshop), c. 1961, The Estate of David Smith

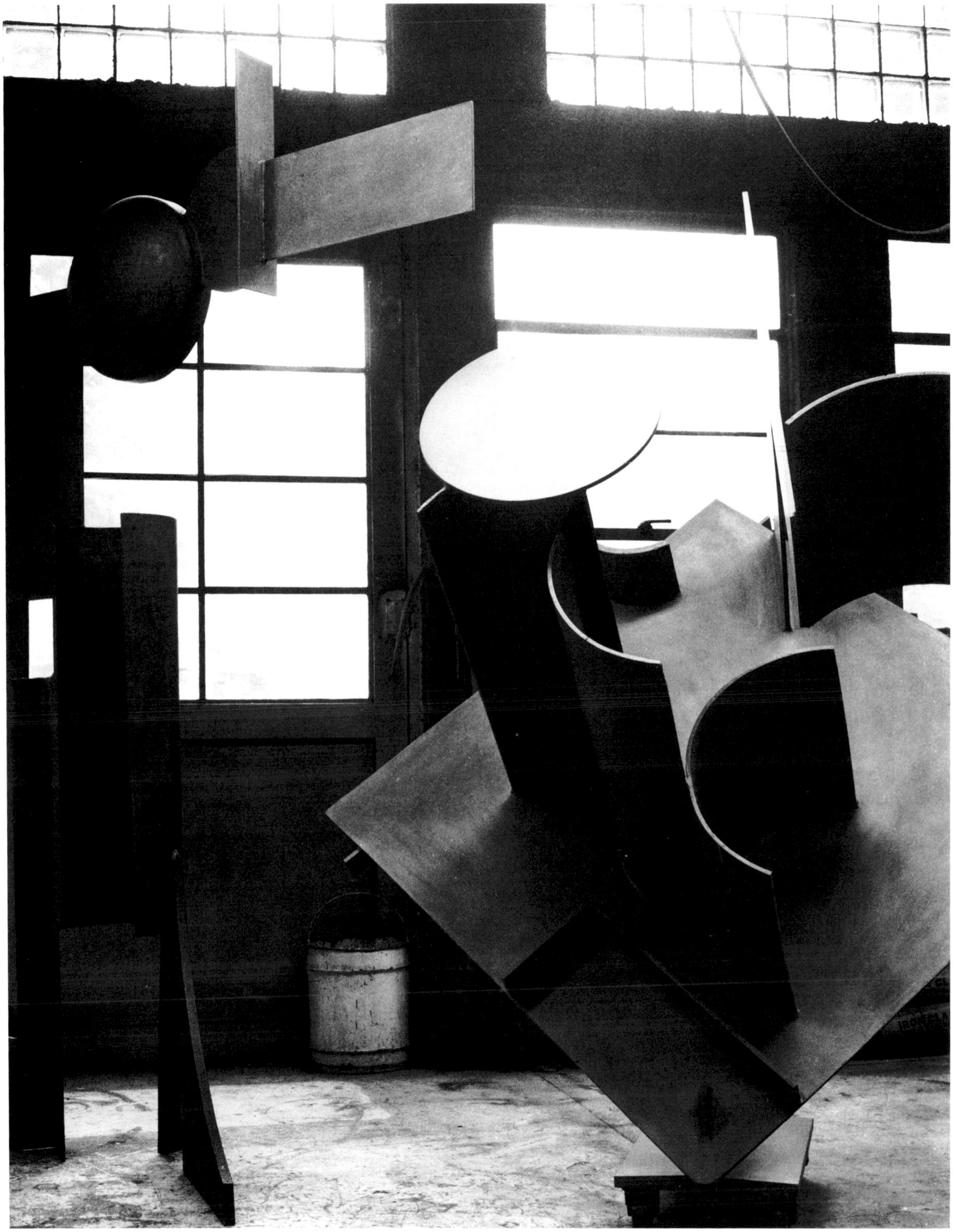

Fig. 12 | Untitled (**Zig V** and **Zig IV** in Bolton Landing workshop), c. 1961, The Estate of David Smith

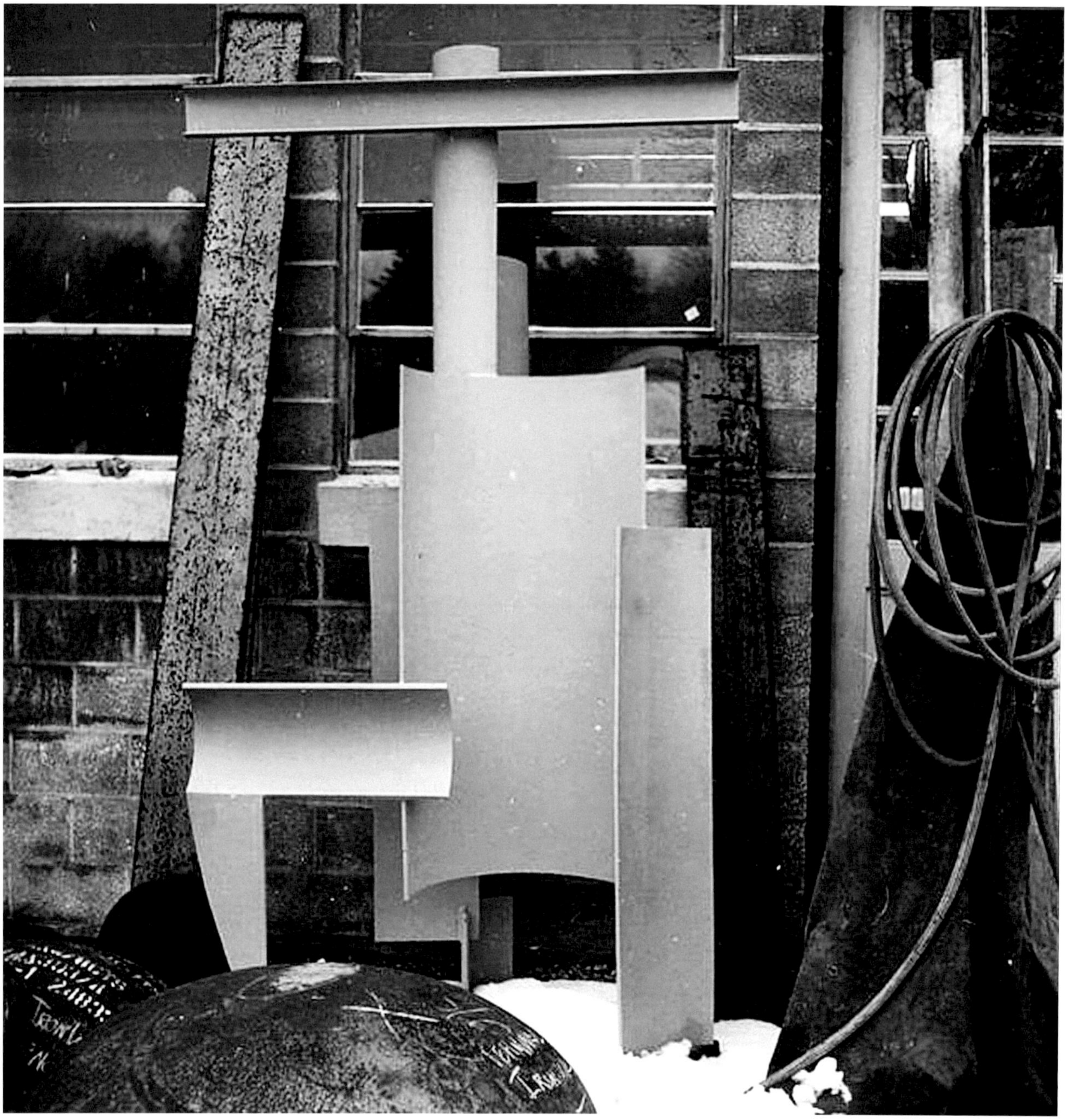

Fig. 13 | Untitled (**Zig II** [unpainted] outside Bolton Landing workshop), c. 1961, The Estate of David Smith

dissolve perfectly into one another, forming a completely plausible sculpture, though one that Smith never realized in plastic form.

Smith declared, "And sculpture can be painting and painting can be sculpture and no authority can overrule the artist in his declaration. Not even the philosopher, the aesthetician, or the connoisseur."[14] In accordance with this belief in the absolute creative agency of the artist—in his right to determine the limits and terms of his own work—Smith manipulated objects in space mindful of the way those spatial relations would be rendered pictorially in a photograph. This suggests that he felt free to use photography as an extension of his practice as a sculptor, and, conversely, to use his compositional skills as a sculptor to produce photographs. The results are works of art that both reject and exceed the designation of "documentary" conventionally applied to them.

As part of Smith's work as a sculptor, and as elaborations on his early interest in found and constructed abstractions, these photographs also reflect Smith's investment in labor as a working principle and as a foundational social ideal. Embedded in the context of their own production, these photographs may not be composed of the utilitarian geometries that define the industrial world, as in his Brooklyn photographs. They record acts of labor nevertheless, and in their desire to forge the new from the old, they are indeed indices of labor in and of themselves. Smith could have simply shot each work in the studio upon completion and considered his documentary duties done. Instead, he transported groups of sculptures to specific sites, installed them and reinstalled them, photographed and rephotographed them, deinstalled them, and then transported the sculptures back to his studio. The specific character of the resultant photographs aside, this arduous process alone belies the designation "documentary," pointing instead to a deliberate, labor-intensive act of creation.

Smith's related beliefs in the generative properties of labor and in the inherent virtue of hard work are most evident in his inability to leave his art alone, and nowhere is that impulse made more literal than in the sculptural collages he created and recorded as photographs in the early 1960s. It is somewhat ironic, then, that it was precisely this restless spirit and drive to experiment that caused a writer for none other than the American Communist Party's *Daily Worker* to express doubts about Smith's practice:

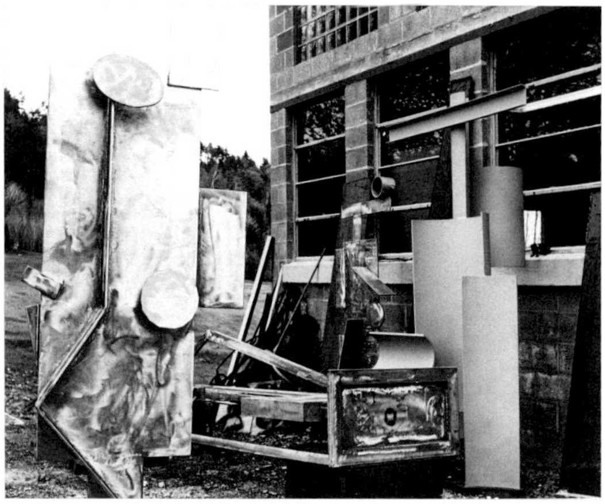

Fig. 14 | Untitled (**March Sentinel** [stainless-steel plates], **Two Box Structure**, **Two Circle Sentinel**, and **Zig II** [unpainted] next to Bolton Landing workshop), c. 1961, The Estate of David Smith

Following spread: **Fig. 15 | Untitled** (**Zig VII** and **Zig VIII**, Bolton Landing) (detail), c. 1964, The Estate of David Smith

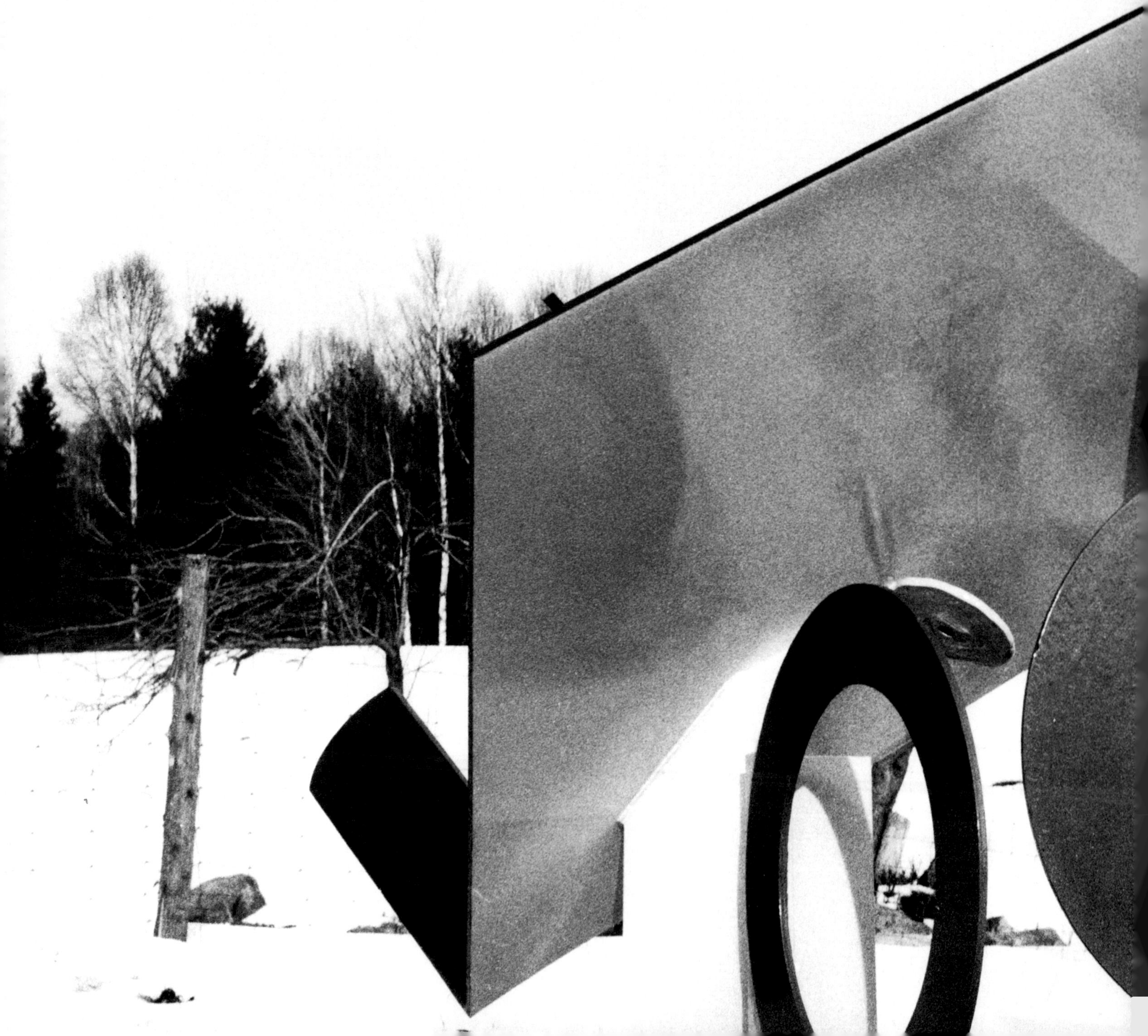

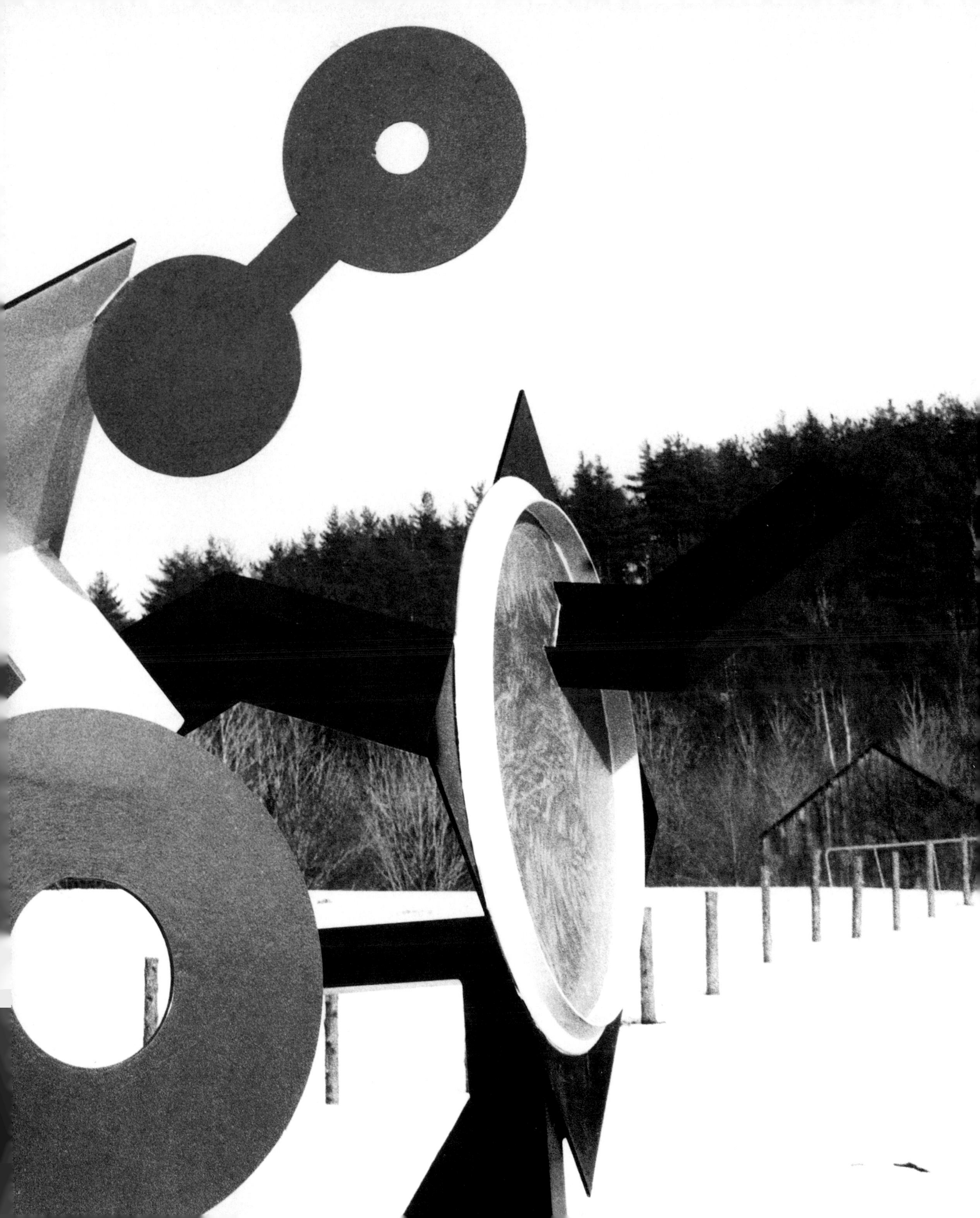

> Even on purely aesthetic grounds, Smith's recent sculpture seems confused. In some cases, he adheres to the concept of the inviolability of the material and allows the material to dictate the nature of the form. In other cases, he turns around and explores the infinite possibilities of the material, even denying its character, making steel look like lace, rope, clay, or plywood. The results, though technically brilliant and artistically imaginative, are disconcerting, unsatisfying, and sometimes even banal.[15]

While the critic objects to the artifice of transforming a material into something it is not, it is precisely the work such transformation entailed that for Smith justified his philosophical alignment with the working man. At the same time, he realized that his gestures should not outpace the society of which he was a part. He notes, "The artist's creative vision cannot go so far beyond the rest of the world that he is not understandable. He is limited by his time. He is dependent upon the past, but he is a contributing factor to the character of his time. His effort is to contribute a unity that has not existed before."[16] Smith's work in all methods and mediums—welding, cutting, painting, drawing, photography, and assemblage—attempts to derive something new from existent materials, to give rise to new unities that once seemed unimaginable.

Though Smith had a way with words, he felt them inadequate to account for his process in anything but the most generalizing terms, and he felt strongly that perception should take precedence over description or intellection in the viewing of a work of art: "There were no words in my mind during its creation, and I'm certain words are not needed in its seeing; and why should you expect understanding when I do not?"[17] Art, in his opinion, should not be understood, it should be seen. Making art was an act not of thinking but of doing. The photographic collages Smith assembled from his own sculptures offer a unique opportunity to see the artist's mind at work. When simple documentation would have sufficed, Smith instead embarked on a new, highly inventive body of work that he surely would have developed further had fate not intervened. As it stands, these photographs are testament to his belief in the value of labor, a belief that was at once a social commitment and *the* concept around which he structured his practice as an artist. As he stated, wasting not a syllable, "The more I work the more it flows."[18] The photographic works discussed here evince Smith's desire and ability to derive something new from something old, even when something new was not required. They are the best "documents" of Smith's beliefs and of his art—his *work*—that one could imagine.

1. David Smith, "Tradition and Identity" (lecture, Ohio University, Athens, OH, April 17, 1959), published in *David Smith,* ed. Garnett McCoy (New York: Praeger, 1973), 146–48.

2. Rosalind E. Krauss, "David Smith's 'New Vision,'" in *David Smith: Photographs, 1931–1965* (New York: Matthew Marks Gallery, 1998), 9.

3. David Smith, letter to Marian Willard, January 23, 1945, Willard Gallery Correspondence, reel 986, Archives of American Art, Smithsonian Institution, Washington, D.C.

4. Carmen Giménez, ed., *David Smith: A Centennial*, exh. cat. (New York: Guggenheim Museum, 2006), 387.

5. Rosalind E. Krauss, "A Photo a Day: Recording the Work of David Smith," in *David Smith: A Centennial*, exh. cat., ed. Carmen Giménez (New York: Guggenheim Museum, 2006), 11.

6. Ibid., 12.

7. See Joan Pachner, "Private Views/Public Images: David Smith's Photographs," in *Sculpture and Photography: Envisioning the Third Dimension*, ed. Geraldine A. Johnson (Cambridge: Cambridge University Press, 1998), 133.

8. Much of this information comes from Joan Pachner's research into Smith's photographic work, published in "Private Views/Public Images: David Smith's Photographs," 131–47.

9. Alex Potts, *The Sculptural Imagination: Figurative, Modernist, Minimalist* (New Haven, CT: Yale University Press, 2000), 160.

10. Garnett McCoy, introduction to *David Smith* (New York: Praeger, 1973), 22.

11. Pachner, "Private Views/Public Images," 132.

12. David Smith, "Notes for *David Smith Makes a Sculpture*," 1951, published in *David Smith*, ed. Garnett McCoy (New York: Praeger, 1973), 75.

13. In the case of the larger groups of sculptures in the fields, Smith likely "staged" his photo compositions by moving his body, not the sculptures themselves. As Susan Cooke, associate director of The Estate of David Smith, notes: "It seems more probable that these images result from Smith moving *himself—his body and his angle of vision*—and that the collaging of forms and the collapsing of space that we see in these photographs [is] a function of his sensitivity to and understanding of his visual *perceptions*: his experience moving around the works in the fields, as he looked at them through the viewfinder, and as he looked at the resulting photographs and then pursued some of the effects that may have originated unconsciously or accidentally. In this sense the later photographs are very different from the Virgin Island photos (in which he did actually assemble still-life arrangements with the intention of photograph[ing] them), even though the visual results are similar. In some ways, Smith's photographs were the least labor-intensive, but most purely perceptually intensive, of his works." Susan Cooke, email message to Carol S. Eliel, March 26, 2010. The italics are Cooke's.

14. Smith, "Tradition and Identity," published in McCoy, *David Smith*, 147.

15. Marion Summers, "A Talented Sculptor," *Daily Worker*, April 18, 1947, 11.

16. David Smith, "The Sculptor's Relationship to the Museum, Dealer, and Public" (lecture, Woodstock Conference of Artists, Woodstock, NY, August 29, 1947), published in *David Smith*, ed. Garnett McCoy (New York: Praeger, 1973), 58.

17. Smith, "Tradition and Identity," published in McCoy, *David Smith*, 148.

18. David Smith, letter to Edgar Levy, September 1, 1945, published in *David Smith*, ed. Garnett McCoy (New York: Praeger, 1973), 196.

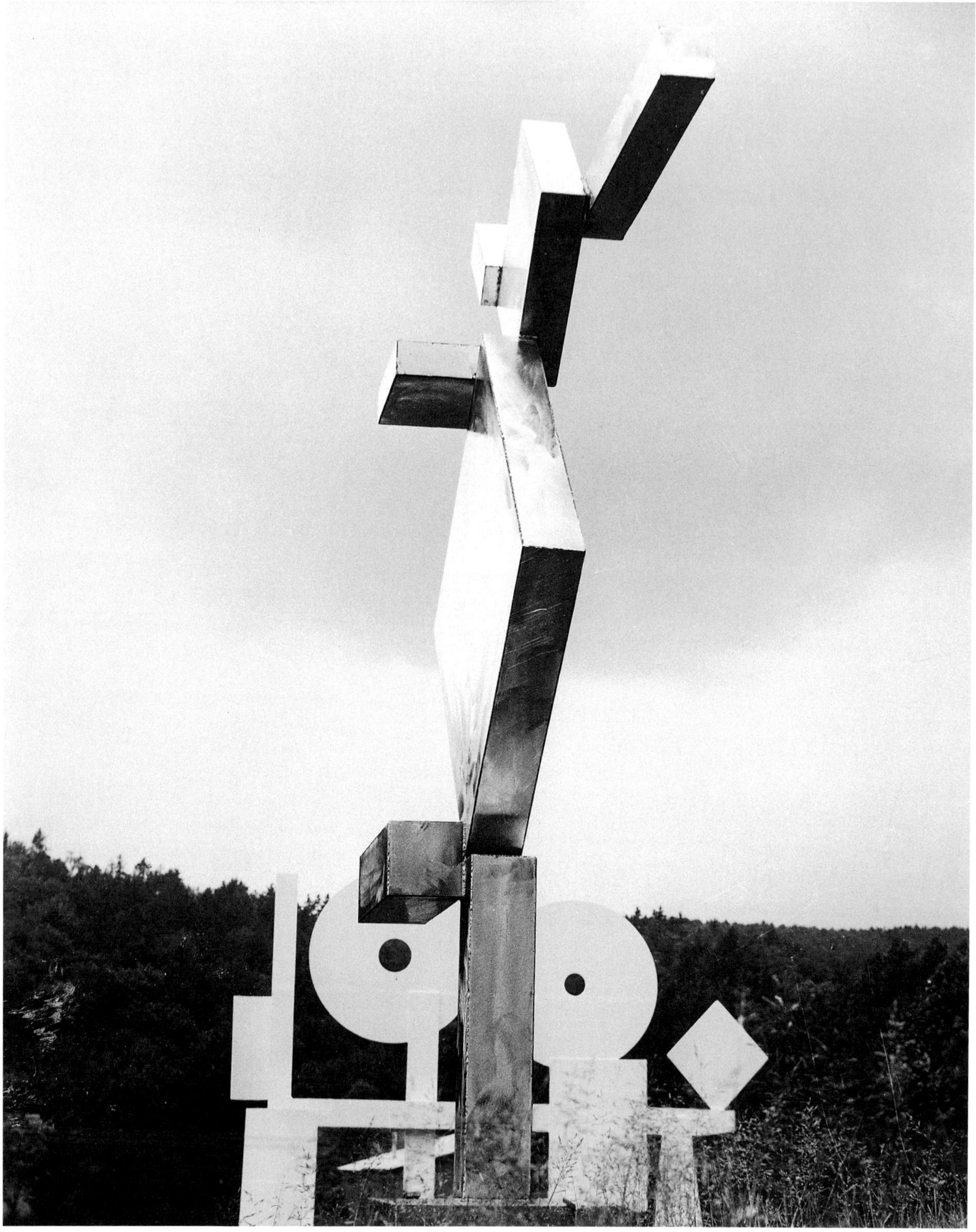

Untitled (**Cubi X** with **Primo Piano**, Bolton Landing),
1963, Richard and Ellen Sandor Family Collection

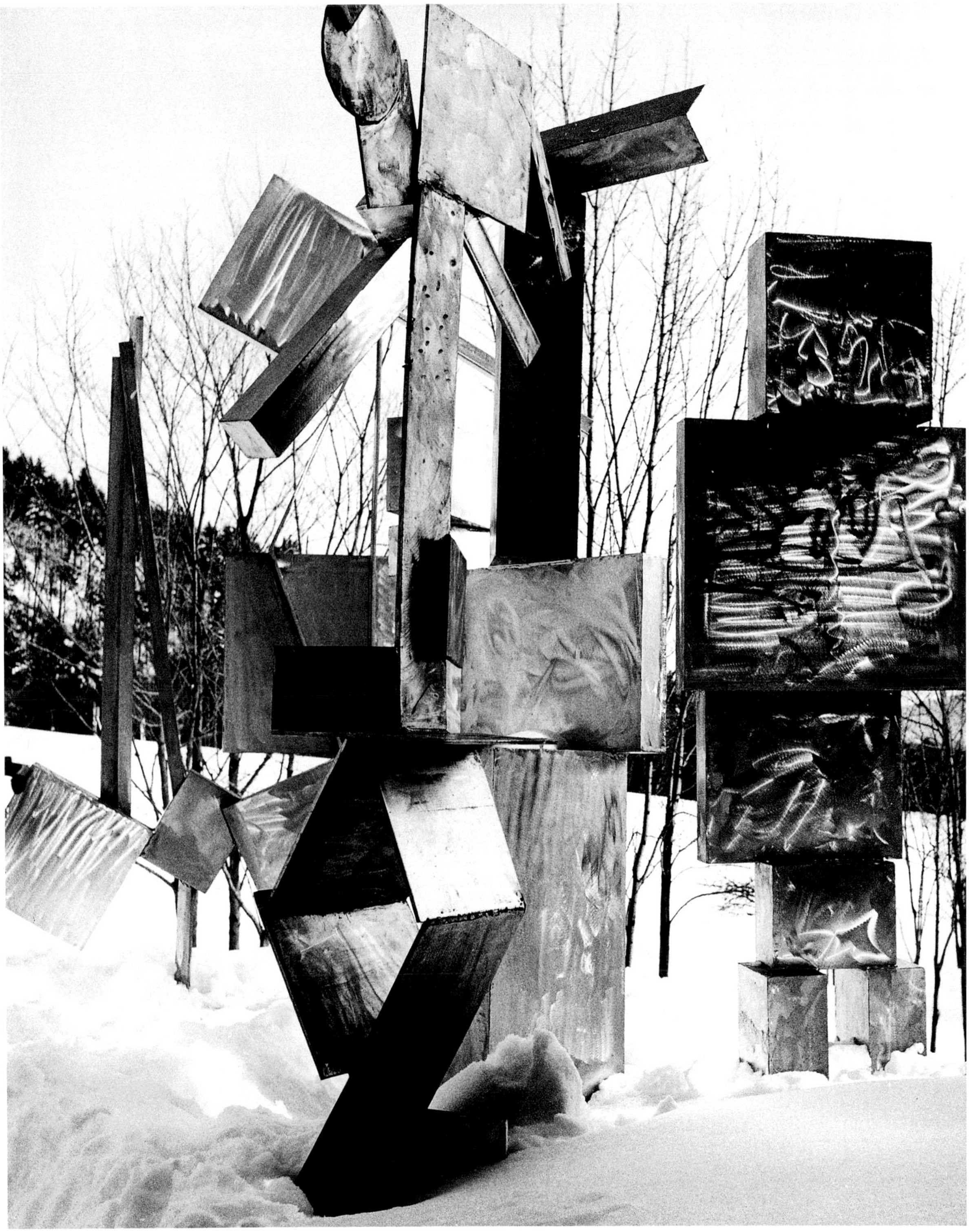

Untitled (**Cube Totem**, **Sentinel**, **Cubi IX**, and **Cubi III**), 1963, The Estate of David Smith

Abstraction and Image Making in David Smith's Sculpture

Alex Potts

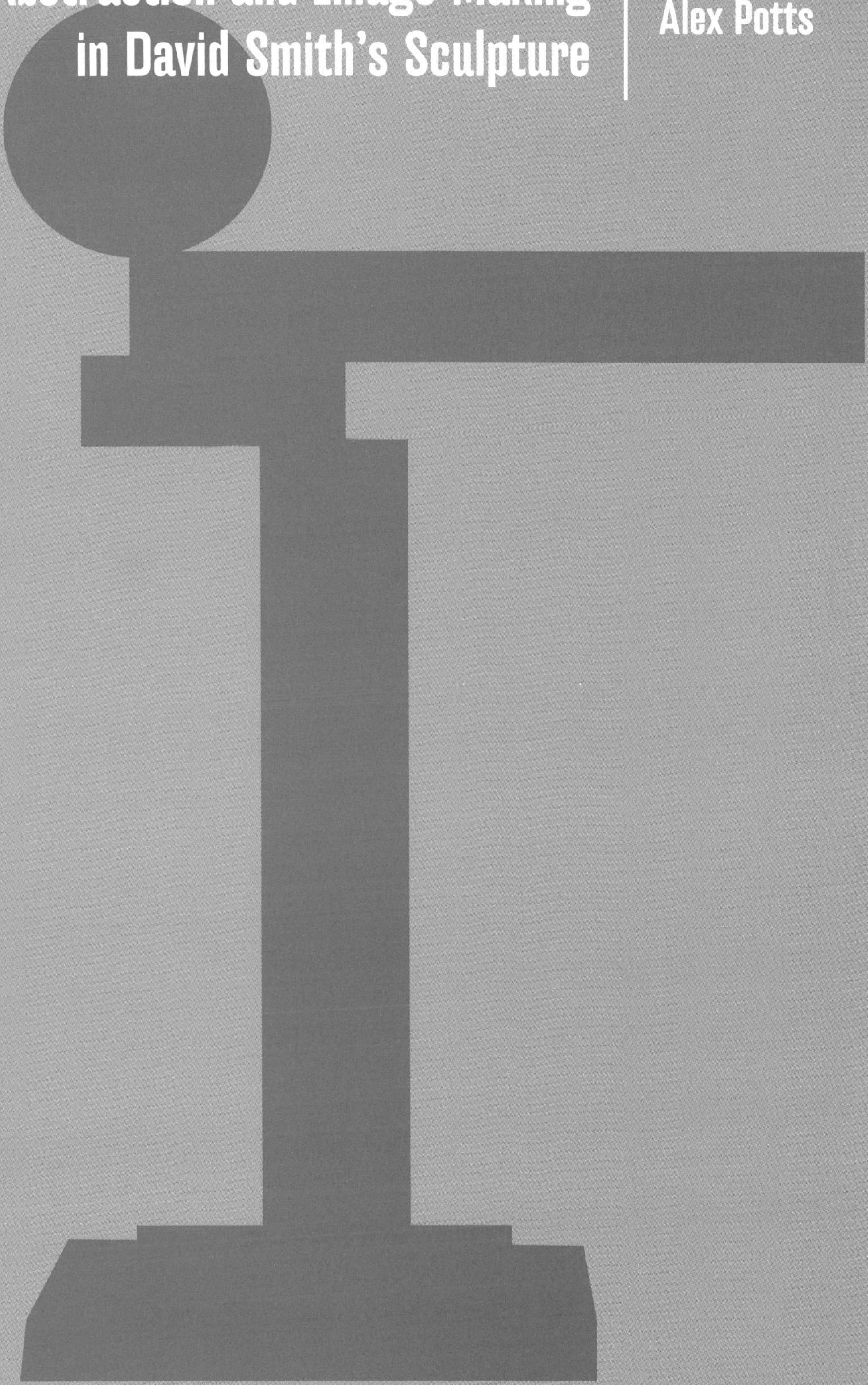

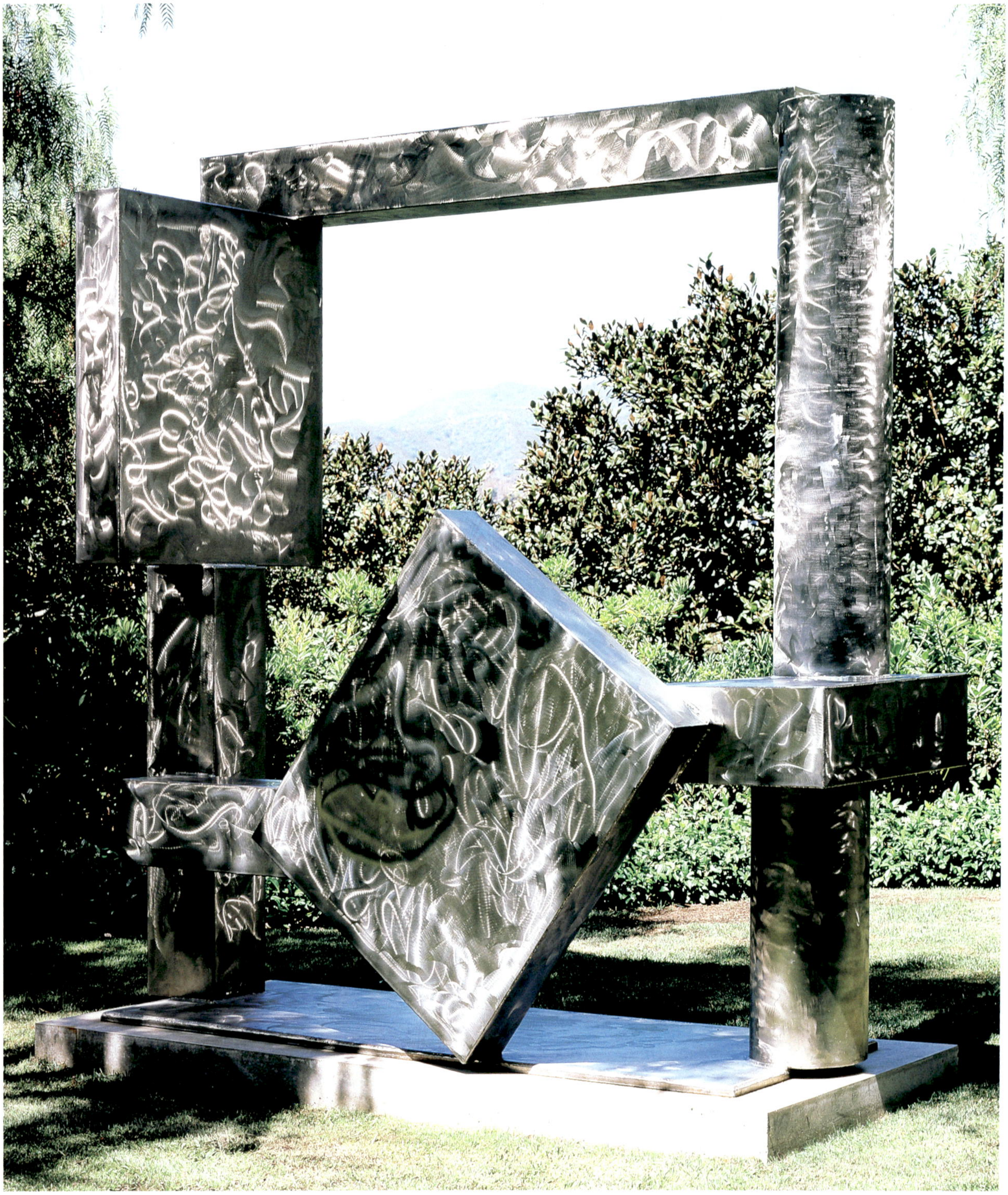

Fig. 1 | Cubi XXVIII, 1965, The Eli and Edythe L. Broad Collection, Los Angeles

In an analysis of David Smith's sculpture published shortly before the artist's death, Clement Greenberg wrote: "I can see that Smith's felicities are won from a wealth of content, of things to say; and this is the hardest, most lasting, way in which they can be won. The burden of content is what keeps an artist going, and the wonderful thing about Smith is the way that burden seems to grow with his years instead of shrinking."[1] What content did Greenberg have in mind? Predictably, it was one for which he was "not able to find words." With a work such as Smith's *Cubi XXVIII* (1965, fig. 1), which makes no evident reference to the figure and eschews such designation in the title, he would be claiming that it is no empty formal exercise. Perhaps the intriguing conflation of rigorous geometric abstraction and residual imagistic shape gives this work its resolutely unspecifiable significance. Not quite a conventional sculpture, it is almost architectonic and sometimes carries the subtitle "Gate." At the same time, though, Smith makes the geometric rationality of architectural form somewhat erratic and unstable by multiple displacements of a regular post-and-lintel structure. On close inspection, the upright shapes with projecting elements at either side can at times suggest vaguely figurative gestures—thrusting, holding, or standing—but then they reinstate themselves as beams and supports of a gateway whose open frame is blocked at the very center by a tipped rectangular slab.

When several *Cubis* are seen together, as in photos taken by Smith himself (fig. 3), they may strike one as virtuoso improvisations in sculptural form, since each array of prefabricated, stainless-steel cubic and rectilinear units is a formal variant configured from similar constituent parts. The works do have a certain autonomy and evocative presence, though. This derives in part from a push-and-pull between suggestions of thrusting and collapsing, as in the precarious tilt of the two longer upward-pointing beams in *Cubi XIX* (1964) that lean against each other. The arrangement of shapes coalesces into an oddly resonant image that resolutely evades identification. This essay aims to explore what kind of image this might be by examining other works by Smith and considering his own complex meditations on artistic abstraction and image making.[2]

Several of the works that Smith produced at the very end of World War II project vivid images with a pointed political significance. *False Peace Specter* (1945, fig. 2), for example, is a deliberately fashioned, monstrously figurative work that recalls the intense anti-capitalist and antifascist polemic against modern warfare evident in Smith's famous series *Medals for Dishonor* (1938–40). The sculpture

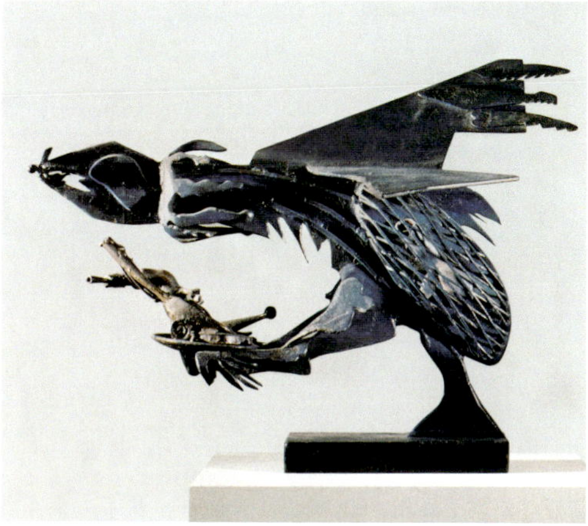

Fig. 2 | False Peace Specter, 1945, bronze and steel, painted, 12 1/2 x 27 1/4 x 10 3/4 in. (31.8 x 69.2 x 27.4 cm), private collection

Following spread: **Fig. 3 |** Installation view of **Cubi XVIII**, **Cubi XVII**, and **Cubi XIX**, Bolton Landing, 1964, photo by David Smith

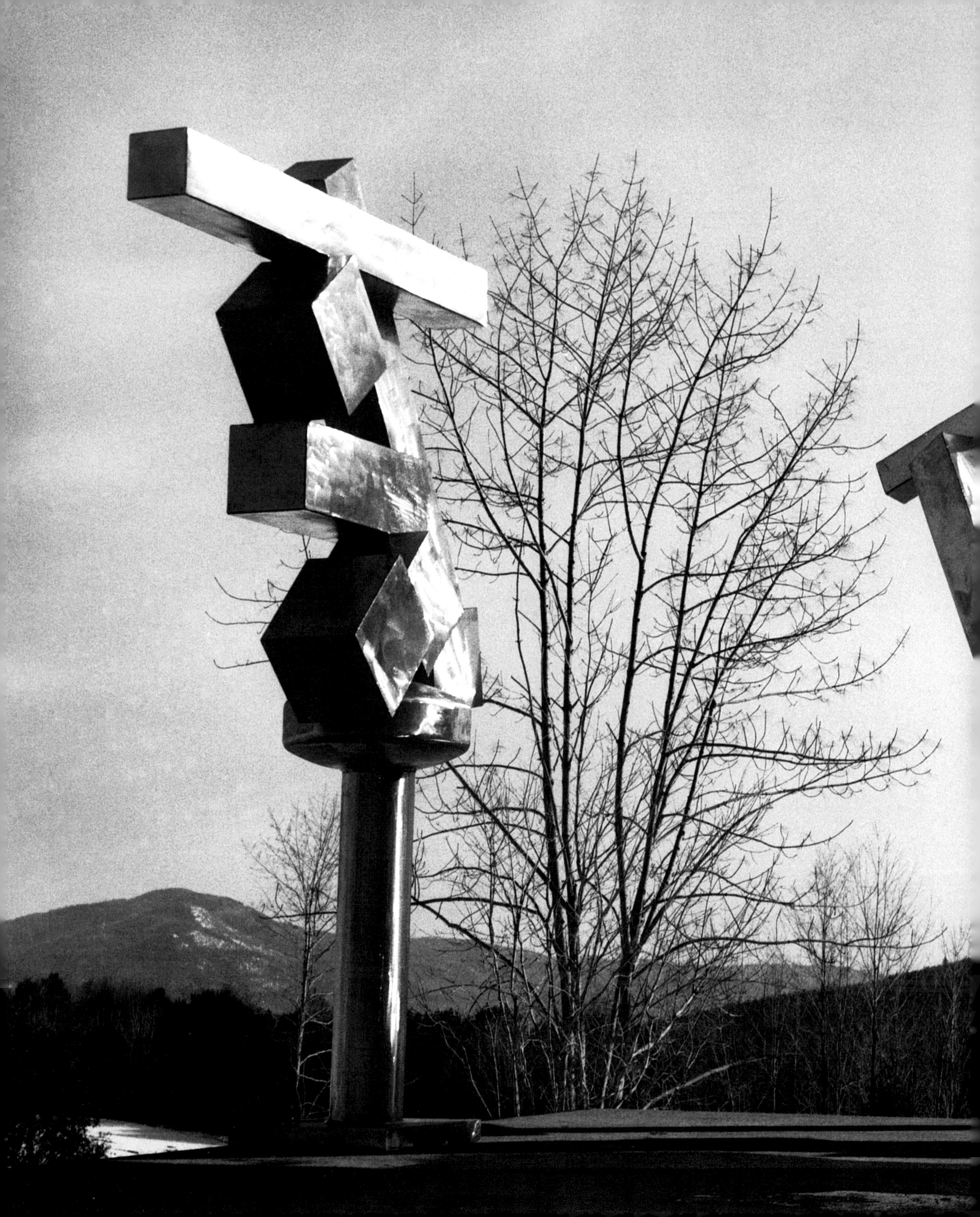

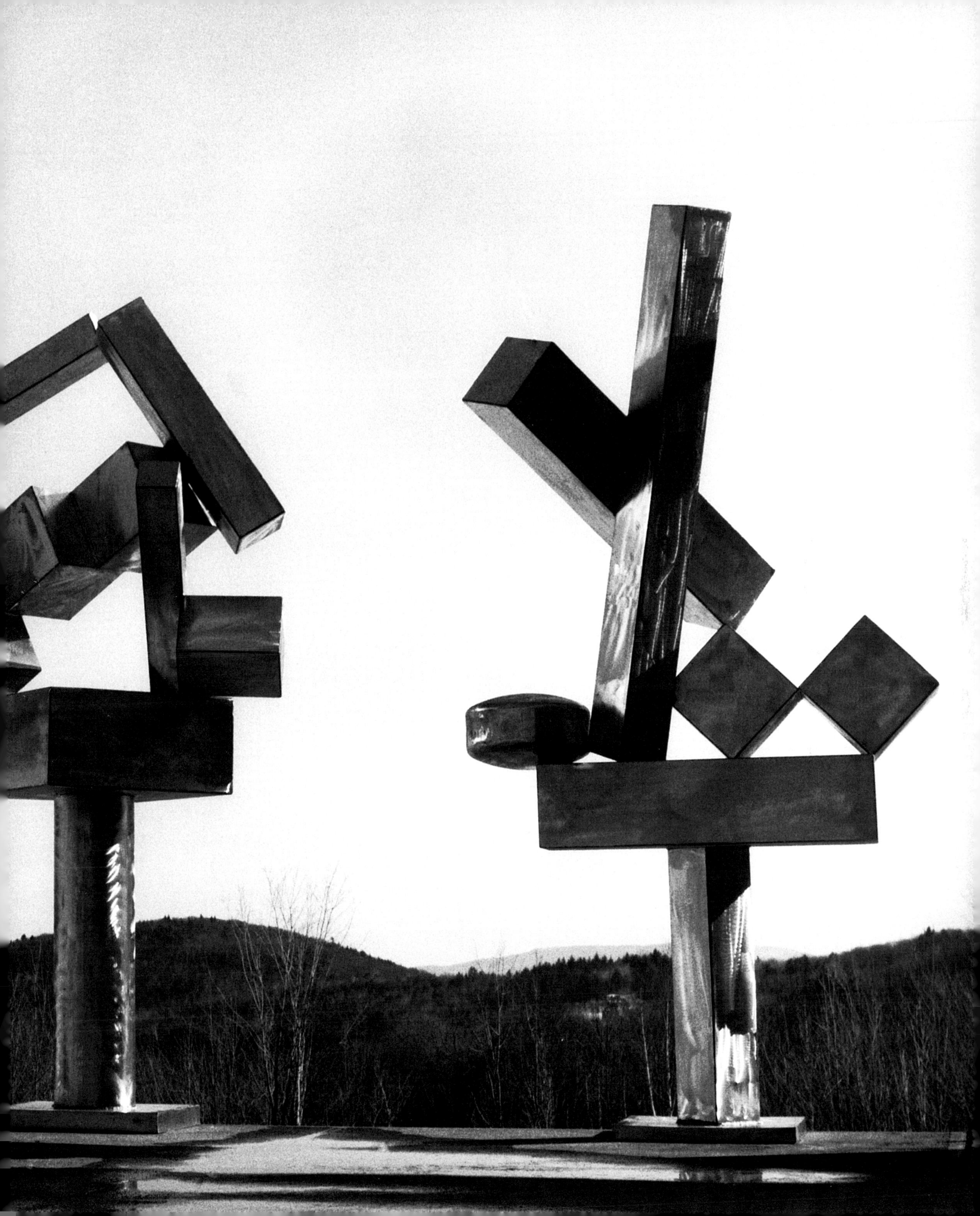

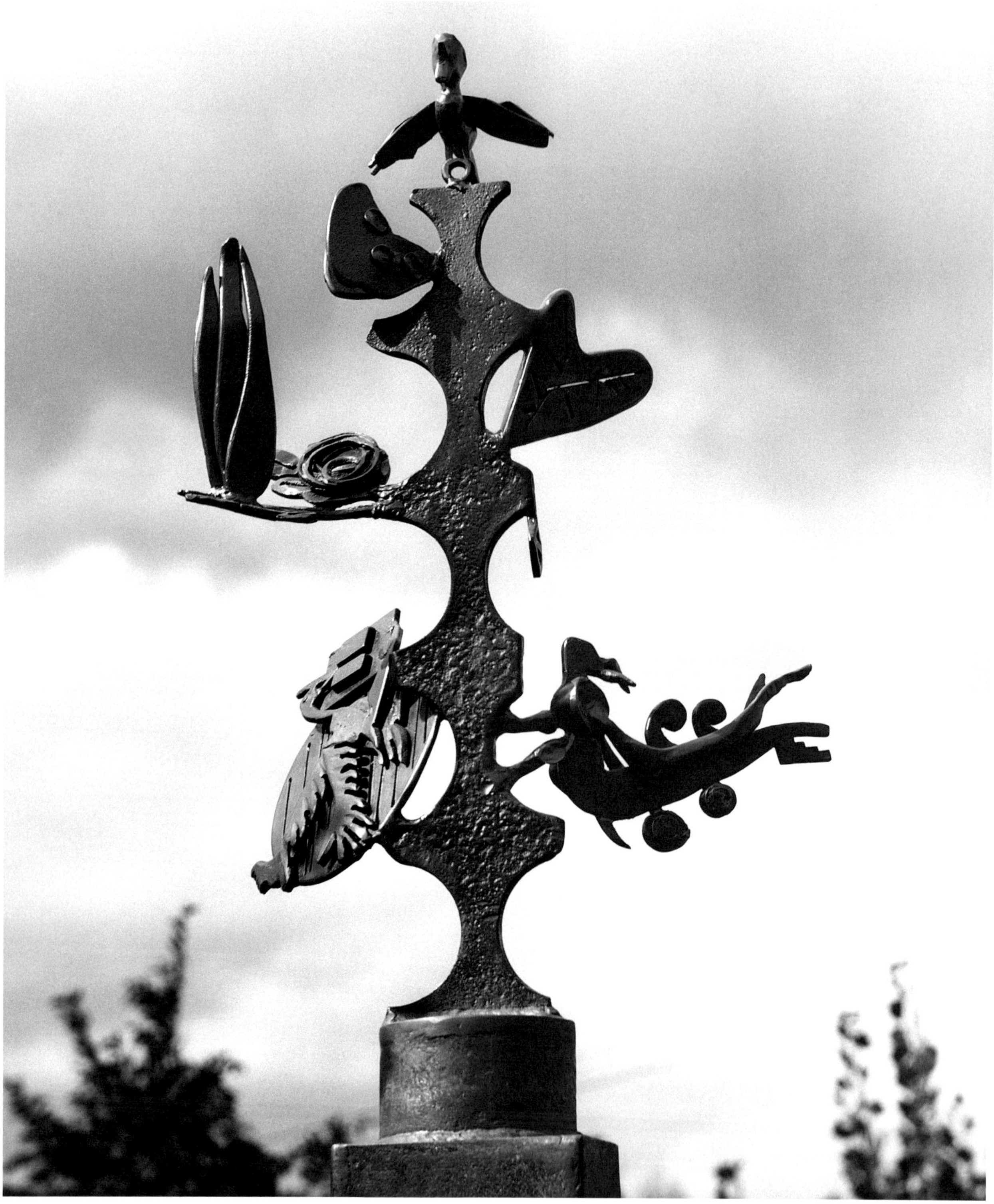

Fig. 4 | Pillar of Sunday, 1945, painted steel, 31 x 16 5/8 x 9 1/2 in. (78.7 x 42.2 x 24.1 cm), Indiana University Art Museum, photo by David Smith

offered a prescient commentary on the false peace negotiated by the United States and the Soviet Union (both dominated by their powerful military-industrial complexes) after the defeat of Germany and Japan in 1945. It also may refer to the devastation wrought by the bombing of Hiroshima and Nagasaki, which had been carried out to force peace upon Japan. Unlike Smith's later, more abstract work assembled from found metal parts, much of *False Peace Specter* was modeled and cast in a relatively traditional way, though its power as an image derives in part from the incongruities between the modeled elements and the found metallic fragments—most notably between the flat, sharp, geometric form of the wings that recall those of a fighter jet[3] and the more biomorphic form of the birdlike creature's body.

Another complex, still figurative work produced the same year—to which Smith gave the ironic title *Pillar of Sunday* (fig. 4)—is closer in conception to the more abstract sculpture for which Smith later became known. No longer forming a single figure, it is an assemblage of vaguely figurative motifs (some of them put together from bits and pieces of metal) attached to a flat, abstractly geometric, treelike or columnlike form. This appears to be a leftover steel sheet from which a series of circular forms was stamped out. Critics have sought to decode the individual motifs as recollections of Sunday rituals in the religious, small-town American environment in which Smith was raised: the chicken dinner at the bottom left; the mermaidlike form on the bottom right, possibly evoking a woman singing in the church choir; the hand of prayer on the left, just above the chicken dinner; various heart shapes; and, at the top, a singing bird that might represent the Sunday preacher. The piety of this scenario is enlivened by suggestions of suppressed erotic charge. Several of the more densely configured forms could be interpreted as sexual symbols, especially the mermaidlike figure and the biomorphic nest or organ beside the upward-flaming motif on the upper left. In the end, the array of images fails to yield any single interpretation. Instead, it generates a flow of semiconscious, shifting associations of the kind that Smith was experimenting with in the poetry he was writing at the time.[4] If one bears in mind the motifs of the drawing (fig. 5) executed in connection with the sculpture and considers the possibility that the flaming form might stand for a burning bush, the work becomes strangely evocative of the violently charged concluding two lines of Smith's poem "Specters Are" that he sent to a friend in 1947:

> Dead birds—limp curls—racist mudball lungfish
> The burning bush and the chicken dinner.[5]

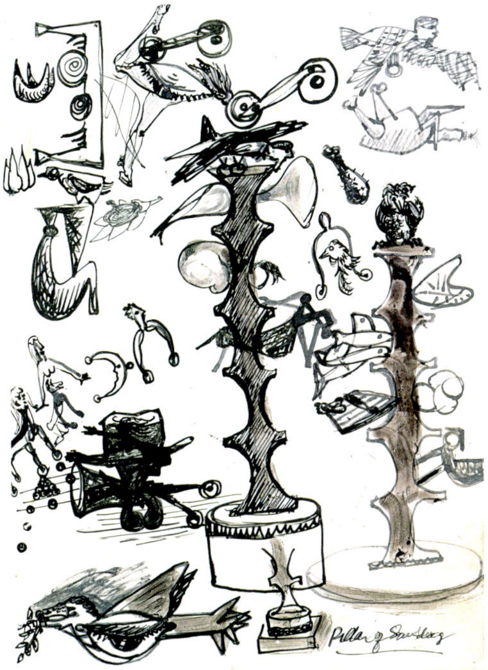

Fig. 5 | Study for Pillar of Sunday, 1945, ink, ink wash, and pencil on paper, 10 x 7 1/4 in. (25.4 x 18.4 cm), The Estate of David Smith

Such associations certainly would be in tune with the irony of the title, and with the less than benign-looking bird crowning the array, which is perhaps not so much a triumphal songster or chanting preacher as a vaguely threatening, if ludicrous, figure of authority. Smith's understanding of how a work like this should resonate with a viewer comes to mind here. "My concept as an artist is a revolt against the well-worn beauties in the form of a statue," he wrote. "Rather I would prefer my assemblages to be the savage idols of basic patterns, the veiled directives, subconscious associations, *the image recall* of orders more true than the object itself, resulting in vision, in aura, rather than object reality."[6]

MATERIALIST ABSTRACTION

For all the figurative references in his work, Smith was unequivocal about his commitment to abstraction. Recalling the full span of his career going back to the 1930s, he maintained in an interview he gave in 1961: "I have been essentially an abstract sculptor."[7] But this did not mean refusal of the image or of representational form. As was the case for many artists of his generation, a commitment to artistic abstraction did not entail a systematic pursuit of purely abstract form. His was a materialist abstract art that he saw as being grounded in the realities of life. "How on earth," he asked, can the artist "know anything he hasn't seen or doesn't exist in his own world? . . . There is no such thing as *truly* abstract. Man always has to work from his life."[8]

He spelled out most fully what this commitment to abstraction meant in some early statements from around 1940, when the status of abstract art was still being strongly contested in the American art world. In his contribution to a forum on abstract art in 1940, organized by Local 60 of the United American Artists, Smith argued that the abstract artist deployed a distinctively modern "art language" that "opposes realism per se, the photographic state of nature and conscious literalism."[9] In other words, abstraction defined a way of working in which the artist no longer sought to portray or copy natural forms but generated new forms impelled by an internal logic of artistic fashioning. Such forms might in the end provoke striking associations with phenomena in the real world, but they were not fashioned with this aim in mind. Here, he articulates an assumption widely held in nontraditional art circles at the time—that the procedures of naturalistic depiction had become so debased, so associated with a stale, bourgeois way of thinking about and imagining things, that they no longer were compatible with the creation of any truly compelling modern art.

Smith also strongly believed that abstract art, because it was not bound by the constraints of naturalistic depiction, affected the viewer at a more suggestive, subconscious level than a literal or naturalistic representation.[10] In abstract sculpture, "form and form associations" would unite in "a statement psychologically decisive, intellectually elevating, and physically unified." The viewer's shifting perceptions of the work's form would stimulate associations whose evocativeness no reference to a real subject could rival. Something vividly actual, then, was brought to mind by way of abstraction. As Smith said, "Instead of a literary message, the mind reacts to a sequence of related forms; the visual result is derived from actuality by abstract association."[11]

One wonders if this way of thinking would have seemed somewhat elitist to those who shared Smith's Communist commitments. He certainly would not have countenanced that a working man's perceptions of and capacities for creativity were in any way inferior to those of the cultivated bourgeois. For him, abstract art was rooted in a "subconscious registry" of psychic realities that cut across class difference. Still, addressing a union audience, he needed to justify politically what might have been misconceived as his rarified commitment to abstract art. Summing up, he insisted that the artist's pursuit of abstraction was no vacuous idealism but rather formed part of labor's struggle for a radically democratic alternative to imperialist capitalism: "The abstract artist admits no mystic process, nor do any union members who paint abstractly live in ivory towers. The problems of the abstract artist in a democratic society are common with those of all men of good will. He rejects participation in the present imperialist war and acknowledges his position with organized labor—to keep America out of war."[12]

Smith's more evidently figurative works, such as *False Peace Specter* and *Pillar of Sunday*, thus should be understood as abstract insomuch as the overall configuration was realized by combining the constituent parts without any particular regard to the representational form of the resulting shape. In short, the driving force was the artist's immersion in the act of juxtaposing and welding the elements together. Abstraction in this sense meant giving precedence to the material realities of artistic process over the rendering of external material realities as they were seen or remembered.

GENERATIVE PROCESS

Smith's commentaries on artistic process were nonformalist in that he made no mention of a formal logic or structure governing how he fashioned his work. What preoccupied him, rather, was the playing out of the immediate impulses and perceptions animating the work's

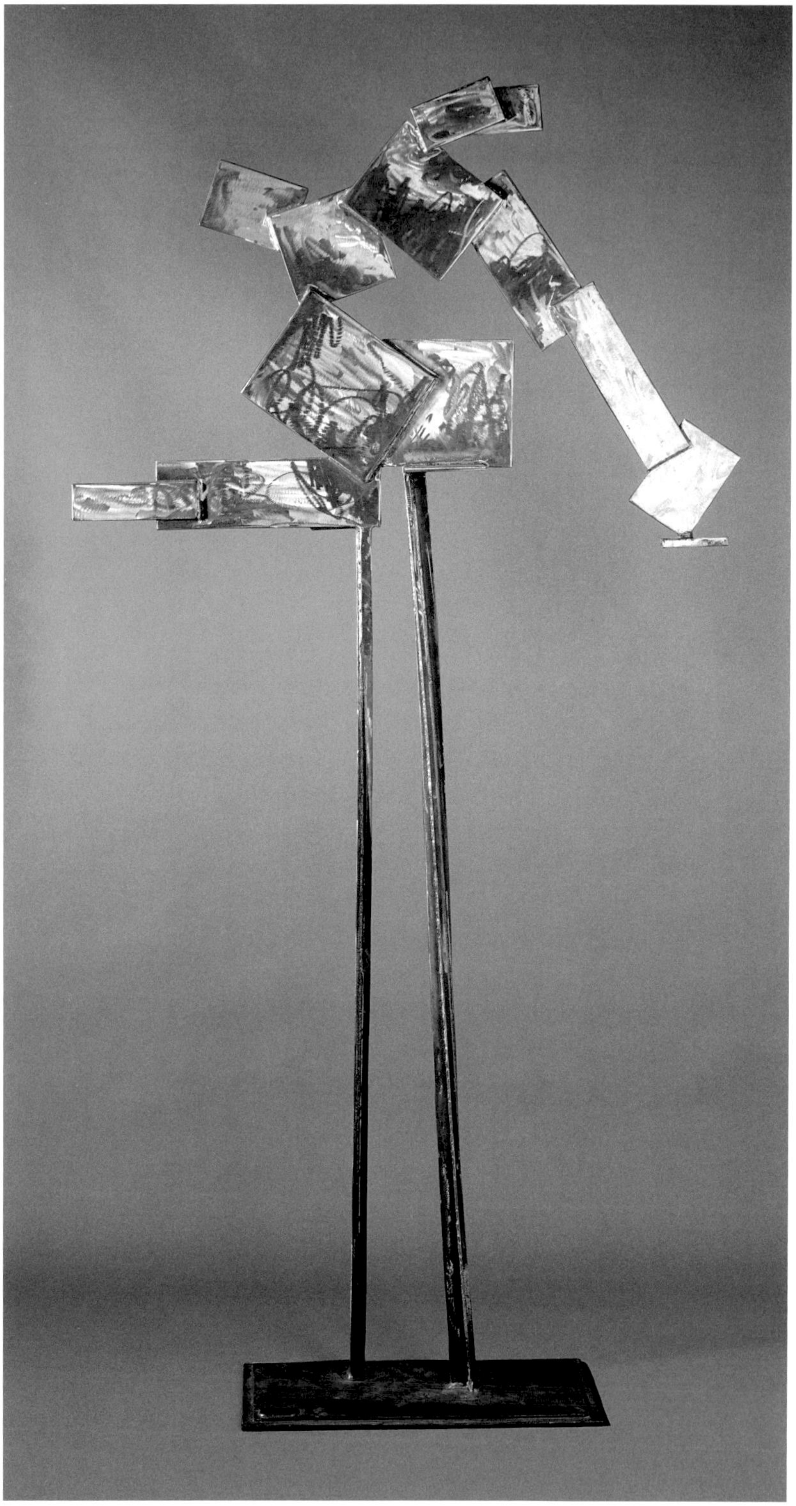

Fig. 6 | Fifteen Planes, 1958, Seattle Art Museum

fabrication. This is evident in the following epigrammatic summation of his conception of artistic creation as a powerfully motivated, ongoing process guided by attending to the changing complexion of the work itself rather than motifs or subjects external to it: “There are trains of form reflections, speeding, to form realization more meaningful to the work of art than conscious action. Reality is the work, there is no subject but the act, reflections in an action of origins. The creative act is in a constant state of movement; even to try to name its parts would stop its action. Visual perception without external subject is a part of all action, a constant and daily involvement.”[13]

Smith also detailed how this understanding of the creative act informed his particular way of working—his abandonment of the modeling or carving of a lump of matter for a process of part-by-part addition in which segments of steel were welded together to form an open array (figs. 6, 7). The work flow involved, he maintained, resulted in part from his experience of the laboring that took place in the manufacture of machinery, where prefabricated parts were assembled and welded together into integrated units. Of fundamental importance to Smith was “the transformation of unit parts into a unified whole from seemingly disparate units, by repeated action . . . [that results] in full order. In fact, my beginning before I knew about art had already been conditioned to the machine—the part of the whole, by addition.” Once the machine tool was mastered, Smith believed, fabrication proceeded almost unconsciously, including the shift from one tool to another as different kinds of joining were required.[14]

Smith had strong ideological grounds for insisting on the parallels between his process of artistic fabrication and that of the skilled welder assembling machines in a factory. He sought to demystify and defetishize traditional understandings of artistic technique. As he claimed in the notes he supplied for an article Elaine de Kooning published on his approach to making sculpture, “I’ve no aesthetic interest in tool marks; my aim in material function is the same as in locomotive building, to arrive at a given functional form in the most efficient manner.”[15]

Clearly, though, the artist was in a very different position from that of the skilled industrial worker. The artist’s way of working was an open and self-determined one, while the worker’s was highly regulated and subject to strictly predetermined, utilitarian ends. Having been employed in a factory that manufactured tanks during World War II, Smith himself was keenly aware of this at a practical level. As someone who politically had been closely associated with the Communist Party,[16]

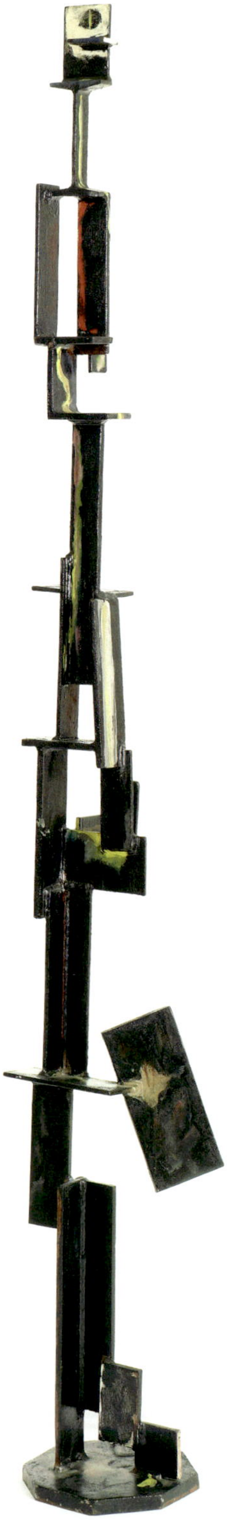

Fig. 7 | Construction in Rectangles, 1955, private collection, courtesy Galerie Gmurzynska, Zurich

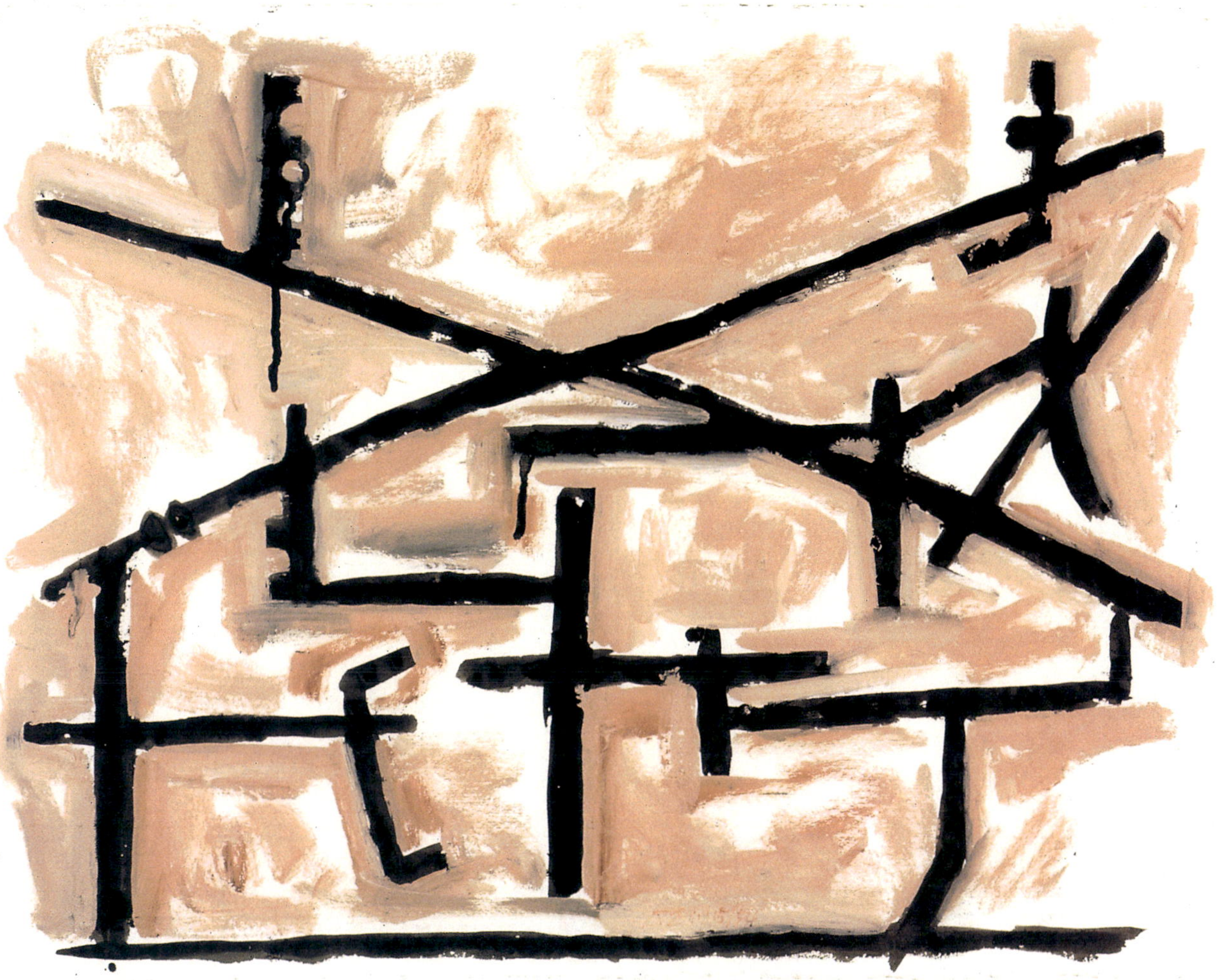

Fig. 8 | ΔΣ 11-15-54, 1954, The Estate of David Smith, courtesy Margo Leavin Gallery, Los Angeles

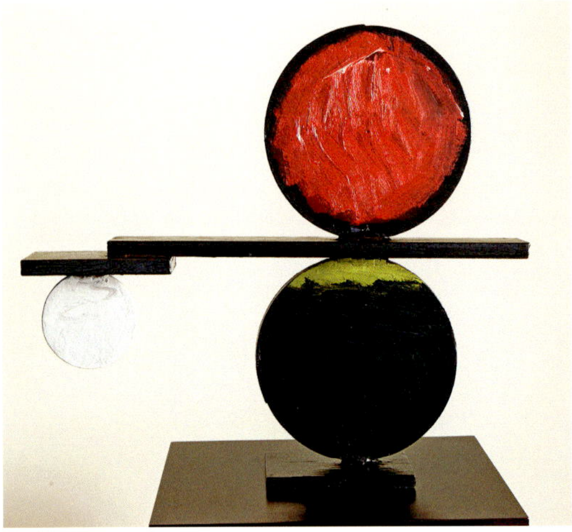

Fig. 9 | Albany IX (Little Albany), 1959–60, The Shidler Family Collection

he also would have been acutely conscious of the very different class connotations of artistic and industrial labor. His public pronouncements on the subject, however, did not go beyond insisting on the honest labor involved in creating sculpture and on making a clear break with traditional bourgeois characterizations of the artist as a mystic creator.[17]

While he evaded drawing attention to real disparities between the relative autonomy of the artist's way of working and the nonautonomous nature of skilled industrial labor, he was quite explicit that welding processes in his case were being deployed to specifically artistic ends. He believed the free flow of arc-welded, part-by-part addition had especially close affinities with the act of drawing (fig. 8).[18] In fact, his most detailed account of the aesthetic logic guiding this type of fabrication came in a lecture he gave on drawing: "The first stroke demands another in complement, the second may demand the third in opposition, and the approach continues, each stroke more free because confidence is built by effort." With practice, "the marks come so easily and move so fast that no time is left to think."[19] Yet the analogy between drawing and fashioning a sculpture was not exact—for the sculptor, faced with a situation in which "the original creative impetus must be maintained during labor, drawing is the fast-moving search which keeps physical labor in balance."[20]

For Smith, the palpable resistance offered by the materials of sculpture meant that realizing a work required more "premeditated and sustained conviction" on the part of the artist than did painting or drawing. There was also something very immediate about making and viewing a sculpture, because it directly incorporated the "physicals" of "gravity, space, and hard objects." In painting, such constants were "illusions," while in sculpture they were material realities integrated into the work's visual fabric (fig. 9).[21]

Moreover, the constituent parts of a welded sculpture stood out more clearly as entities with their own weight and substance than strokes in a drawing did, and this could potentially interrupt the sense of a freely composed flow from one part to the other. Smith's awareness of this helps explain his insistence on the key role played by the found object. Foundness, he claimed, operated at two levels, most obviously in relation to the preformed metal components he incorporated, such as wheels, tool parts, and bits of scrap. But he also saw basic geometric forms, "triangles, circles, and spheres"—and presumably cubic and rectangular volumes—as found rather than created. As a sculptor, he created work from such shapes in the same way that painters composed their still lifes and landscapes from found motifs. Their "trees . . . flowers, fruit, everything" in his view were "found objects," not invented ones.[22]

The question of what integrity the found elements retain in the final work, and of whether awareness of their past functions is effaced in the "transformation of unit parts into a unified whole," comes very much to the fore with his *Agricola* series from the early 1950s (fig. 10). These works were assembled from parts of discarded agricultural tools and machinery. Smith insisted that he chose particular elements based on how their abstract geometric form would fit with the larger configuration he was generating, not by his sense of their original function. At the same time, though, he acknowledged "a certain romantic relationship in my mind to the old handmade objects that have ceased to function."[23] For anyone seeing these works today, individual component elements still register to some degree, but their original function is mostly obscured, except perhaps for someone knowledgeable about American agricultural machinery. The effect is very different in Smith's late *Volton* series (fig. 12), where recognizable tools such as massive pliers and wrenches can be clearly distinguished from the array of more abstract metal forms.

Particularly striking in the *Agricolas* is the virtuosity of the assembling and configuring of constituent elements. The impression that this was a process of free improvisation is accentuated when several

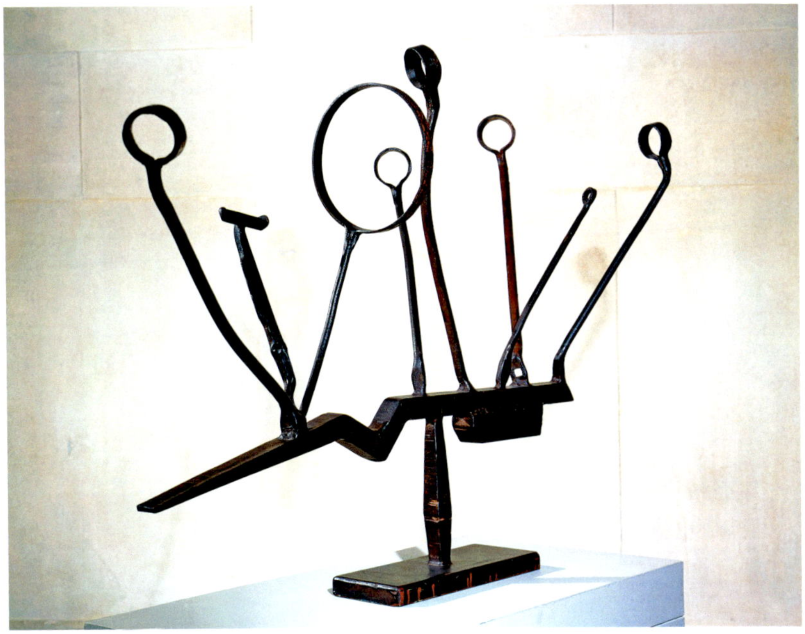

Fig. 10 | Agricola IX, 1952, steel, 36 5/8 x 55 1/4 x 18 in. (93 x 140.3 x 45.7 cm), Tate, London, lent by The Estate of David Smith, promised gift, 2000

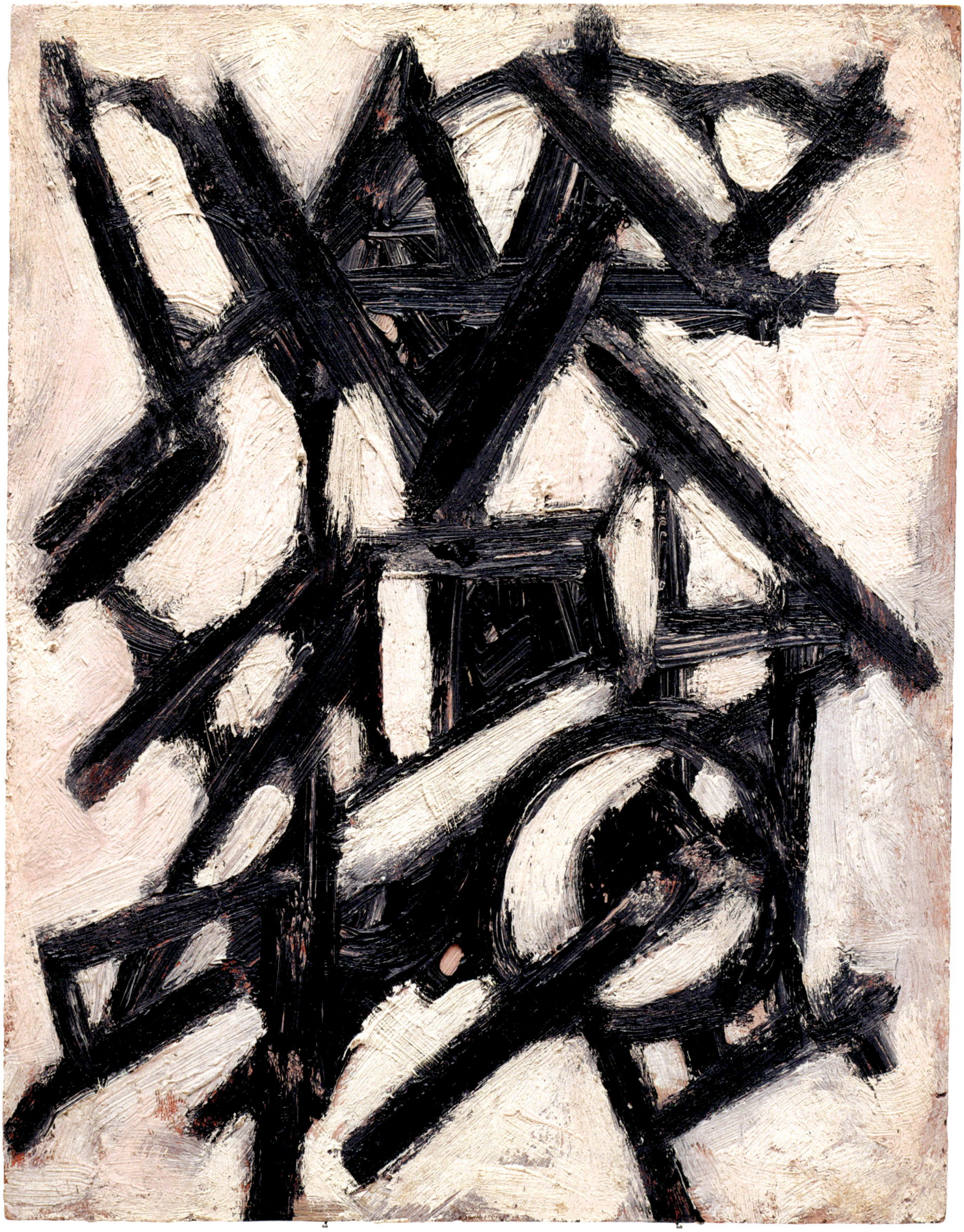

Fig. 11 | Untitled, 1957, The Estate of David Smith,
courtesy Margo Leavin Gallery, Los Angeles

such works are seen together. It is almost as if they were generated in one continuous process, with individual sculptures standing as provisional, fluidly conceived configurations rather than stable, definitive works. Smith's dramatization of his artistic process might apply almost literally in this case: "The creative act is in a constant state of movement . . . The work of art is not premeditated. There is movement and cycles of associative influences which are involved right up until the end. The end may represent only a superficial detachment until it picks up again in the next work. There was a certain culminating stage reached, but it was not anticipated before the work started."[24]

At the same time, the impact these works make as intriguing, somewhat awkward, and unstable-looking presences comes in part from one's sense of the material substance and integrity of the forged- and cast-steel elements held forcibly in place by welding. They are not just formal structures. The images they form have a striking character and individuality, while stubbornly resisting one's impulse to identify them as recognizable objects.

IMAGE MAKING

For Smith, the commitment to abstraction existed alongside, and was in no way incompatible with, fashioning powerful images. As he made clear in his address to an art-historical audience at a 1954 College Art Association meeting, a preoccupation with the images was central to his artistic project: "Images are part of the values in the work of art, profundities for which there are no identifications."[25] The kinds of images he had in mind were more powerful for being "abstract" rather than directly representational: "The image is the aura in space, after the subject is gone—starting a sequence of origins more pointed than auras." He worked on the assumption that "the eidetic image, the after-image, is more important than the object."[26]

The visual qualities of such images could set off a train of proliferating associations. Even a simple quality such as blackness (fig. 11), he suggested, might have this effect: "Is it . . . good or evil, positive or negative? Is it life or death? Is it the superficial scientific explanation about the absence of light? Is it a solid wall or is it space? Is it paint, a man, a father? Or does it come out blank having been censored out by some unknown or unrecognizable association?"[27] Such proliferation, he believed, was heightened by his particular way of working—open forms, as opposed to solid masses, could superimpose themselves in the viewer's field of vision and activate a multiplicity of simultaneous associations; "In vision the overlay of shapes seen through each other not only permits each shape to retain its individual intent but in juxtaposition highly multiplies the associations of the new and more complex unity."[28]

In Smith's view, the images constituted by his works arose out of, and in turn activated, a dialectic of variegated associations operating across several different registers of experience, from recollections of very ordinary material things to apprehensions of "wonders" and "specters." As he said:

> My realities giving impetus to a work which is a train of hooked visions arise from very ordinary locales—the arrangement of things under an old board; stress patterns; fissures; the structure pattern of growth; stains; tracks of men, animals, machines . . . accidental evidences such as spilled paint, patched sidewalks, broken parts, structural faults . . . Realistic all, made by ancient pattern or unknown force . . . Some works are the celebrations of wonders. After several of these a specter.[29]

The resonances of images that made a particularly powerful impact often were dramatized by Smith in terms of extreme dualities between "monster" or "specter" and "grace," between "brutality" and "cloud-longing," and between "beauty" and "destruction and degeneration." His works, he suggests, activated responses that kept shifting between such polarities—for "the poetic statement in the form of cloud-longing is always menaced by brutality . . . Form will flower with spikes of steel."[30]

Even Clement Greenberg, with his high-formalist take on art, suggested that some such dialectic was operating in Smith's work: "As he turned increasingly abstract in latter years . . . the human figure became more and more the one constant attaching him to nature. It was the soar of the human figure that held him, the uncompromising upward thrust it makes, the fight it carries on with the force of gravity."[31] Such a characterization seems particularly apt when considering several of Smith's very late works, such as *Volton XVIII* (1963, fig. 12). It seems both to soar and to collapse—the bold dramatic arc on one side contrasting with the precarious array of small fragments on the other. Something more charged than a gravitational balancing act is involved, as well, which is not reducible to a clichéd humanist interplay between upward-thrusting aspiration and the downward drag of material reality. Smith's dualities between monster and grace, though, do not seem quite appropriate either.[32] When one sees the imposing metal

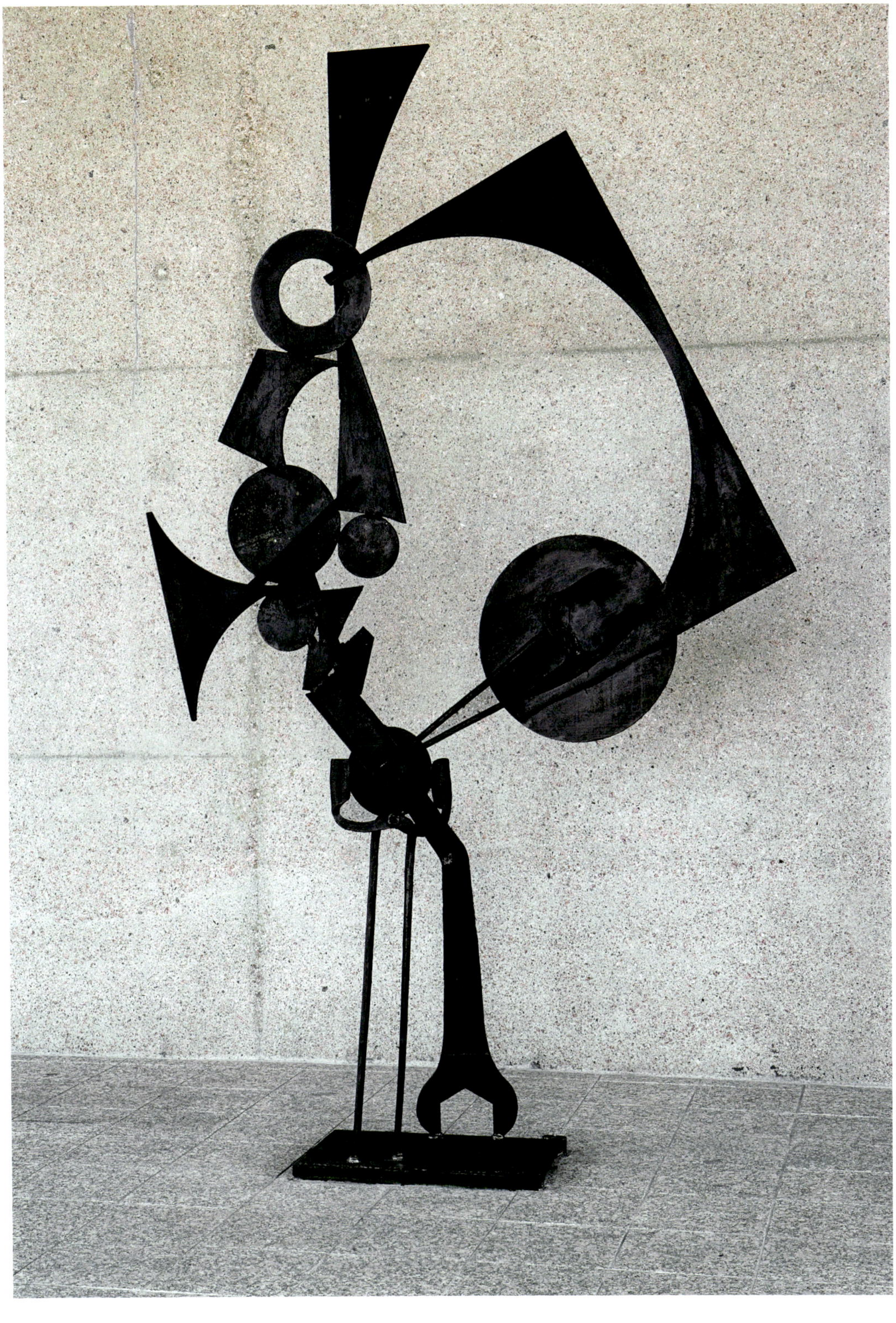

Fig. 12 | Volton XVIII, 1963, steel, 109 1/2 x 67 x 15 in. (278.1 x 170.2 x 38.1 cm), Empire State Plaza Collection, Albany, New York

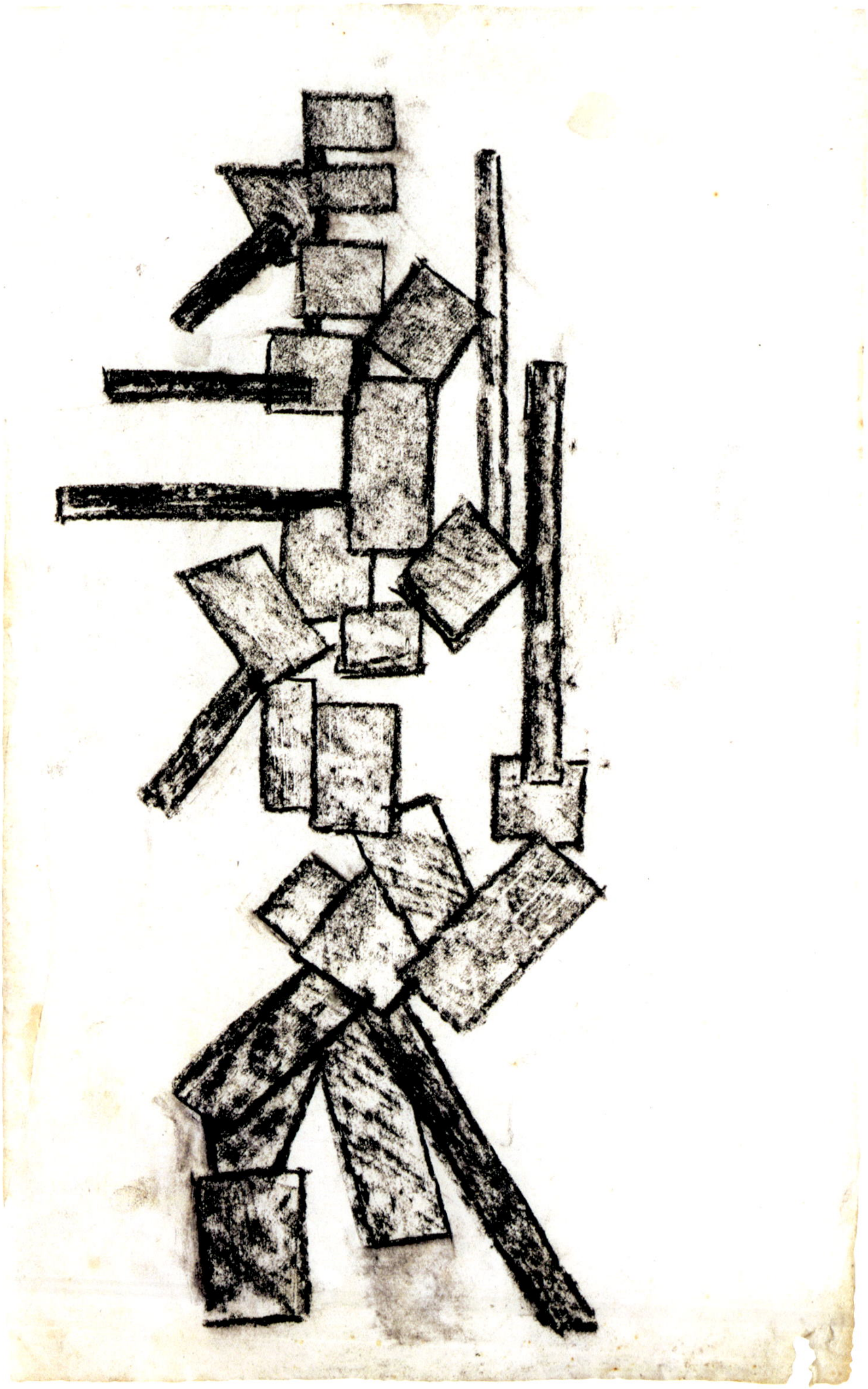

Fig. 13 | Untitled, 1958, The Estate of David Smith

construction as evoking a standing figure of some kind, it also seems somewhat comic and ludicrous. This effect operates both abstractly and concretely, as happens with a drawing in which a configuration of lines suddenly coalesces into a striking caricature (fig. 13).

A similar, if less dramatic but more complex, disparity between contrary associations is at play in *Voltri XVII* (1962, figs. 14, 15). This work too has a powerfully configured presence—standing there as a curiously awkward yet emphatically upright figure, improvised from segments of heavy steel. Its core is a gratelike element (cannibalized from a smelting furnace) set on an elementary, post-and-lintel steel stand. Into this basic structure Smith slotted large slats of steel with rounded edges—the discarded ends, or what he called "clouds," produced when rolled steel was cut to a rectangular shape. Like *Volton XVIII*, this is an integrated configuration, but one in which the found elements (such as the central grate) stand out, even if their original source is not immediately identifiable, and give the work a certain heterogeneous, discontinuous aspect.

As an image, it strikes one as a large, almost dominating presence but also as a ludicrous caricature on simple peg legs. It is spare and austerely rectilinear, quite nonhuman from some points of view but oddly bodylike—its shape amplified by sensuous, almost biomorphic curves—from others. Critics have remarked on how the work invites contradictory associations and resists being seen as a single, stable motif. For E. A. Carmean Jr., writing in the catalogue of a Smith exhibition held in 1982, the "post-and-lintel structure" has a "rigid," "column-like" identity, while the "curving shapes" displayed a "feminine" quality.[33] Particularly suggestive are Rosalind Krauss's responses in her study of Smith published more than ten years earlier. Like Carmean, she identified "something magnificently Doric" about the work when seen from the front, and then went on to comment that, in a profile view, "an almost blowsy biomorphism, a swollen sensuousness . . . seems to come from nowhere."[34] For her, the sculpture's disjunctive formalization of sculptural shape entailed a complete negation of ideas of totality or centered identity. What makes the work so compelling, though, is not its disjunctiveness as such, but its curiously unstable coherence as an entity both vulgarly figurelike and austerely abstract. As with many of Smith's more striking works, the incongruous yet vividly configured assemblage of found and prefabricated steel elements has a presence that is, to use the artist's own words, "both humorous and profound."[35]

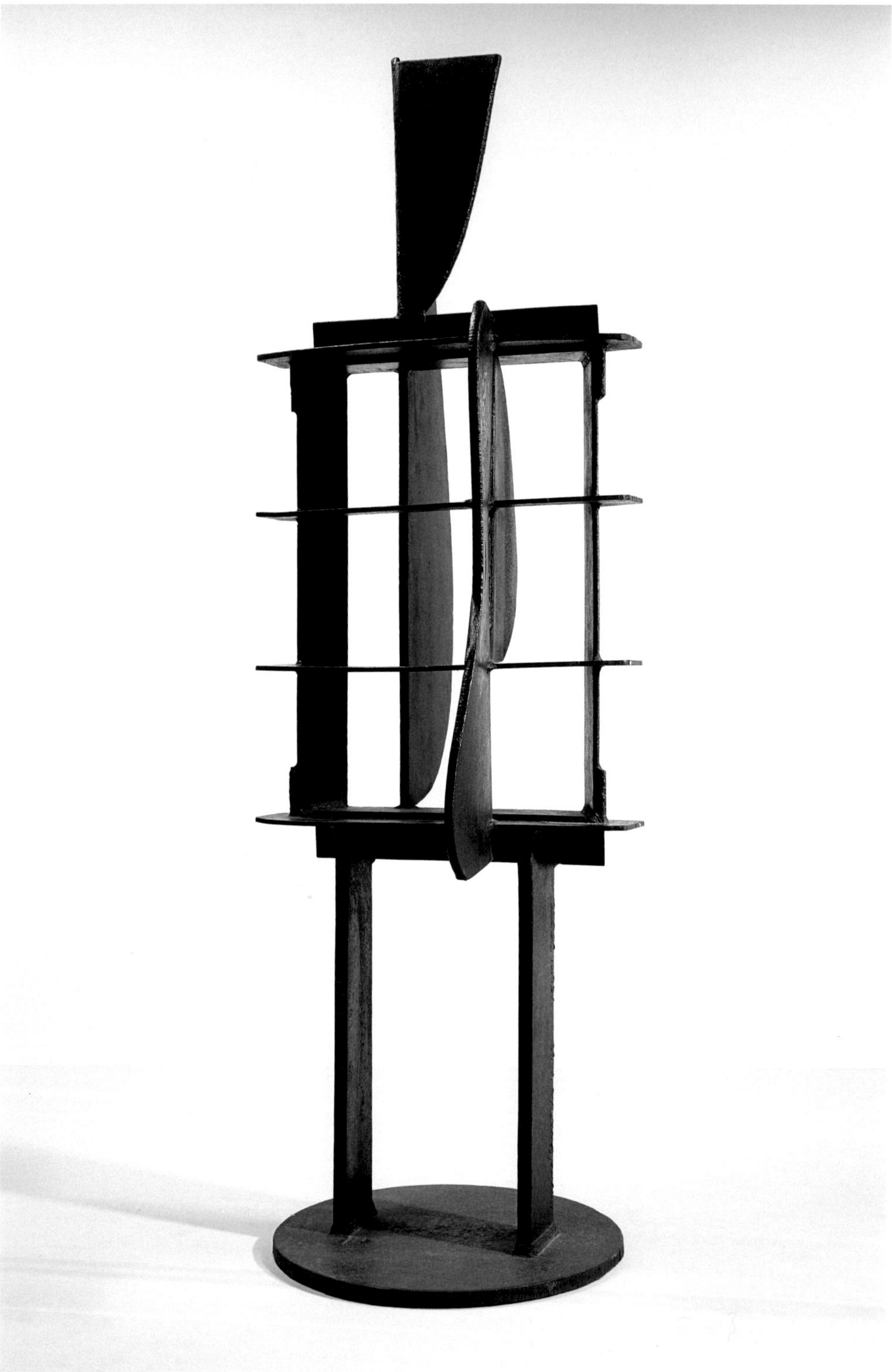

Fig. 14 | Voltri XVII, 1962, steel, 95 x 31 3/8 x 30 3/4 in. (241.3 x 79.7 x 78.1 cm), collection of Lois and Georges de Menil, New York

Fig. 15 | Installation view of Voltri XVII (on left), **Voltri IV**, and **Voltri** in the Anfiteatro Romano, Spoleto, Italy, June 1962, photo by David Smith

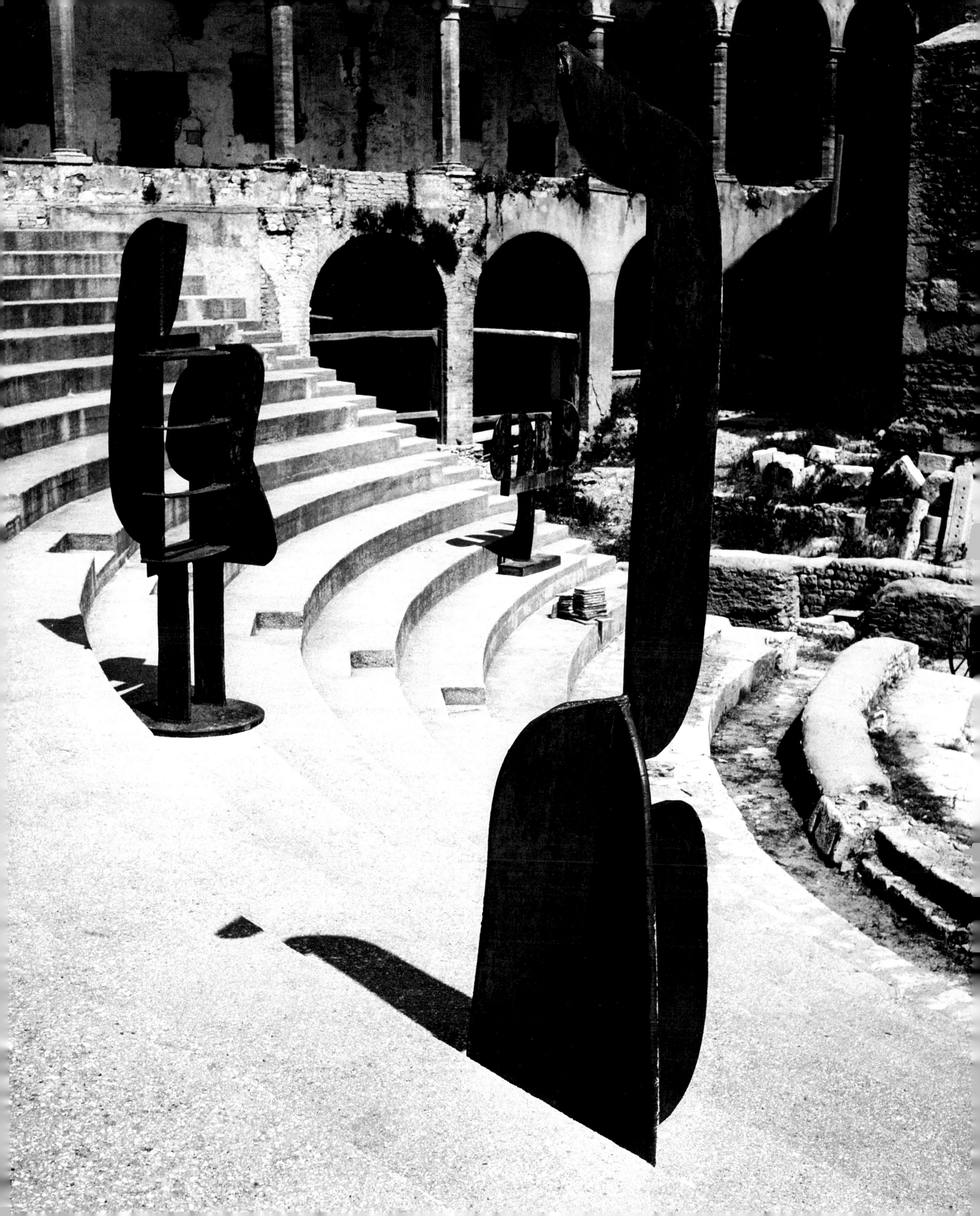

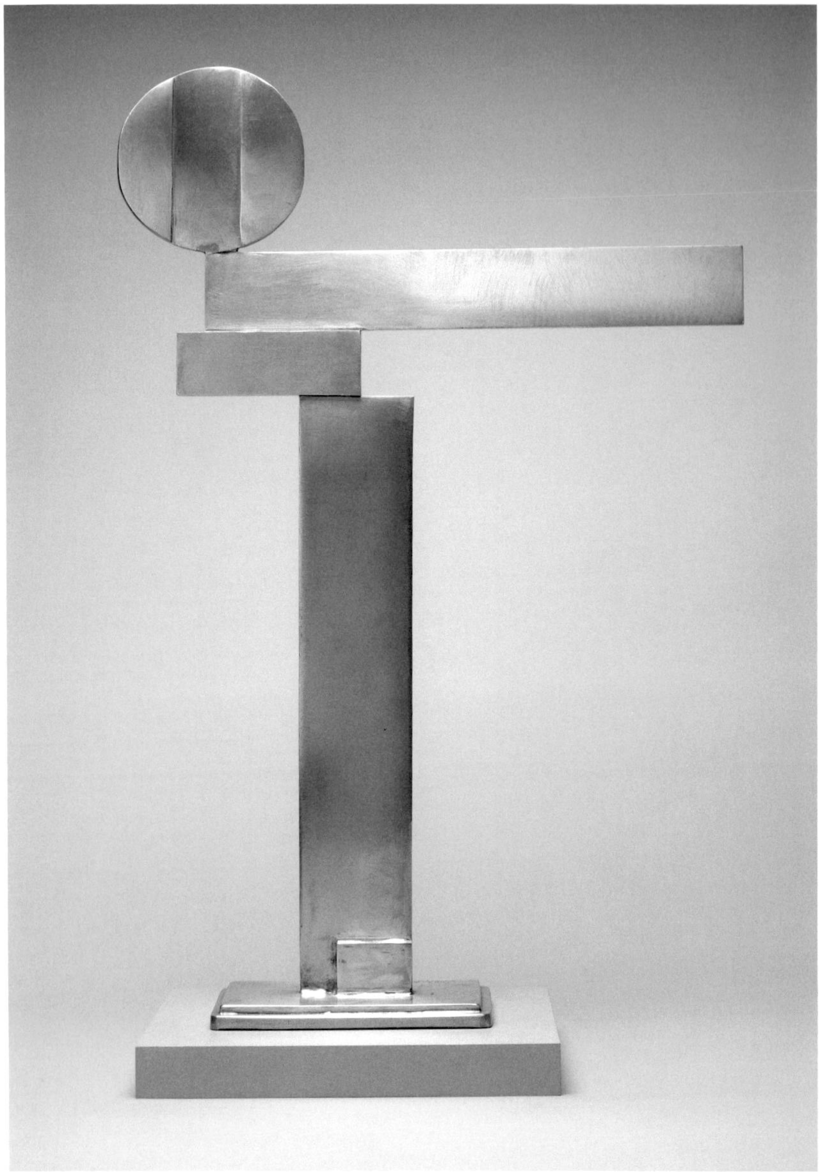

Books and Apple, 1957, Harvard Art Museums/Fogg Museum

Quotations by David Smith are taken from the collection of his writings published by Garnett McCoy, ed., in *David Smith* (New York: Praeger, 1973), as are the references in the notes that cite the original sources of Smith's writings.

1. Clement Greenberg, "America Takes the Lead, 1945–1965," 1965, reprinted in *The Collected Essays and Criticism*, vol. 4, ed. John O'Brian (Chicago: University of Chicago Press, 1993), 192.

2. I discuss these issues as they inform the conception of Smith's more figurelike works in my essay "Personages Imperfect and Persistent," in *David Smith: Personage* (New York: Gagosian Gallery, 2006), 7–19.

3. At the time of the sculpture's creation, one of the only fighter jets with swept wings was the German Messerschmitt, which came into service in 1944.

4. Sarah B. Kianovsky, "Annotated Checklist of Sculptures," in *David Smith: A Centennial*, exh. cat., ed. Carmen Giménez (New York: Guggenheim Museum, 2006), 296.

5. David Smith, "Specters Are," 1947, published in McCoy, 200.

6. David Smith, "Perception and Reality" (speech, Williams College, Williamstown, MA, December 17, 1951), published in McCoy, 78. Italics are Smith's.

7. David Sylvester, "Tape-Recorded Interview with David Smith, Sculptor, at the International Building, New York City, June 16, 1961; Interviewer: David Sylvester, of the British Broadcasting Corp." (transcript, The Estate of David Smith, Archives, box 12), reprinted as "Interview" in McCoy, 169.

8. Ibid., 171. Italics are Smith's.

9. David Smith, "On Abstract Art" (lecture, United American Artists Forum on Abstract Art, New York, February 15, 1940), excerpted in David Smith, "Abstract Art," *The New York Artist*, April 1940, published in McCoy, 37.

10. Ibid., 39–40.

11. David Smith, "Modern Sculpture and Society" (essay written at the request of the Federal Arts Project for the proposed publication *Art for the Millions*, 1940), published in McCoy, 42.

12. Smith, "On Abstract Art," published in McCoy, 40.

13. David Smith, "The Artist's Image" (paper, College Art Association meeting, Philadelphia, January 30, 1954), published in McCoy, 115.

14. David Smith, "The New Sculpture" (paper, The Museum of Modern Art, New York, February 21, 1952), published in McCoy, 84–85. See also David Smith's statement on arc welding, "Design for Progress—*Cockfight*," c. 1947, published in McCoy, 60.

15. David Smith, "Notes for *David Smith Makes a Sculpture*," 1951, published in McCoy, 74.

16. For information on Smith's political involvements in the late 1930s and early 1940s, see Paula Wisotzki, "Strategic Shifts: David Smith's China Medal Commission," *Oxford Art Journal* 17, no. 2 (1994): 63–77.

17. For information on Smith's self-image as a worker artist, see Paula Wisotzki, "Artist and Worker: The Labor of David Smith," *Oxford Art Journal* 28, no. 3 (2005): 347–70.

18. David Smith, "Atmosphere of the Early Thirties" (notes from a sketchbook, c. 1952), published in McCoy, 85.

19. David Smith, "Drawing" (lecture, Sophie Newcomb College, Tulane University, New Orleans, LA, March 21, 1955), published in McCoy, 137. He also drew some very suggestive analogies between his approach to sculptural fabrication and the techniques of Japanese pen drawing (Smith, "The New Sculpture," published in McCoy, 83).

20. Smith, "Drawing," published in McCoy, 137.

21. Smith, "The New Sculpture," published in McCoy, 82.

22. Thomas B. Hess, "The Secret Letter: An Interview with David Smith, June 1964" (transcript with handwritten edits, The Estate of David Smith, Archives, box 12), n.p., published in *David Smith*, exh. cat. (New York: Marlborough-Gerson Gallery, 1964), n.p.; reprinted in McCoy, 175.

23. Ibid.

24. Smith, "The Artist's Image," published in McCoy, 115.

25. Ibid.

26. David Smith, "The Artist and Nature" (address, University of Mississippi, Oxford, March 8, 1955), published in McCoy, 117.

27. David Smith, "The Sculptor and His Problems" (speech, Woodstock Conference of Artists, Woodstock, NY, August 23, 1952), published in McCoy, 87.

28. Smith, "The New Sculpture," published in McCoy, 83–84.

29. David Smith, "The Language Is Image," *Arts and Architecture*, February 1952, reprinted in McCoy, 80.

30. Smith, "The New Sculpture," published in McCoy, 85.

31. Clement Greenberg, "David Smith: Critical Comment," 1966, reprinted in *The Collected Essays and Criticism*, vol. 4, ed. John O'Brian (Chicago: University of Chicago Press, 1993), 228.

32. Smith saw his late *Wagons* as "monsters" but also potentially as "graces." David Smith, "Memories to Myself" (speech, Eighteenth Conference of the National Committee on Art Education, The Museum of Modern Art, New York, May 5, 1960), published in McCoy, 155.

33. E. A. Carmean Jr., *David Smith*, exh. cat. (Washington, D.C.: National Gallery of Art, 1982), quoted in *David Smith: A Centennial*, exh. cat., ed Carmen Giménez (New York: Guggenheim Museum, 2006), 93.

34. Rosalind E. Krauss, *Terminal Iron Works: The Sculpture of David Smith* (Cambridge, MA: MIT Press, 1971), 152.

35. Smith, "The Artist's Image," published in McCoy, 115.

Checklist of the Exhibition

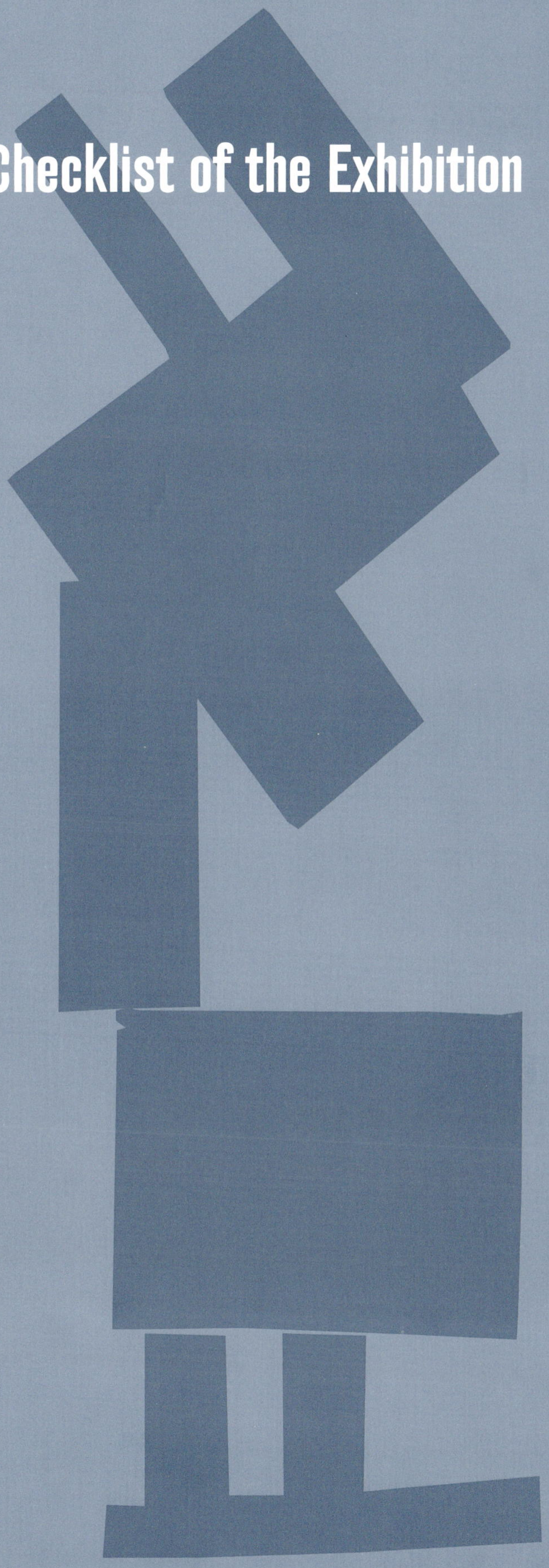

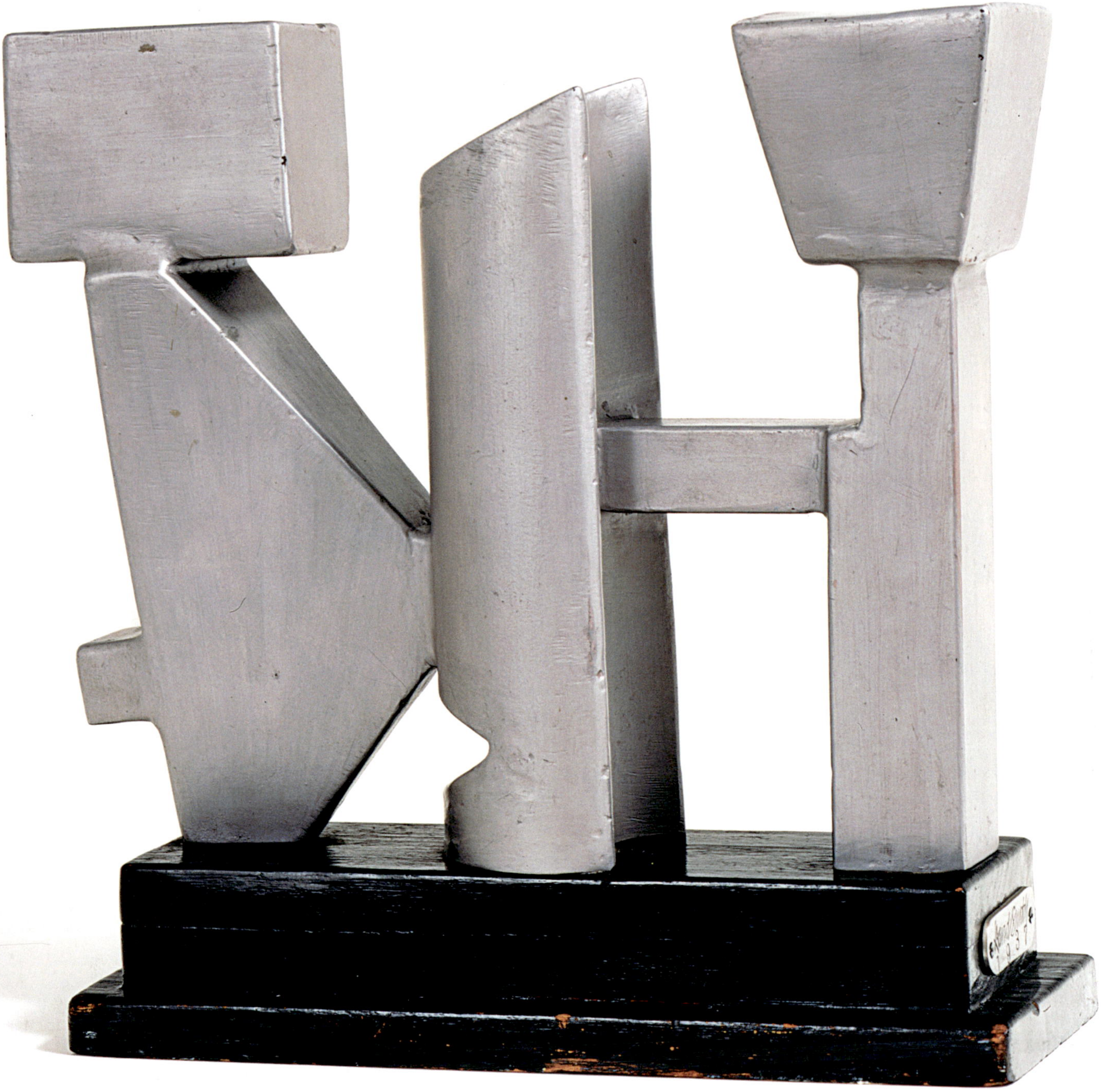

Unity of Three Forms, 1937

The checklist is complete as of October 1, 2010. Height precedes width, which precedes depth.

Sculptures

Construction, 1932
Wood and plaster, painted, on wood base
11 x 11 x 9 1/2 in. (27.9 x 27.9 x 24.1 cm)
The Estate of David Smith
p. 30

Saw Head, 1933
Iron and bronze, painted
18 1/2 x 12 x 8 1/4 in. (47 x 30.5 x 21 cm)
The Estate of David Smith, courtesy Tate, London
p. 22

Unity of Three Forms, 1937
Steel and painted wood base
14 x 17 1/2 x 5 in. (35.6 x 44.5 x 12.7 cm)
Private collection, courtesy The Estate of David Smith

Blue Construction, 1938
Sheet steel with baked-enamel finish
36 1/4 x 28 1/2 x 30 in. (92.1 x 72.4 x 76.2 cm)
The Estate of David Smith, courtesy National Gallery of Art, Washington
p. 33

Suspended Cube, 1938
Painted steel
23 x 16 x 20 1/4 in. (58.4 x 40.6 x 51.4 cm)
Private collection, courtesy The Estate of David Smith
p. 27

Untitled, 1938
Steel and paint, on artist's wood base
9 x 5 3/4 x 2 in. (22.9 x 14.6 x 5.1 cm)
Private collection
p. 73

Growing Forms, 1939
Aluminum on wood base
69 15/16 x 13 x 13 in. (177.6 x 33 x 33 cm)
University of Michigan Museum of Art, Ann Arbor, bequest of Charles E. Palmer in honor of Jean Paul Slusser
p. 38

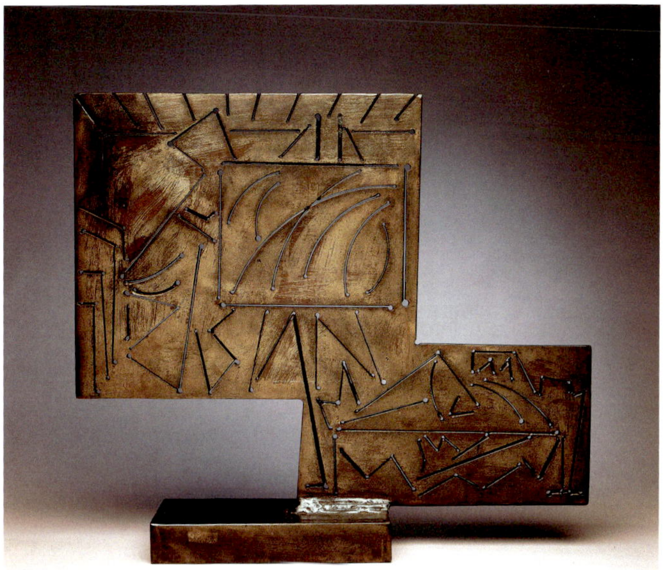

Steel Drawing I, 1945

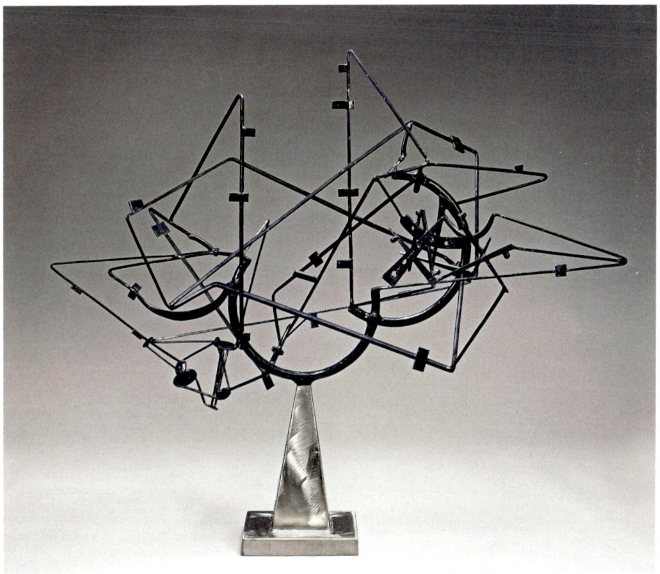

Star Cage, 1950

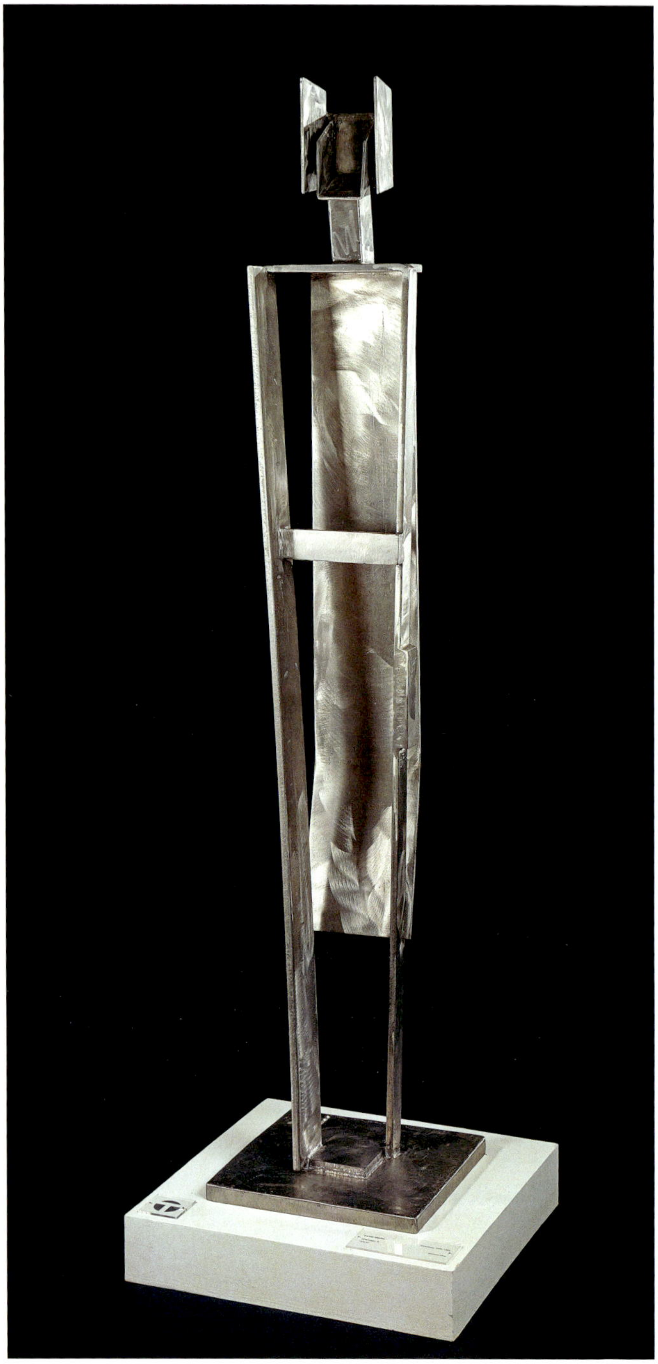

Sentinel II, 1956–57

Vertical Structure–Vertical Construction, 1939
Steel with copper
45 7/8 x 33 1/2 x 28 3/8 in. (116.5 x 85.1 x 72.1 cm)
The Estate of David Smith, courtesy Museo Nacional Centro de Arte Reina Sofía, Madrid
p. 35

Steel Drawing I, 1945
Steel
22 1/4 x 26 x 6 in. (56.5 x 66.1 x 15.3 cm)
Hirshhorn Museum and Sculpture Garden, Smithsonian Institution, Washington, D.C., gift of Joseph H. Hirshhorn, 1966
p. 145

17 h's, 1950
Painted steel
44 1/2 x 29 x 12 1/2 in. (113 x 73.7 x 31.8 cm)
The Estate of David Smith
p. 48

Star Cage, 1950
Painted and brushed steel
44 7/8 x 51 1/4 x 25 3/4 in. (114 x 130.2 x 65.4 cm)
Frederick R. Weisman Art Museum, University of Minnesota, Minneapolis, the John Rood Sculpture Collection
p. 145

The Hero, 1951–52
Painted steel
73 3/4 x 25 1/2 x 11 3/4 in. (187.2 x 64.8 x 29.8 cm)
Brooklyn Museum, Dick S. Ramsay Fund, 57.185
p. 41

Big Diamond, 1952
Painted steel
28 1/8 x 27 5/8 x 8 7/8 in. (71.4 x 70.2 x 22.5 cm)
Memorial Art Gallery of the University of Rochester; The Charles Rand Penney Collection of the Memorial Art Gallery
p. 37

The Sitting Printer, 1954–55
Bronze
87 x 15 3/4 x 17 in. (221 x 40 x 43.2 cm)
Storm King Art Center, Mountainville, New York, gift of the Ralph E. Ogden Foundation, Inc.
p. 68

Construction in Rectangles, 1955
Painted steel
78 x 10 7/8 x 10 1/2 in. (198.1 x 27.6 x 26.7 cm)
Private collection, courtesy Galerie Gmurzynska, Zurich
p. 128

5 1/2, 1956
Painted steel
81 3/4 x 18 1/4 x 14 in. (207.6 x 46.3 x 35.6 cm)
Harvard Art Museums/Fogg Museum, gift of
Lois Orswell
p. 148

Sentinel II, 1956–57
Stainless steel
71 3/8 x 14 1/2 x 14 1/2 in. (181.3 x 36.8 x 36.8 cm)
Hirshhorn Museum and Sculpture Garden, Smithsonian
Institution, Washington, D.C., gift of Joseph H. Hirshhorn,
1966

Books and Apple, 1957
Silver
30 x 21 x 4 7/8 in. (76.2 x 53.3 x 12.4 cm)
Harvard Art Museums/Fogg Museum, gift of
Lois Orswell
p. 140

Lonesome Man, 1957
Silver
28 x 9 1/2 x 4 1/2 in. (71.1 x 24.1 x 11.4 cm)
The Estate of David Smith

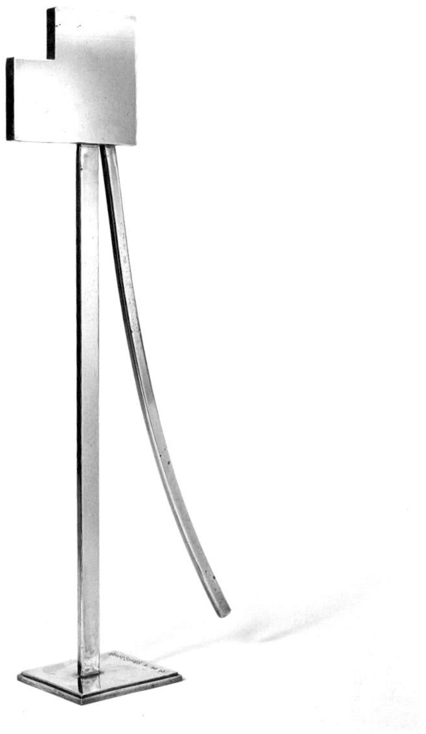

Lonesome Man, 1957

Fifteen Planes, 1958
Stainless steel
113 3/4 x 59 1/16 x 16 in. (288.9 x 150 x 40.6 cm)
Seattle Art Museum, gift of the Virginia Wright Fund
p. 126

Albany I, 1959
Painted steel
25 x 25 3/4 x 7 1/4 in. (63.5 x 65.4 x 18.4 cm)
Storm King Art Center, Mountainville, New York,
gift of the Ralph E. Ogden Foundation, Inc.
p. 149

XI Books III Apples, 1959
Stainless steel
94 x 35 x 16 1/4 in. (238.8 x 88.9 x 41.3 cm)
Storm King Art Center, Mountainville, New York,
gift of the Ralph E. Ogden Foundation, Inc.
p. 86

Albany IX (Little Albany), 1959–60
Painted steel
18 x 20 1/2 x 4 1/4 in. (45.7 x 52.1 x 10.8 cm)
The Shidler Family Collection
p. 130

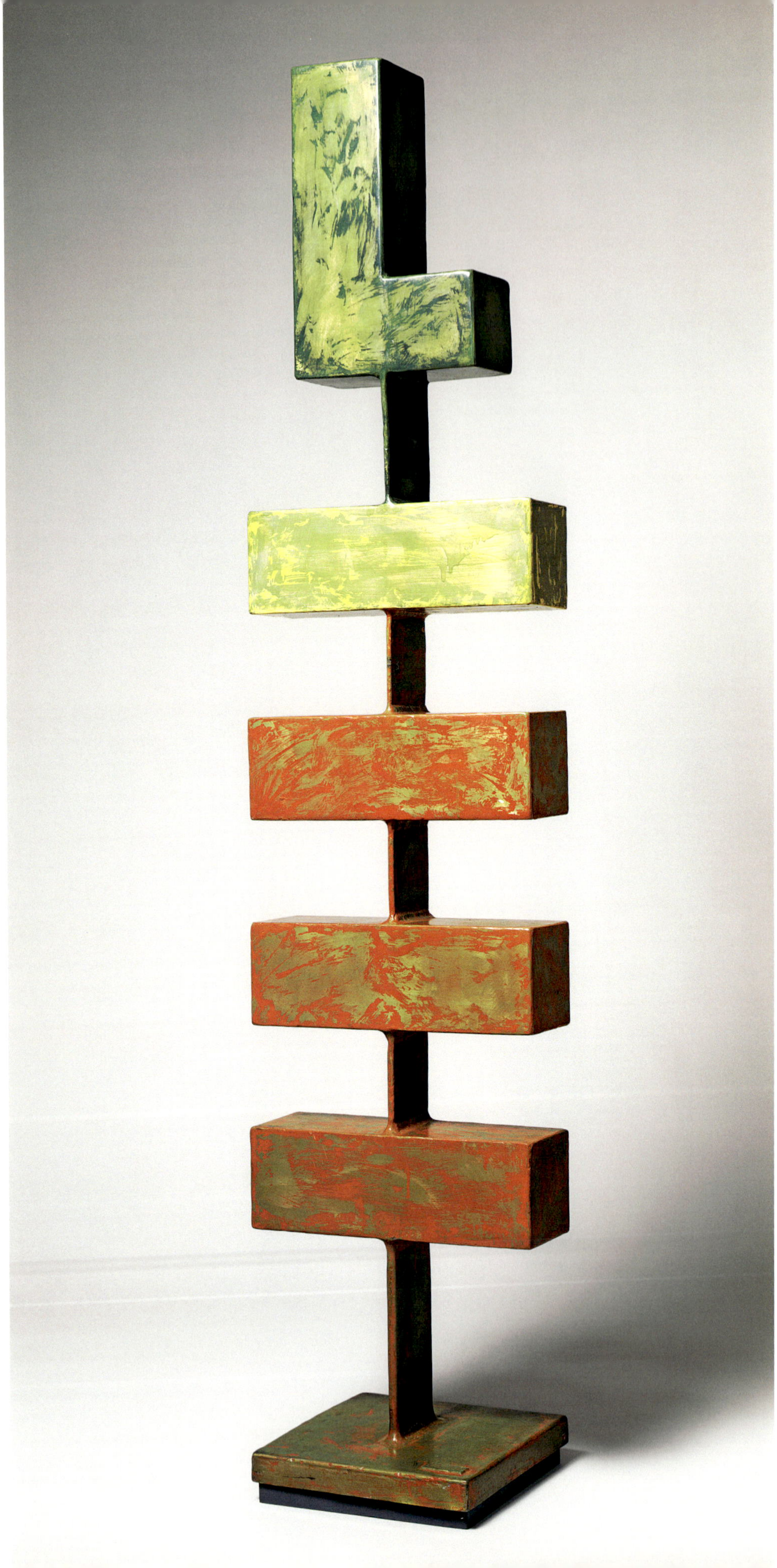

$5^1/_2$, 1956

Four Units Unequal, 1960
Stainless steel
70 1/2 x 28 1/4 x 14 1/4 in. (179.1 x 71.8 x 36.2 cm)
Frederick R. Weisman Art Foundation, Los Angeles
p. 84

Tanktotem VII, 1960
Painted steel
84 1/2 x 37 x 14 1/8 in. (214.6 x 94 x 35.9 cm)
Storm King Art Center, Mountainville, New York,
gift of the Ralph E. Ogden Foundation, Inc.
p. 78

Tanktotem IX, 1960
Painted steel
90 x 33 x 24 1/8 in. (228.6 x 83.8 x 61.3 cm)
The Estate of David Smith
p. 79

Three Planes, 1960–61
Painted steel
90 1/4 x 15 1/8 x 16 1/2 in. (229.2 x 38.4 x 41.9 cm)
Collection Museo Tamayo INBA-CONACULTA,
Mexico City
p. 43

Black White Forward, 1961
Painted steel
88 1/8 x 48 x 38 in. (223.8 x 121.9 x 96.5 cm)
The Estate of David Smith, courtesy National Gallery
of Art, Washington
p. 151

Lectern Sentinel, 1961
Stainless steel
101 3/4 x 33 x 20 1/2 in. (258.5 x 83.8 x 52.1 cm)
Whitney Museum of American Art, New York, purchase,
with funds from the Friends of the Whitney Museum of
American Art
p. 85

Untitled, 1961
Stainless steel
12 x 10 x 3 in. (30.5 x 25.4 x 7.6 cm)
The Estate of David Smith
p. 150

Zig III, 1961
Painted steel
93 x 124 x 61 in. (236.2 x 315 x 154.9 cm)
The Estate of David Smith, courtesy Gagosian Gallery
pp. 28 and 10, 51 (details)

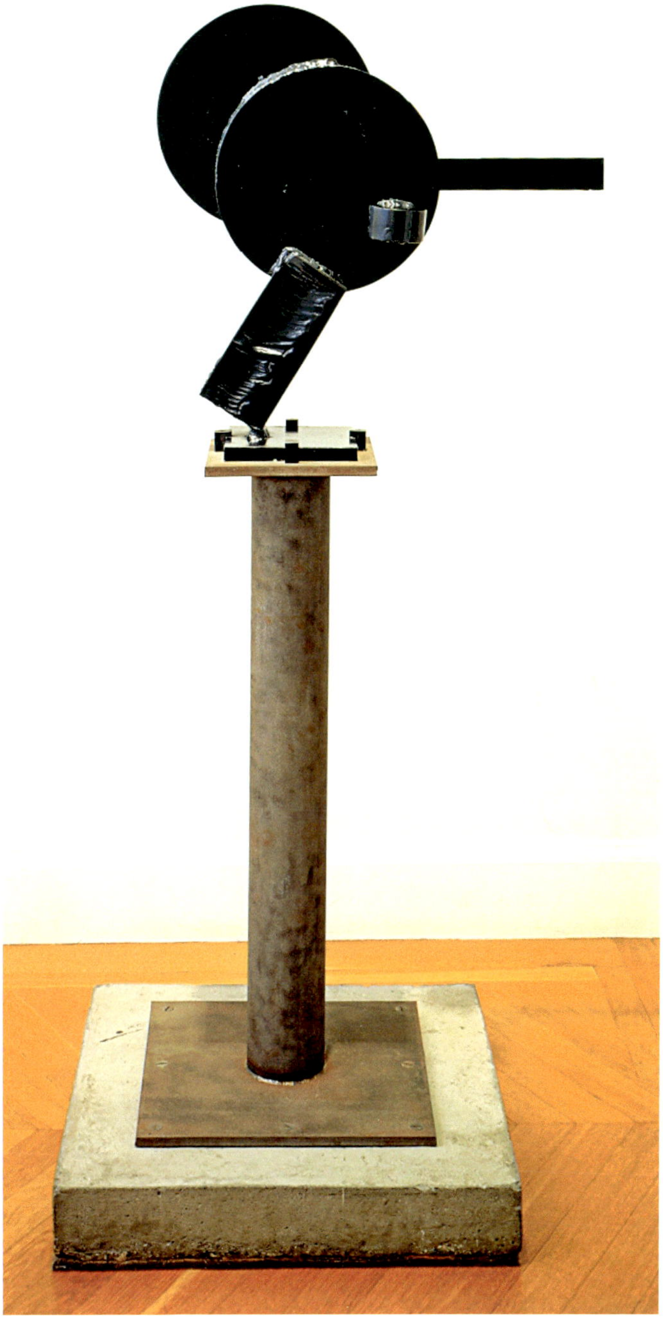

Albany I, 1959

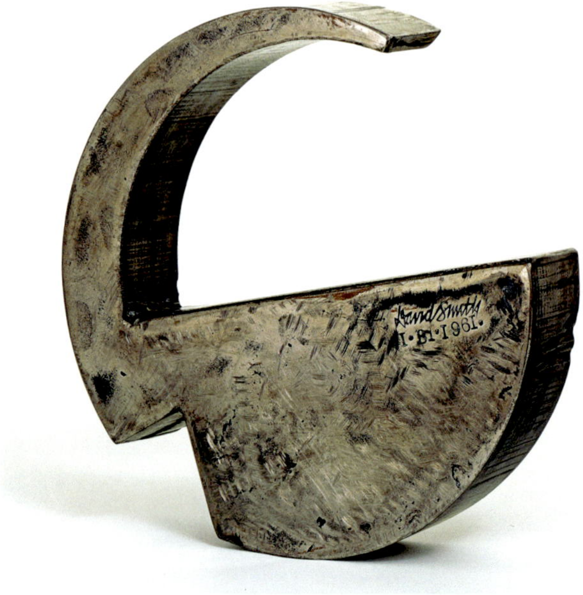

Untitled, 1961

Zig IV, 1961
Painted steel
95 3/8 x 84 1/4 x 76 in. (242.3 x 214 x 193 cm)
Lincoln Center for the Performing Arts, Inc., New York, gift of Mr. and Mrs. Howard Lipman
p. 31

Circle III, 1962
Painted steel
95 1/2 x 71 15/16 x 18 in. (242.5 x 182.7 x 45.7 cm)
National Gallery of Art, Washington, Ailsa Mellon Bruce Fund, 1977.60.3
p. 52

Circle IV, 1962
Painted steel
85 x 59 3/4 x 15 in. (215.9 x 151.8 x 38.1 cm)
The Estate of David Smith, courtesy Gagosian Gallery
p. 53

Cubi VIII, 1962
Stainless steel
91 3/4 x 38 x 34 in. (233 x 96.5 x 86.4 cm)
Meadows Museum, SMU, Dallas, gift of The Meadows Foundation, MM.1969.07
p. 18

Primo Piano III, 1962
Painted steel
124 x 146 x 19 in. (315 x 370.8 x 48.3 cm)
The Estate of David Smith, courtesy Gagosian Gallery
p. 54

Bec-Dida Day, 1963
Painted steel
89 x 65 x 18 in. (226.1 x 165.1 x 45.7 cm)
Yale University Art Gallery, Charles B. Benenson, BA 1933, Collection
p. 50

Cubi I, 1963
Stainless steel
124 x 34 1/2 x 33 1/2 in. (315 x 87.6 x 85.1 cm)
Detroit Institute of Arts, Founders Society Purchase, Special Purchase Fund
p. 16

Cubi V, 1963
Stainless steel
96 x 73 x 22 in. (243.8 x 185.4 x 55.9 cm)
Jon and Mary Shirley
p. 42

Cubi XXIII, 1964
Stainless steel
76 1/4 x 172 7/8 x 32 in. (193.7 x 439.1 x 81.3 cm)
Los Angeles County Museum of Art, Modern and Contemporary Art Council Fund, M.67.26
pp. 44–45

Untitled, 1964
Stainless steel
117 1/2 x 62 1/2 x 16 3/4 in. (298.5 x 158.8 x 42.6 cm)
Collection of the Newark Museum, purchase 1967 Charles Engelhard Foundation
p. 55

Becca, 1965
Stainless steel
113 1/4 x 123 x 30 1/2 in. (287.7 x 312.4 x 77.5 cm)
The Metropolitan Museum of Art, New York, purchase, bequest of Miss Adelaide Milton de Groot (1876–1967), by exchange, 1972 (1972.127)
p. 90

Cubi XXVIII, 1965
Stainless steel
108 x 110 x 45 in. (274.3 x 279.4 x 114.3 cm)
The Eli and Edythe L. Broad Collection, Los Angeles
p. 118

Untitled (Candida), 1965
Stainless steel
103 x 120 x 31 in. (261.6 x 304.8 x 78.7 cm)
The Estate of David Smith
p. 92

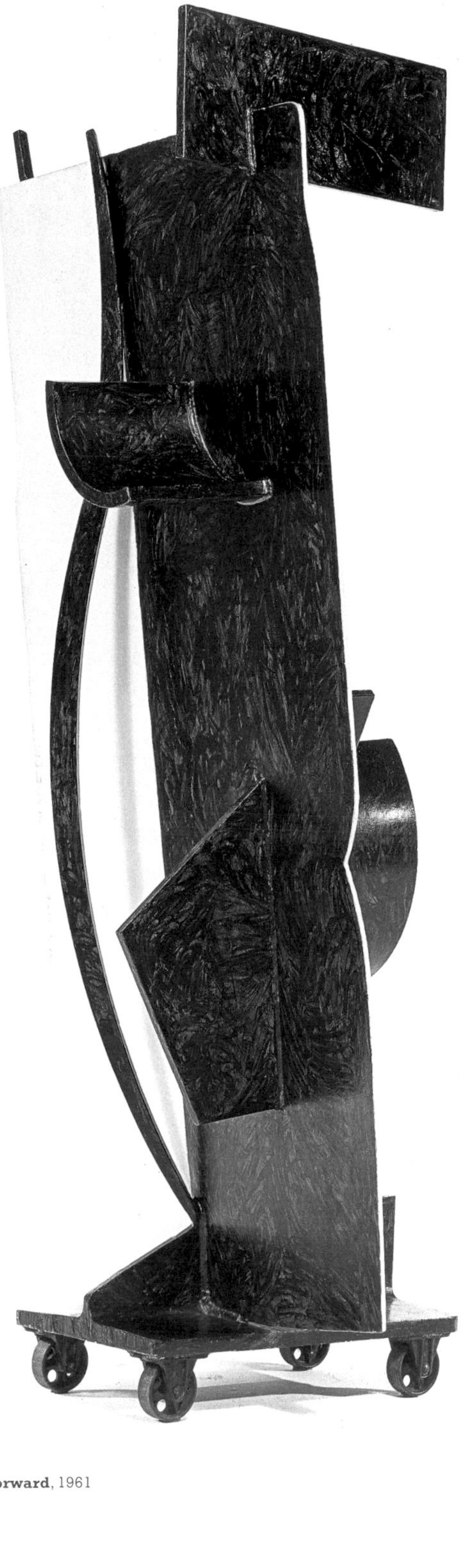

Black White Forward, 1961

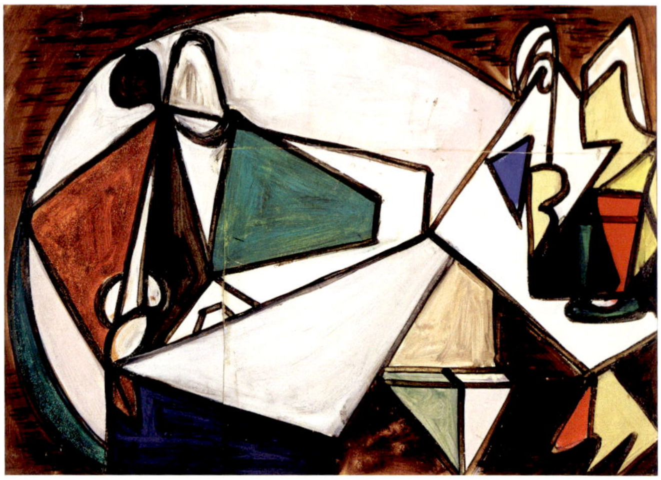

Untitled (2 drawings), 1930–31

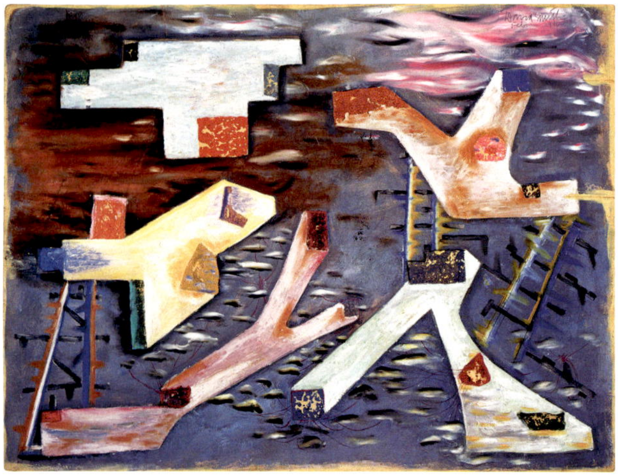

Untitled, 1946

Paintings and Works on Paper

Untitled (2 drawings), 1930–31
Tempera on paper
10 x 13 5/8 in. (25.4 x 34.6 cm)
The Estate of David Smith

Page from Sketchbook #23, 1933–45
Pencil on paper
10 1/2 x 8 in. (26.7 x 20.3 cm)
The Estate of David Smith
p. 32

Untitled, c. 1937–38
Ink, pastel, and watercolor on paper
17 x 22 1/16 in. (43.2 x 56 cm)
Whitney Museum of American Art, New York, purchase, with funds from Joel and Anne Ehrenkranz
p. 29

Spread, c. 1938, from Sketchbook #23, 1933–45
Pencil on paper
10 1/2 x 16 in. (26.7 x 40.6 cm)
The Estate of David Smith
p. 34

Untitled, c. 1938
Ink on paper
14 x 9 3/4 in. (35.6 x 24.8 cm)
The Estate of David Smith
p. 34

Untitled (Study for Widow's Lament), c. 1942
Ink on paper
3 15/16 x 5 15/16 in. (10 x 15.1 cm)
The Estate of David Smith

Page, c. 1945–50, from Sketchbook #41, 1944–54
Pencil on paper
12 x 9 in. (30.5 x 22.9 cm)
The Estate of David Smith

Untitled, 1946
Oil on paper mounted on Masonite
22 3/8 x 30 5/16 in. (56.8 x 77 cm)
The Estate of David Smith

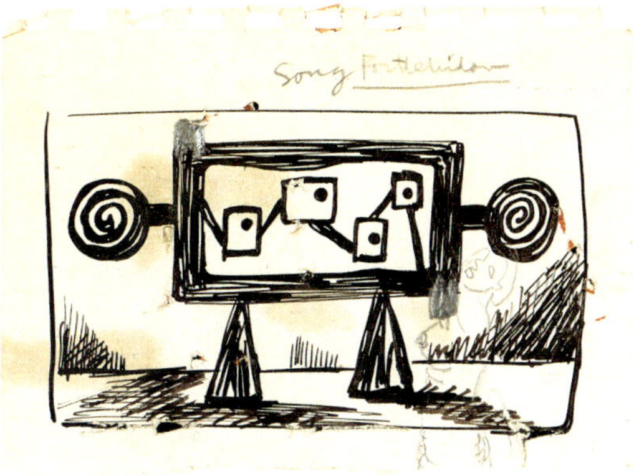

Untitled (Study for Widow's Lament), c. 1942

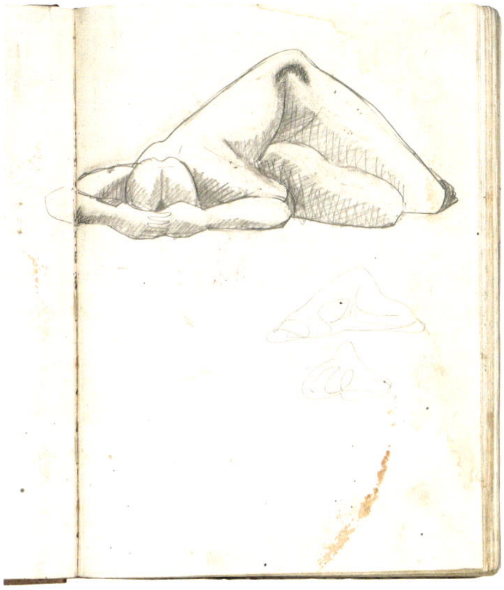

Page, c. 1945–50, from Sketchbook #41, 1944–54

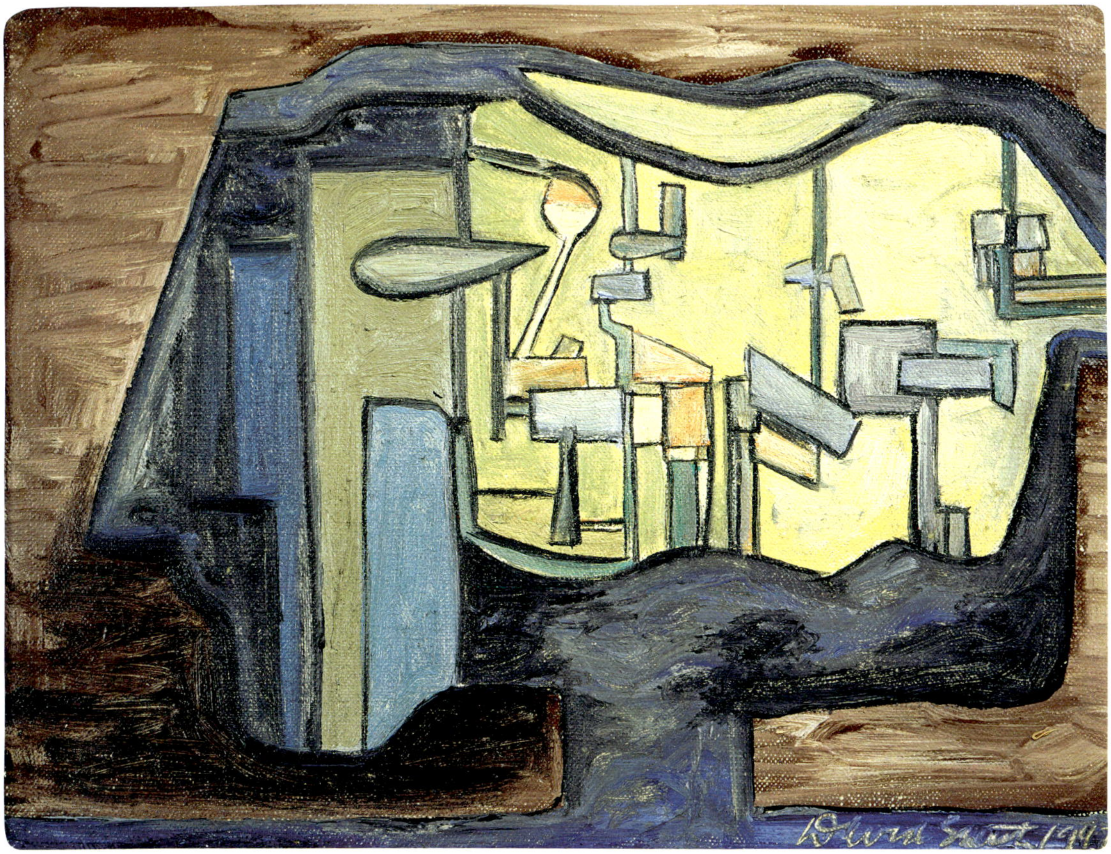

Untitled, 1947

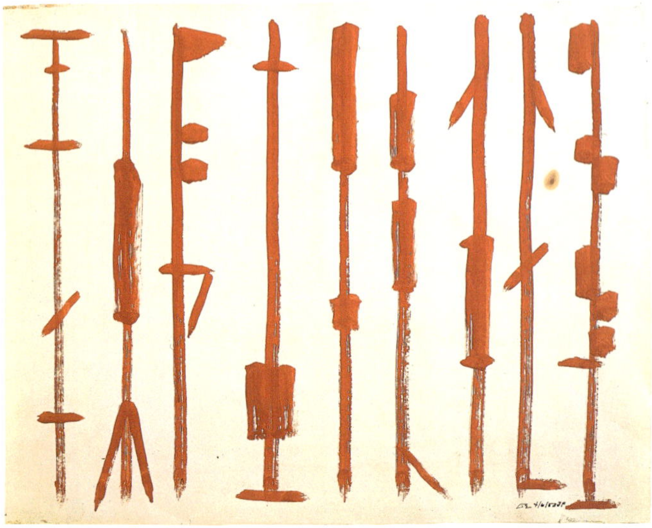

DS 4/6/53 JF, 1953

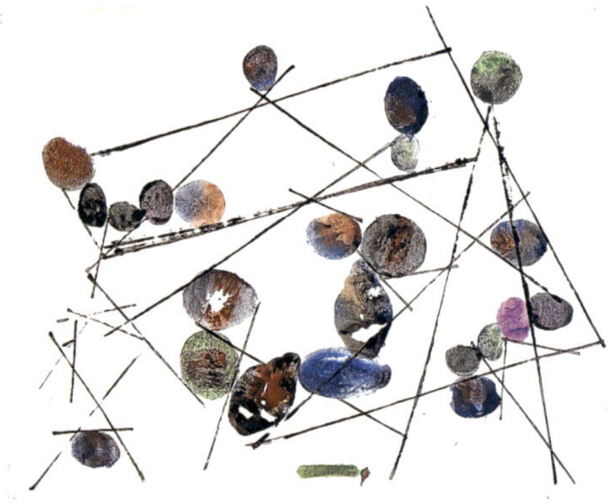

DS 11/7/54 1, 1954

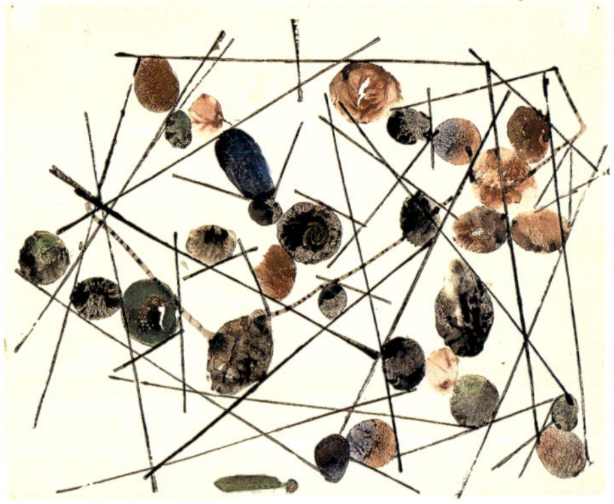

DS 11/7/54 2, 1954

Untitled, 1946
Gouache and conté crayon on paper
29 x 22 7/8 in. (73.7 x 58.1 cm)
The Estate of David Smith
p. 40

Untitled, 1947
Oil on canvas
9 x 12 in. (22.9 x 30.5 cm)
The Estate of David Smith
p. 153

Untitled, 1951
Tempera and egg ink on paper
22 3/4 x 18 in. (57.8 x 45.7 cm)
The Estate of David Smith, courtesy Galerie Gmurzynska, Zurich
p. 49

Spread, c. 1951, from Sketchbook #41, 1944–54
Pencil and ink on paper
12 x 18 in. (30.5 x 45.7 cm)
The Estate of David Smith
p. 36

Page from Sketchbook #39, 1952–54
Pencil on paper
5 1/2 x 3 1/2 in. (14 x 8.9 cm)
The Estate of David Smith
p. 49

Page, c. 1952–54, from Sketchbook #40, 1950–54
Ink on paper
11 x 8 1/4 in. (27.9 x 21 cm)
The Estate of David Smith
p. 49

DS 4/6/53 JF, 1953
Tempera on paper
17 1/2 x 22 1/2 in. (44.5 x 57.2 cm)
The Estate of David Smith

ΔΣ 10/31/54 3, 1954
Egg ink on paper
17 x 21 in. (43.2 x 53.3 cm)
Gail and Tony Ganz, Los Angeles

DS 11/7/54 1, 1954
Egg ink and gouache on paper
17 x 21 1/4 in. (43.2 x 54 cm)
The Estate of David Smith

DS 11/7/54 2, 1954
Egg ink and gouache on paper
16 7/8 x 21 1/4 in. (42.9 x 54 cm)
Private collection, courtesy Gagosian Gallery

ΔΣ 11-15-54, 1954
Egg ink and tempera on paper
15 3/4 x 20 1/4 in. (40 x 51.4 cm)
The Estate of David Smith, courtesy Margo Leavin Gallery, Los Angeles
p. 129

Study for Fifteen Planes, 1957
Oil and board on board
11 x 8 3/4 in. (27.9 x 22.2 cm)
Private collection
p. 166

Untitled, 1957
Oil on cardboard
10 x 8 in. (25.4 x 20.3 cm)
The Estate of David Smith
p. 155 (top)

Untitled, 1957
Oil on Masonite
10 x 8 in. (25.4 x 20.3 cm)
The Estate of David Smith, courtesy Margo Leavin Gallery, Los Angeles
p. 132

Untitled, 1957
Paper, board, and oil on board
10 3/16 x 7 3/4 in. (25.9 x 19.7 cm)
Private collection
p. 155 (bottom)

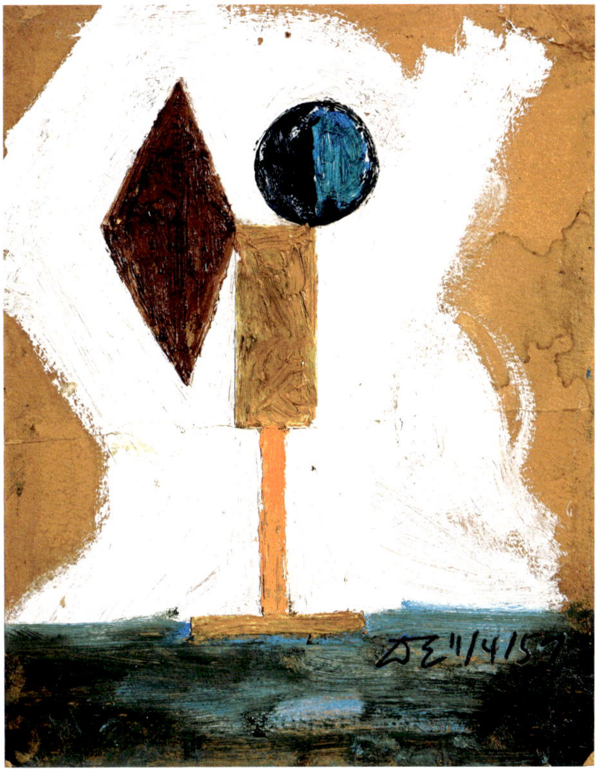

Untitled, 1957

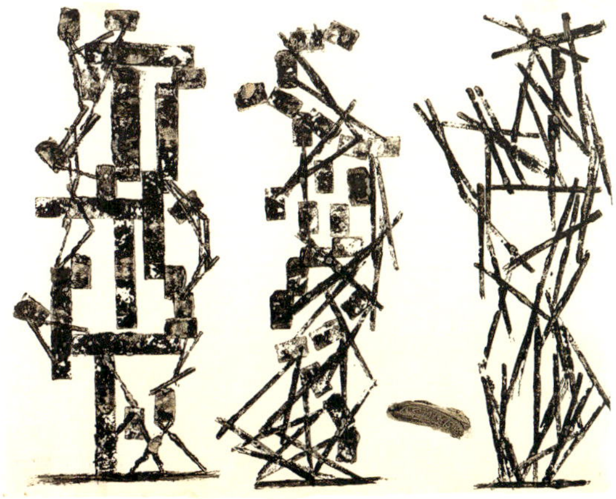

ΔΣ 10/31/54 3, 1954

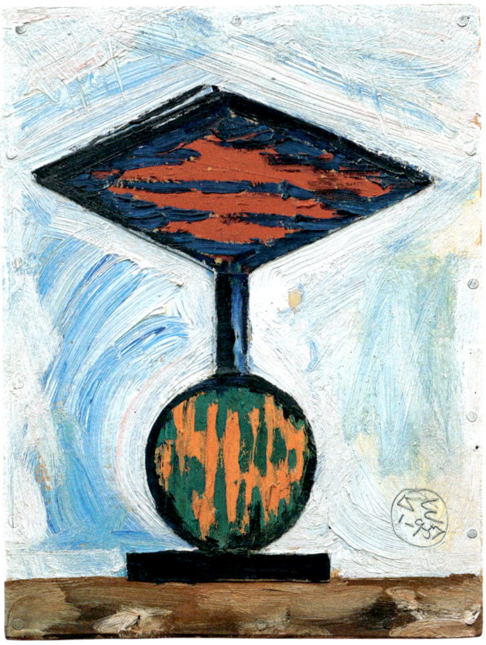

Untitled, 1957

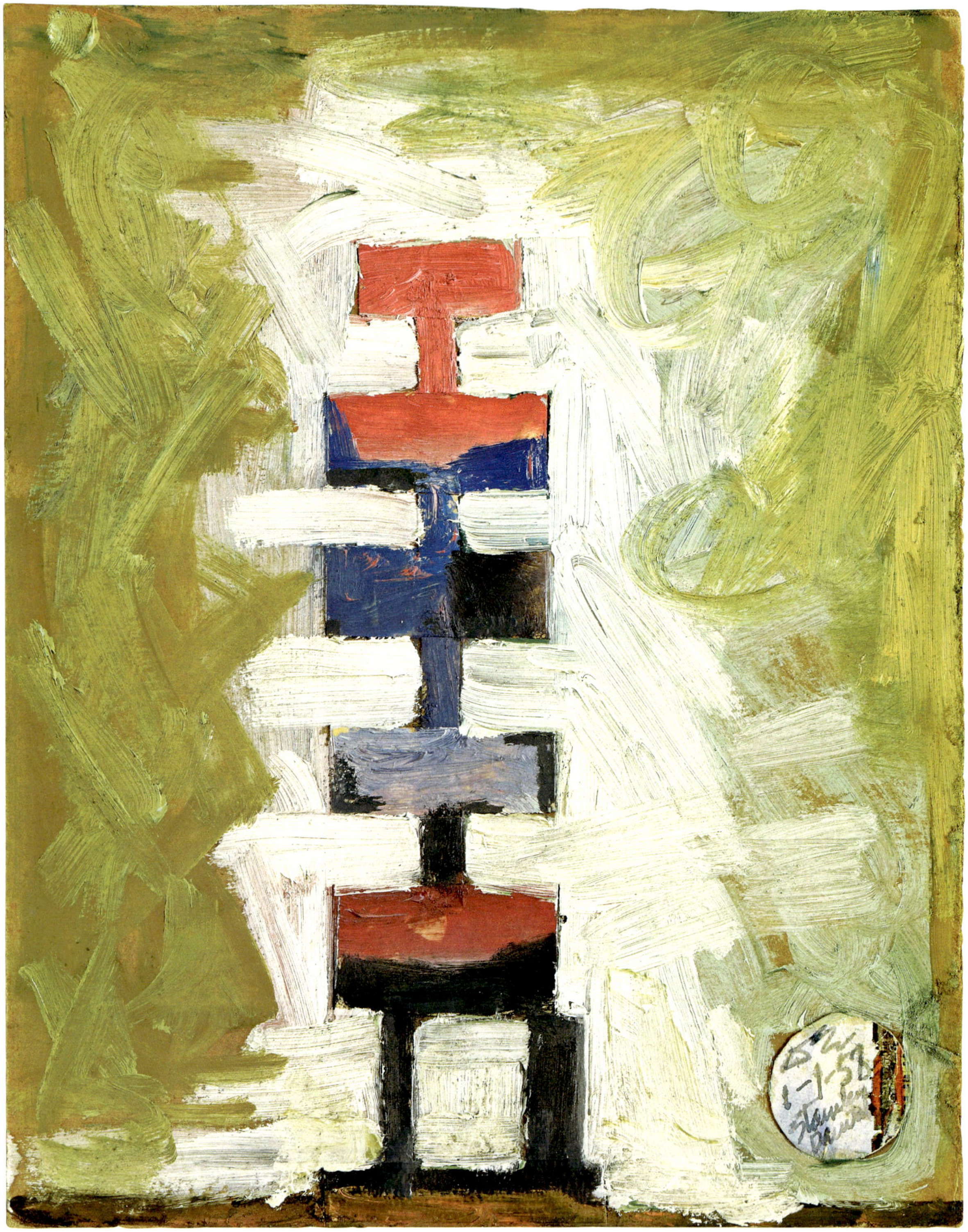

Five Units Unequal, 1958

DS 1958, 1958
Spray enamel on paper
17 1/2 x 11 1/2 in. (44.5 x 29.2 cm)
The Metropolitan Museum of Art, New York, gift of Candida and Rebecca Smith, 1994 (1994.399)
p. 57

Five Units Unequal, 1958
Oil and board on board
10 x 8 in. (25.4 x 20.3 cm)
The Estate of David Smith, courtesy Galerie Gmurzynska, Zurich

Untitled, 1958
Oil and board on board
10 x 8 in. (25.4 x 20.3 cm)
The Estate of David Smith
p.157 (top)

Untitled, 1958
Charcoal on japan paper
17 3/8 x 11 1/4 in. (44.1 x 28.6 cm)
The Estate of David Smith
p. 136

Untitled, 1958
Oil on canvas
38 x 35 in. (96.5 x 88.9 cm)
The Estate of David Smith
p. 157 (bottom)

Untitled, 1958
Colored paper on paper
19 3/4 x 13 in. (50.2 x 33 cm)
The Estate of David Smith
p. 158

Untitled, 1959
Spray enamel on canvas
96 1/8 x 13 1/4 in. (244.2 x 33.7 cm)
Private collection, Lake Forest, Illinois
p. 159

Untitled, 1962
Spray enamel on paper
13 x 19 in. (33 x 48.3 cm)
Dallas Museum of Art, Contemporary Art Fund, general acquisitions
p. 56

Untitled (Three Cubi Studies), 1962–63
Spray enamel on paper
11 1/2 x 16 3/8 in. (29.2 x 41.6 cm)
The Estate of David Smith
p. 46

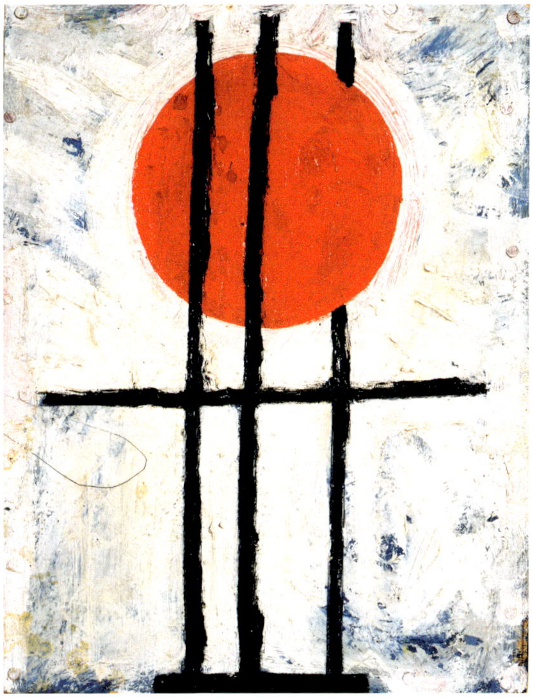

Untitled, 1958

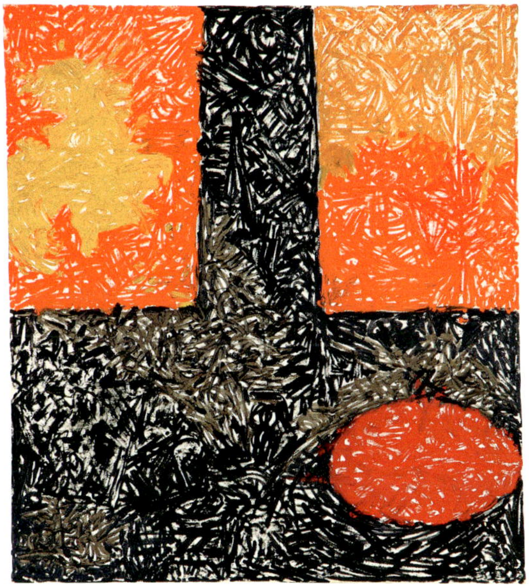

Untitled, 1958

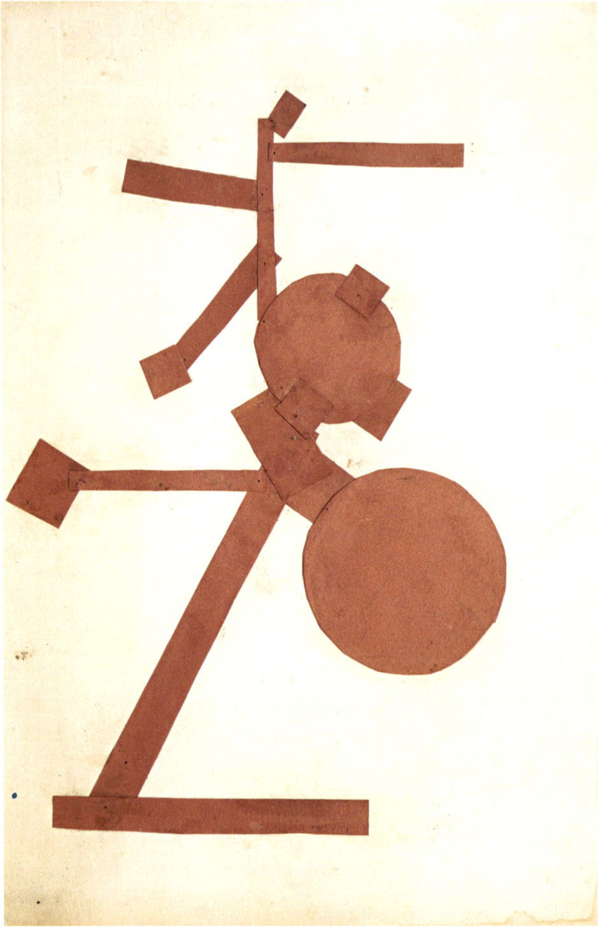

Untitled, 1958

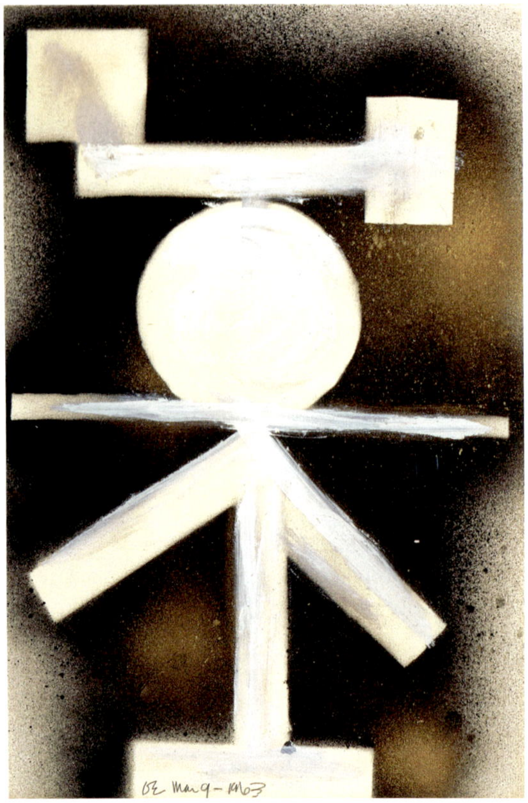

ΔΣ Mar. 9-1963, 1963

ΔΣ Mar. 9-1963, 1963
Spray enamel and oil on paper
17 1/2 x 11 1/2 in. (44.5 x 29.2 cm)
The Estate of David Smith

Untitled, 1963
Spray enamel on paper
14 x 19 in. (35.6 x 48.3 cm)
Jon and Mary Shirley
pp. 58 and 2–3 (detail)

Untitled (Study for Cubi), 1963
Spray enamel on paper
17 1/4 x 12 in. (43.8 x 30.5 cm)
Private collection

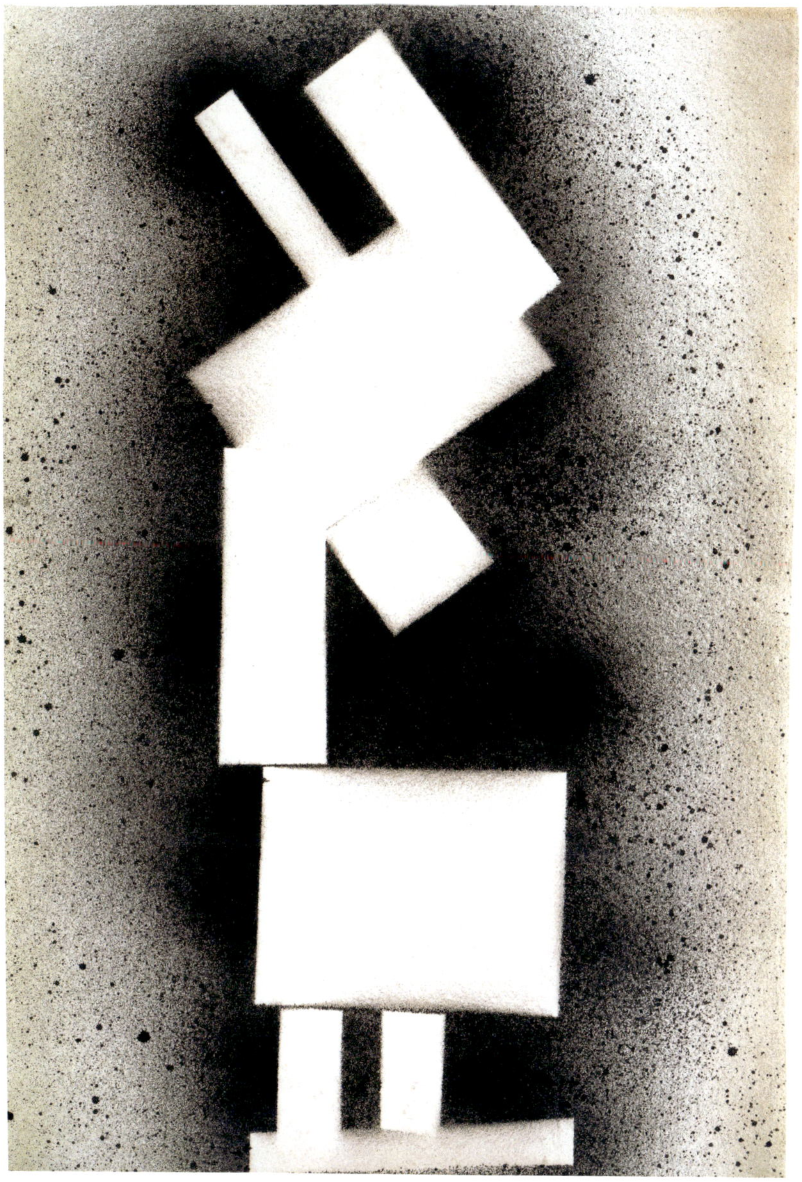

Untitled (Study for Cubi), 1963

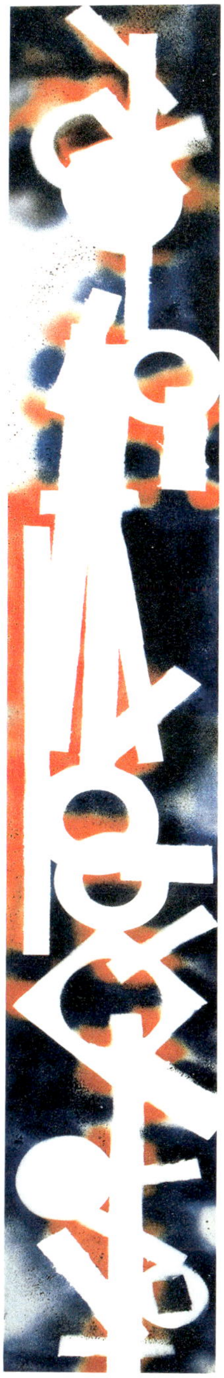

Untitled, 1959

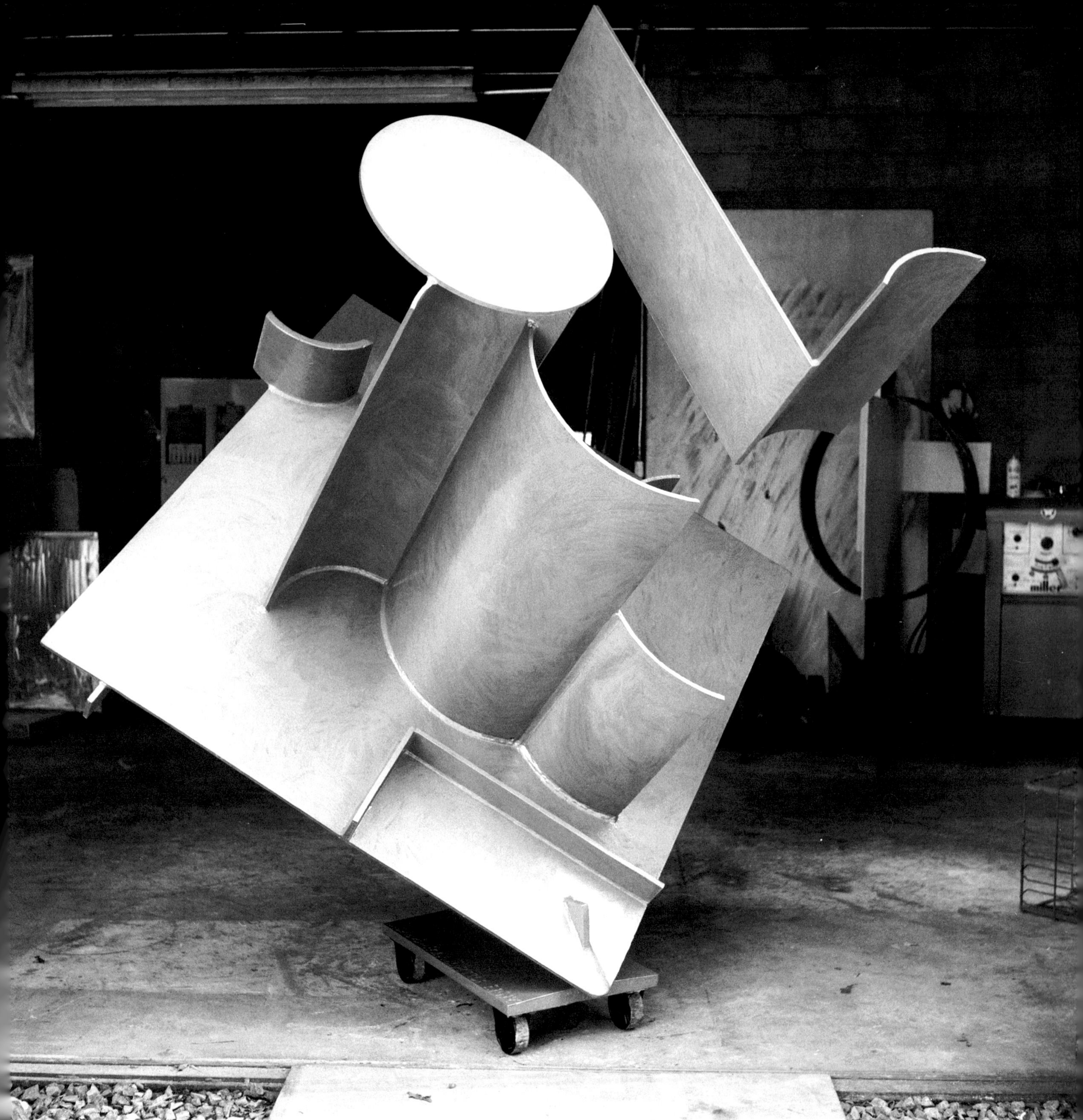

Untitled (**Zig IV** in workshop doorway,
Bolton Landing), c. 1961

Photographs

Untitled (dock montage), c. 1930
Gelatin silver print from multiple-exposure negative
9 1/2 x 6 1/8 in. (24.1 x 15.6 cm)
The Estate of David Smith
p. 97

Untitled, c. 1932–35
Gelatin silver print
6 1/2 x 4 3/4 in. (16.5 x 12.1 cm)
Private collection
p. 98

Untitled (on ship), c. 1932–35
Gelatin silver print
9 9/16 x 6 7/8 in. (24.3 x 17.5 cm)
The Estate of David Smith
p. 100

Untitled (Brooklyn), 1933–35
Gelatin silver print
9 15/16 x 6 7/8 in. (25.2 x 17.5 cm)
The Estate of David Smith
p. 101

Untitled (4/28/61, Bolton Landing workshop), 1961
Exhibition print from existing negative
The Estate of David Smith
p. 70

Untitled (**Hirebecca, Hi Candida, Untitled** [1959], and **Noland's Blues** [circular segments from] in Bolton Landing workshop), 1961
Gelatin silver print
9 9/16 x 7 11/16 in. (24.3 x 19.5 cm)
The Estate of David Smith
p. 103

Untitled (**Hirebecca**, **Untitled** [1959], **Hi Candida**, and **Noland's Blues** [circular segments from] in Bolton Landing workshop), 1961
Gelatin silver print
7 3/4 x 8 3/4 in. (19.7 x 22.2 cm)
The Estate of David Smith

Untitled (**Dida's Circle on a Fungus** with **Zig I**, Bolton Landing workshop), c. 1961
Exhibition print from existing negative
The Estate of David Smith
p. 104

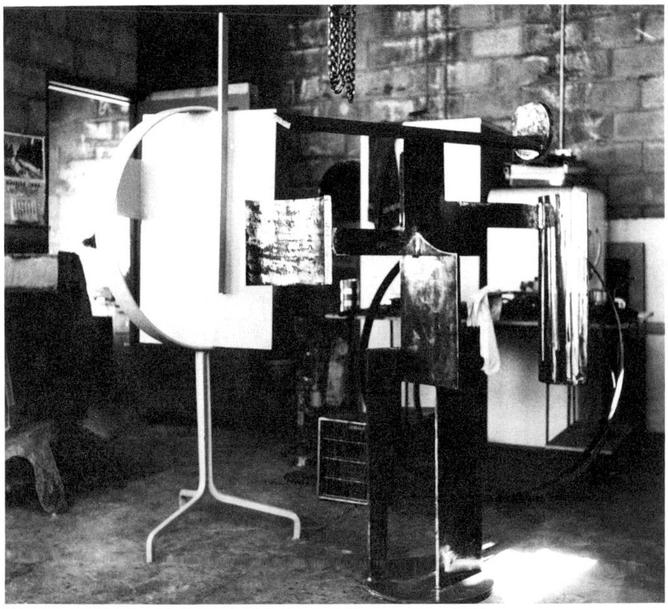

Untitled (**Hirebecca**, **Untitled** [1959], **Hi Candida**, and **Noland's Blues** [circular segments from] in Bolton Landing workshop), 1961

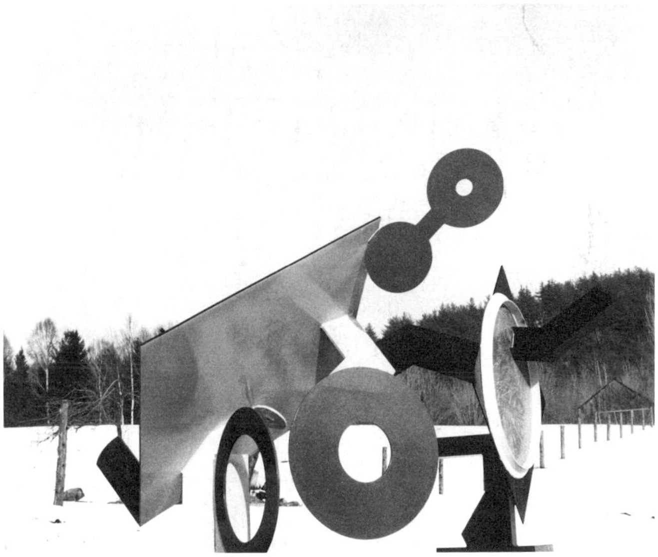

Untitled (**Zig VII** and **Zig VIII**, Bolton Landing) c. 1964, The Estate of David Smith

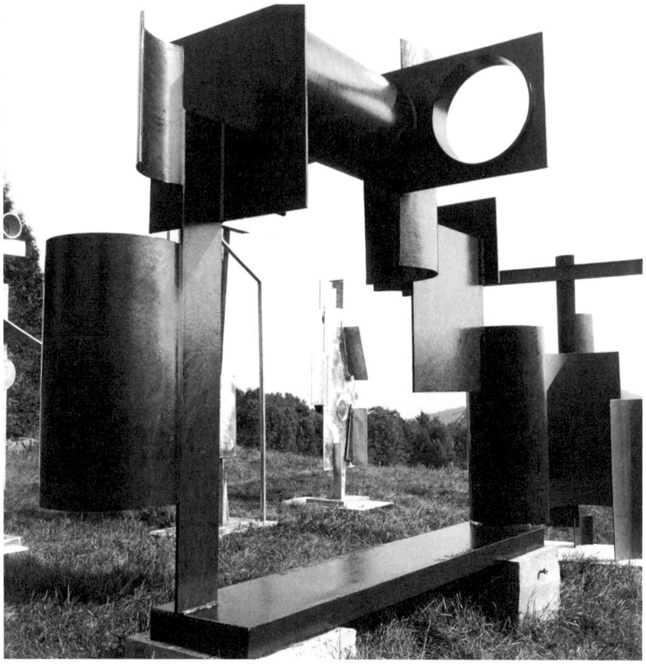

Untitled (**Zig III** with **Two Circle Sentinel**, **Two Box Structure**, and **March Sentinel**, Bolton Landing), c. 1961

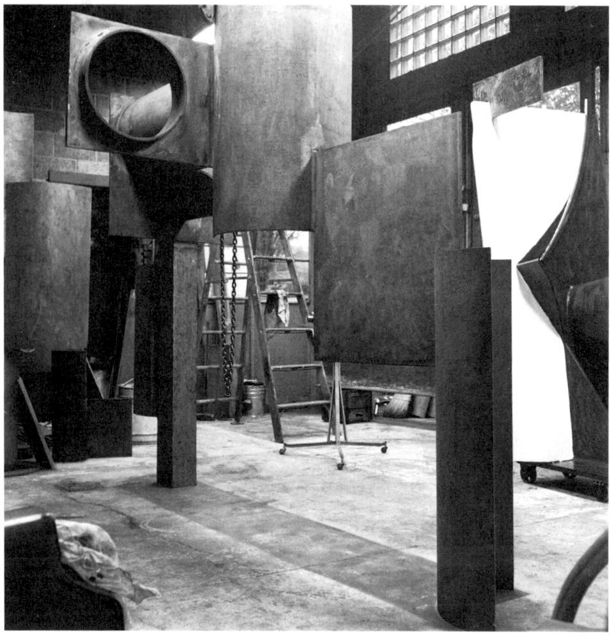

Untitled (**Zig III** and **Black White Forward**, Bolton Landing workshop), c. 1961

Untitled (**March Sentinel** [stainless-steel plates], **Two Box Structure**, **Two Circle Sentinel**, and **Zig II** [unpainted] next to Bolton Landing workshop), c. 1961
Gelatin silver print
7 5/8 x 9 5/8 in. (19.4 x 24.4 cm)
The Estate of David Smith
p. 109

Untitled (**Zig II** [unpainted] outside Bolton Landing workshop), c. 1961
Exhibition print from existing negative
The Estate of David Smith
p. 108

Untitled (**Zig III** and **Black White Forward**, Bolton Landing workshop), c. 1961
Exhibition print from existing negative
The Estate of David Smith

Untitled (**Zig III** with **Black White Backward**[?], **Ninety Father**, **Ninety Son**, and **Black White Forward**, Bolton Landing workshop), c. 1961
Exhibition print from existing negative
The Estate of David Smith
p. 106

Untitled (**Zig III** with **Two Circle Sentinel**, **Two Box Structure**, and **March Sentinel**, Bolton Landing), c. 1961
Exhibition print from existing negative
The Estate of David Smith

Untitled (**Zig IV** in workshop doorway, Bolton Landing), c. 1961
Gelatin silver print
9 9/16 x 7 3/4 in. (24.3 x 19.7 cm)
The Estate of David Smith
p. 66

Untitled (**Zig IV** in workshop doorway, Bolton Landing), c. 1961
Exhibition print from existing negative
The Estate of David Smith
p. 160

Untitled (**Zig IV** in workshop doorway, Bolton Landing), c. 1961
Gelatin silver print
9 1/2 x 7 3/4 in. (24.1 x 19.7 cm)
The Estate of David Smith
p. 64

Untitled (**Zig V** and **Zig IV** in Bolton Landing workshop), c. 1961
Gelatin silver print
9 5/8 x 7 5/8 in. (24.5 x 19.4 cm)
The Estate of David Smith
p. 107

Untitled (**Cube Totem**, **Sentinel**, **Cubi IX**, and **Cubi III**), 1963
Gelatin silver print
9 9/16 x 7 13/16 in. (24.3 x 19.8 cm)
The Estate of David Smith
p. 115

Untitled (**Cubi X** with **Primo Piano**, Bolton Landing), 1963
Gelatin silver print
8 7/8 x 8 in. (22.5 x 20.3 cm)
Richard and Ellen Sandor Family Collection
p. 114

Untitled (**Voltri-Bolton I**, **Voltri-Bolton VII**, **Voltri-Bolton II**, **Voltri-Bolton VIII**, **Voltri-Bolton III**, **Voltri-Bolton IX**, and **Voltri-Bolton VI** at Bolton Landing), 1963
Gelatin silver print
7 9/16 x 9 1/2 in. (19.2 x 24.1 cm)
The Estate of David Smith
pp. 163 and 4–5 (detail)

Untitled (**Tower I** outside Bolton Landing workshop), c. 1963
Exhibition print from existing negative
The Estate of David Smith

Untitled (**Voltri-Boltons** in snow, Bolton Landing), c. 1963
Exhibition print from existing negative
The Estate of David Smith
pp. 164–65

Untitled (**Zig VII** and **Zig VIII**, Bolton Landing), c. 1964
Gelatin silver print
7 11/16 x 9 7/16 in. (19.5 x 23.9 cm)
The Estate of David Smith
pp. 161 and 110–11 (detail)

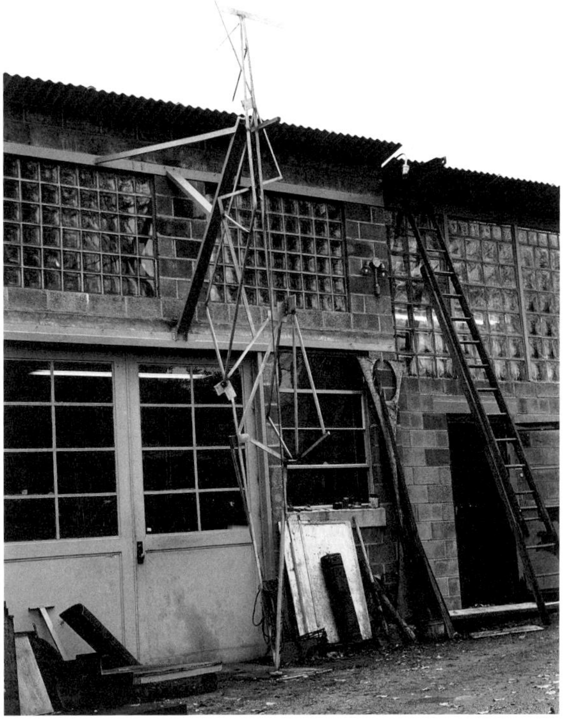

Untitled (**Tower I** outside Bolton Landing workshop), c. 1963

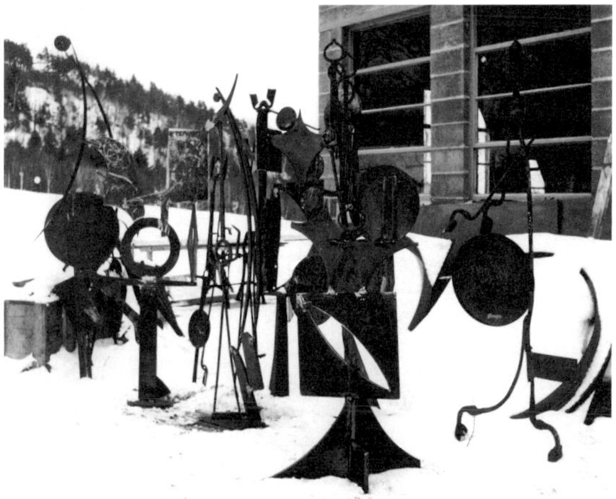

Untitled (**Voltri-Bolton I**, **Voltri-Bolton VII**, **Voltri-Bolton II**, **Voltri-Bolton VIII**, **Voltri-Bolton III**, **Voltri-Bolton IX**, and **Voltri-Bolton VI** at Bolton Landing), 1963

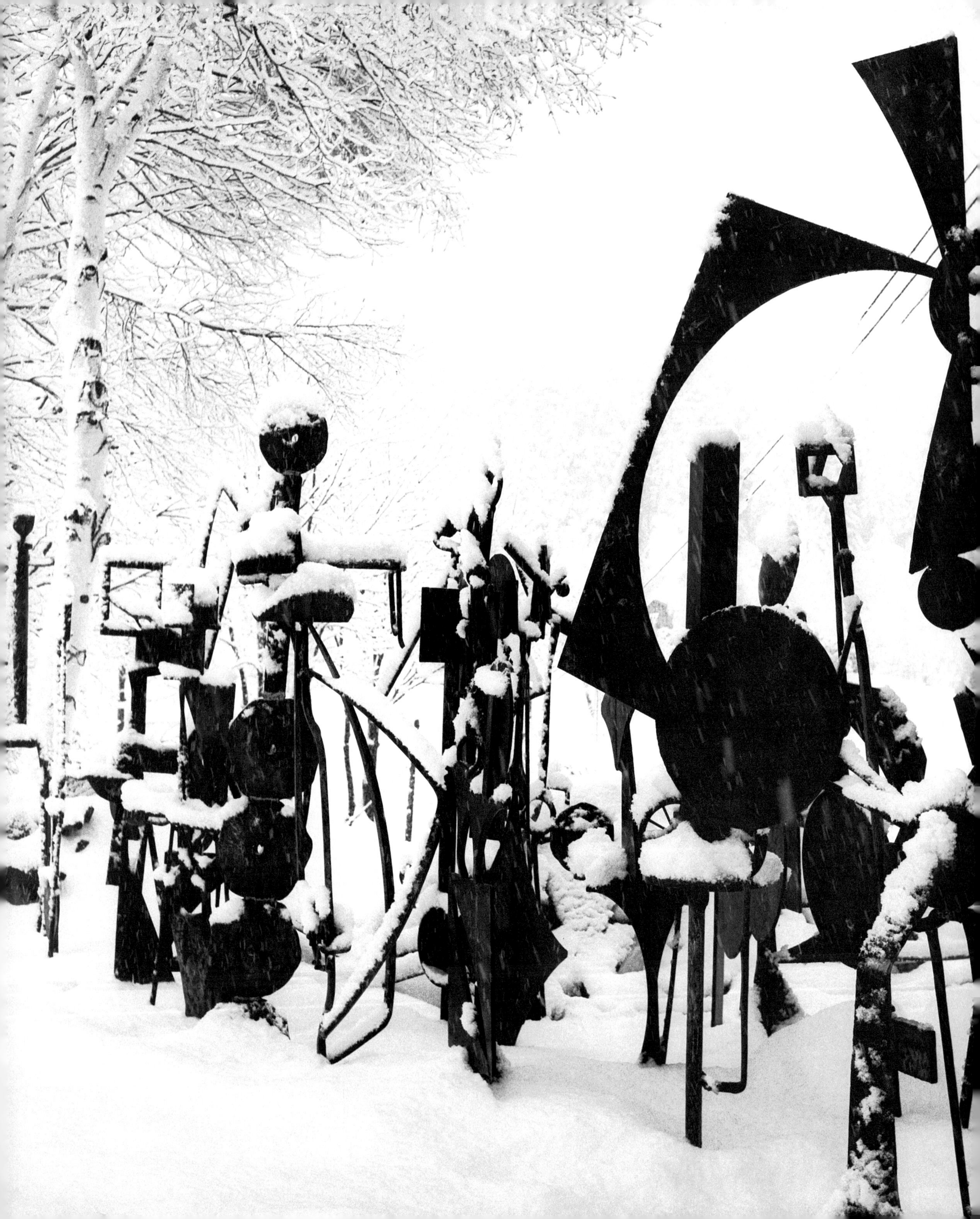

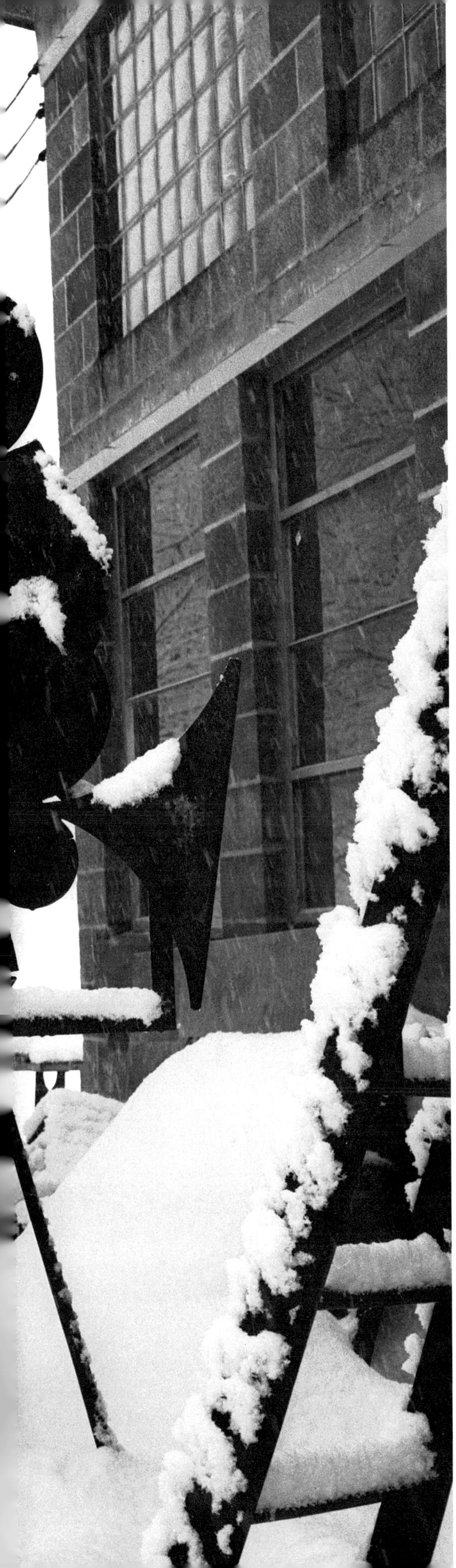

Untitled (**Voltri-Boltons** in snow, Bolton Landing),
c. 1963

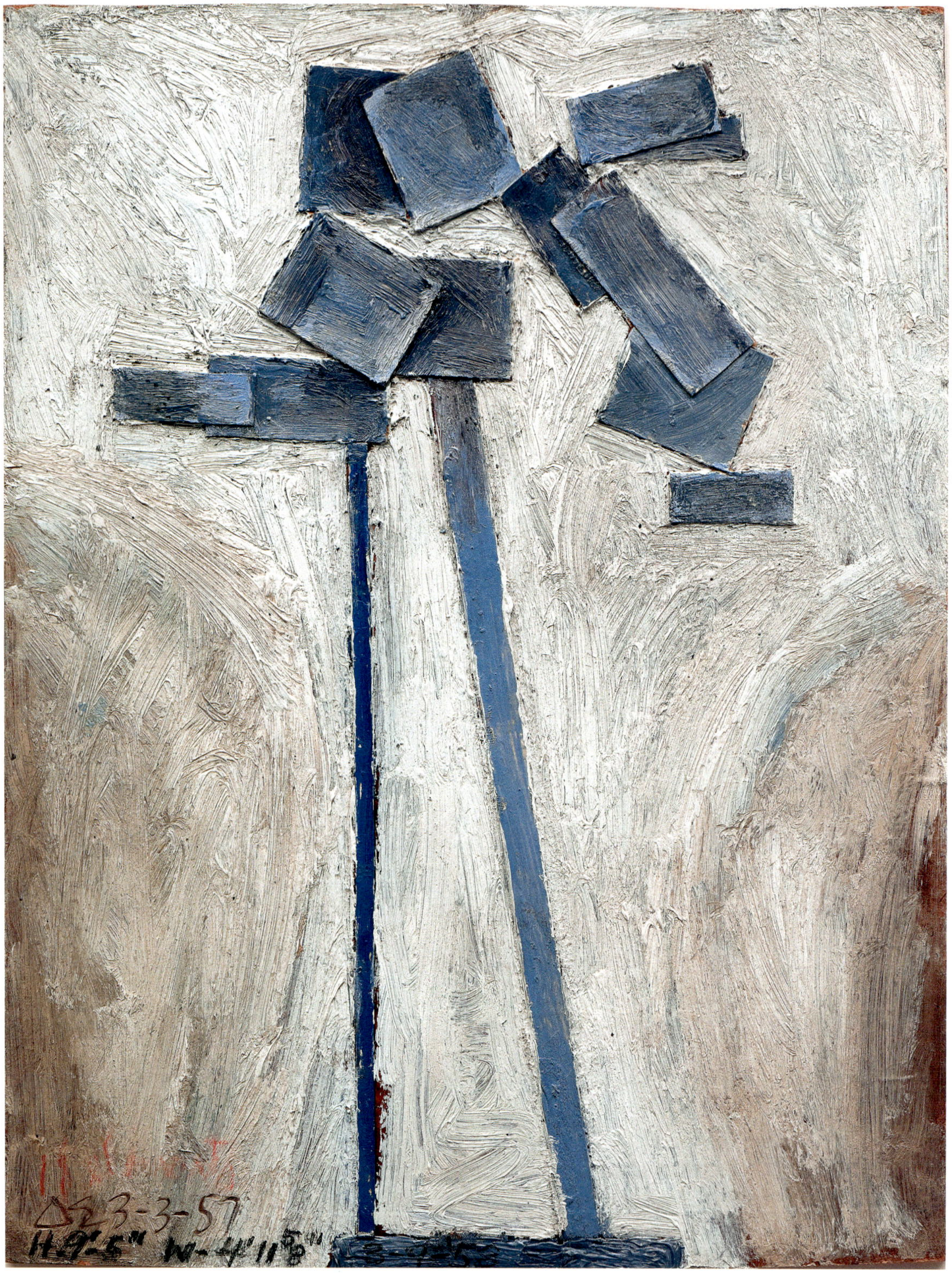

Study for Fifteen Planes, 1957, private collection

Acknowledgments

It takes a village to organize an exhibition, although—when successfully completed—the “villagers” tend to become invisible. Without them, however, this show would never have happened. I would first and foremost like to thank Peter Stevens, executive director of The Estate of David Smith, and Susan Cooke, associate director. Their unflagging interest, support, kindness, and good cheer, along with their generosity in making all of the estate’s resources available to me (notebooks and sketchbooks, archives, works in storage, and more), were invaluable, as were their broad and deep knowledge of and love for Smith’s art. No one has looked at or thought about Smith as closely, and I am grateful for their willingness to share their extraordinary insights. I also want to acknowledge Candida Smith and Rebecca Smith, without whose support a major project devoted to David Smith would not be possible. Tony Ganz provided the initial introduction to Peter Stevens; I thank him for opening the door to a long and fruitful collaboration.

Many colleagues across the country and beyond gave of their time and assistance in varying ways. I would like to acknowledge Tracey Bashkoff, Michael Darling, Karen Davidson, Elizabeth Easton, Valerie Fletcher, Jennifer Gross, Susan Frank, Sarah B. Kianovsky, Roxana Marcoci, Liliana Martínez Dominguez, Helen Molesworth, Nu Nguyen, George Shackelford, Peter Shelton, Beth Venn, and MaryAnn Wilkinson. Jay Jensen in particular went far beyond the call of duty, and I thank him for his assistance. Emily Braun always provides me with a willing ear, a sharp intellect, and a home-away-from-home in New York, for which I am eternally grateful. I would also like to thank the Getty Research Institute here in Los Angeles; their library—with its wonderful staff—offered the perfect haven in which I could read and think about Smith.

Nina Berson, Paul Zelevansky, and the Art Historians of Southern California provided the opportunity to present a session on Smith at the 2009 College Art Association annual conference in Los Angeles. I am grateful to Christopher Bedford for co-organizing the session with me, and to participants David J. Getsy, Alex Potts, Kenneth E. Silver, and Anne M. Wagner. The texts in this catalogue by Bedford, Potts, and Wagner, each of which makes a significant contribution to the Smith literature, grew out of that very productive session.

Numerous gallerists over the years collaborated with David Smith and/or continue to show his work, and I called on the expertise and archives of many of them. Margo Leavin and Wendy Brandow of the Margo Leavin Gallery have been welcoming, helpful, and generous at every step. Ann Freedman and Edye Weissler gave me access to wonderful research materials at Knoedler & Company; Miani Johnson similarly opened the Willard Gallery archives to me. I would like to salute Deborah McLeod and John Good (assisted by Jillian Murphy) at Gagosian Gallery for their always speedy and cheerful responses to my requests. Thanks are due also to Frish Brandt and Jennifer Larsen of the Fraenkel Gallery and Gabriel Catone of Ruth|Catone. I am extremely grateful as well to Nina del Rio and Leslie Prouty of Sotheby's for their invaluable assistance.

There are likewise many colleagues (and a few—sadly—former colleagues) at LACMA without whom this exhibition would not have come to fruition. Director Michael Govan has been enthusiastic about this show since he came to the museum in 2006 (although the project was initiated before his arrival in Los Angeles). Nancy Thomas, deputy director, was an ongoing source of encouragement. Curatorial colleagues (current and former) have provided critical support, both intellectual and moral, especially Stephanie Barron, Ilona Katzew, Lynn Zelevansky, and Christopher Bedford. Chris worked closely with me on the project, particularly on the early development of the exhibition concept and checklist. Tracy Serur Kerr in LACMA's library facilitated numerous interlibrary loans, which were critical for research on Smith. Tiffany Daneshgar (and, before her, Megan Hawley Mastroianni) ably and cheerfully handled the voluminous administrative needs of the show; I am grateful for the efficiency and good energy they brought to the process. LACMA's exhibitions department—Irene Martín, Sarah Minnaert, Marciana Broiles, and more recently Zoe Kahr and Liz Andres—navigated many organizational thickets on behalf of the project. I want to thank LACMA's development department for assistance in securing funding for the project, in particular Terry Morello, Melissa Bomes, Stephanie Dyas, Chelsea Hadley, and Amanda Lipsey. Registrars Erika Franek and Emily Horton coordinated exceptionally challenging and complex shipping arrangements, while Renée Montgomery, with the assistance of Jonathan Alfi, managed complicated insurance issues. Fred Goldstein and Sue Ellen Smyle facilitated legal paperwork. It was a pleasure to work once again with Brenda Levin and Robert Stone of Levin & Associates Architects, who designed a striking installation for the show, with support from LACMA's own John Bowsher and senior exhibition designer Victoria Behner. Conservators John Hirx, Chail Norton, and Virginia Rasmussen addressed issues large and small. Jeff Haskin and his art preparation staff carefully installed Smith's wonderful—and often physically challenging—work. I similarly appreciate Christine Choi and Brooke Fruchtman, whose efforts bring attention and visitors to LACMA's exhibitions. I am also grateful for Mary Lenihan's enthusiasm in planning public programs related to the show.

Any exhibition catalogue is a labor of love unto itself, and this book is no exception. I wish to thank Nola Butler and Thomas Frick in LACMA's publications department for their sage advice and assistance all along the way. Working with editor Jennifer MacNair was a pure pleasure. She has a deft touch and an incisive mind, a wonderful combination that will be evident to any reader of this book. Piper Severance put in long hours to procure the photographic materials for the catalogue. Peter Brenner both evaluated existing images and shot beautiful new ones. Paul Wehby created an exciting and elegant design for the book as well as for the exhibition graphics; I also wish to thank Amy McFarland for her thoughtful contributions to the design process.

I am exceptionally grateful to those whose financial support—all the more striking given the challenging economic times—made the exhibition possible. My dear friends Alice and Nahum Lainer are inspiring and stalwart supporters; thank you. I salute the Steven F. Roth Family Foundation; it has been a pleasure to begin to know Steve in the context of this show. I also want to acknowledge the gratifying support and friendship of Judy and Steaven Jones (The Steaven K. and Judith G. Jones Foundation), Myron Laskin, Agnes Gund, Dorothy R. Sherwood, Terri and Michael Smooke, and Ellie and Mark Lainer. The National Endowment for the Arts continues to be an important and positive force in American cultural life, and I am proud to have its support. I am likewise thankful for the indemnity provided by the Federal Council on the Arts and the Humanities. I also wish to thank Gagosian Gallery, the Dedalus Foundation, the Lipman Family Foundation, and Contemporary Collectors–Orange County for their generosity.

I am profoundly grateful to the many lenders to the exhibition, listed on the following page, who graciously agreed to part temporarily with extraordinary works by David Smith so that the visitors to this exhibition could enjoy and learn from them.

Finally, I wish to thank "my boyz," Tom, Ben, and Sam Muller. They always provide me with perspective, laughter, and love.

Carol S. Eliel
Curator of Modern Art

Lenders to the Exhibition

Brooklyn Museum
Dallas Museum of Art
Detroit Institute of Arts
The Eli and Edythe L. Broad Collection, Los Angeles
The Estate of David Smith
Frederick R. Weisman Art Foundation, Los Angeles
Frederick R. Weisman Art Museum, University of Minnesota, Minneapolis
Gail and Tony Ganz, Los Angeles
Harvard Art Museums/Fogg Museum
Hirshhorn Museum and Sculpture Garden, Smithsonian Institution, Washington, D.C.
Lincoln Center for the Performing Arts, Inc., New York
Los Angeles County Museum of Art
Meadows Museum, SMU, Dallas
Memorial Art Gallery, University of Rochester
The Metropolitan Museum of Art, New York
Museo Tamayo INBA-CONACULTA, Mexico City
National Gallery of Art, Washington
Newark Museum
Richard and Ellen Sandor Family Collection
Seattle Art Museum
The Shidler Family Collection
Jon and Mary Shirley
Storm King Art Center, Mountainville, New York
University of Michigan Museum of Art, Ann Arbor
Whitney Museum of American Art, New York
Yale University Art Gallery

And those who wish to remain anonymous

About the Authors

Carol S. Eliel is Curator of Modern Art at the Los Angeles County Museum of Art. Educated at Yale and the Institute of Fine Arts, New York University, she has organized numerous exhibitions, including *Annette Messager*; *L'Esprit Nouveau: Purism in Paris, 1918–1925*; and *SoCal: Southern California Art of the 1960s and 70s from LACMA's Collection*. In 1999 she was named a Chevalier de l'Ordre des Arts et des Lettres by the French government.

Christopher Bedford is Chief Curator at the Wexner Center for the Arts, The Ohio State University, where his exhibitions include a recent survey of Mark Bradford's work. His writing has appeared in numerous exhibition catalogues as well as in *Artforum*, *Art in America*, *Frieze*, *October*, and *Word & Image*.

Alex Potts is Max Loehr Collegiate Professor in the Department of History of Art, University of Michigan. His publications include *Flesh and the Ideal: Winckelmann and the Origins of Art History* (1994 and 2000); *The Sculptural Imagination: Figurative, Modernist, Minimalist* (2000); and the coedited anthology *The Modern Sculpture Reader* (2007).

Anne M. Wagner, professor in the Department of History of Art at the University of California, Berkeley, from 1988 to 2010, is currently Henry Moore Foundation Research Curator at Tate Britain. Her books include *A House Divided: On American Art since 1955* (2011) and *Behaving Globally* (forthcoming).

Illustration Credits

Front and back cover, 6–7 (silhouette), 145 bottom: courtesy the Frederick R. Weisman Art Museum at the University of Minnesota; **endpapers, 4–5, 16, 64, 66, 70, 89 (silhouette), 95, 96, 97, 100, 101, 103, 104, 106, 107, 108, 109, 110–11 (detail), 120–21, 122, 139, 160, 161, 162, 163, 164–65:** photo by David Smith, courtesy The Estate of David Smith, NY; **2–3 (detail), 22, 24, 33, 48, 58, 92, 155 bottom left:** courtesy The Estate of David Smith, NY; **10 (detail), 28, 51 (detail), 54, 147:** photo by Jerry L. Thompson, courtesy Gagosian Gallery; **12–13:** photo © Dan Budnik; **14–15 (silhouette), 44–45, 65, 73:** © 2011 Museum Associates/LACMA; **18:** photo by Michael Bodycomb, courtesy Meadows Museum, SMU, Dallas; **23:** © Julio González Estate, Paris; **26:** photo by Karoly Szelenyi; **27, 76:** photo by Ellen Page Wilson, courtesy The Estate of David Smith, NY; **29 left:** © Whitney Museum of American Art, by Geoffrey Clements; **29 right, 47 bottom:** © Estate of El Lissitzky/Artists Rights Society (ARS), New York/VG Bild-Kunst, Bonn; **30 right, 31, 135, 138:** photo by David Heald, courtesy The Estate of David Smith, NY; **32 top, 34, 36, 49 top left, 49 top middle, 80, 153 top:** photo by Tim Pyle, Light Blue Studio, Fairfield, CT; **32 bottom left:** courtesy the United States Postal Service, designed by C. Dale Badgeley; **35:** photo by Ken Cohen, courtesy The Estate of David Smith; **37:** courtesy the Memorial Art Gallery of the University of Rochester, Rochester, NY; **38:** © The University of Michigan Museum of Art, by Patrick Young; **39 top:** © Estate of Constantin Brancusi/Artists Rights Society (ARS), New York/ADAGP, Paris, photo credit: Musée national d'Art Moderne, Centre Georges Pompidou, Paris/Brancusi Bequest, 1957; **39 bottom:** © Estate of Constantin Brancusi/Artists Rights Society (ARS), New York/ADAGP, Paris, photo © National Gallery of Art, Washington, by Philip A. Charles; **40, 43, 46, 53, 123, 136, 143 (silhouette), 144, 150, 151, 152, 153 bottom, 154 top, 155 top, 157 top, 158, 159:** photo by Robert McKeever, courtesy Gagosian Gallery; **41:** courtesy Brooklyn Museum; **42:** courtesy Jon and Mary Shirley; **47 top:** digital image © The Museum of Modern Art/Licensed by SCALA/Art Resource, NY (ART162719); **49 top right:** © HCR International, digital image © The Museum of Modern Art/Licensed by SCALA/Art Resource, NY (ART164658); **49 bottom, 79, 128, 156:** courtesy Galerie Gmurzynska, Switzerland; **50:** courtesy Yale University Art Gallery; **52:** courtesy the National Gallery of Art, Washington; **55:** © Newark Museum, by Richard Goodbody; **56 top, 56 bottom left:** © Estate of Vasily Kandinsky/Artists Rights Society (ARS), New York/ADAGP, Paris, photo © Solomon R. Guggenheim Museum, NY; **56 bottom right:** © Dallas Museum of Art; **57:** © The Metropolitan Museum of Art/Art Resource, NY (ART403820); **63, 72, 85:** © Whitney Museum of American Art, by Jerry L. Thompson; **68, 78, 86, 149:** © Storm King Art Center, Mountainville, NY, by Jerry L. Thompson; **74 left:** photo by Robert McAfee, courtesy The Estate of David Smith, NY; **74 right:** © 1942 Worldwide Photo, courtesy The Estate of David Smith, NY; **75, 131:** © Tate, London 2011; **83:** © Estate of Marcel Duchamp/ARS, NY, digital image © The Museum of Modern Art/Licensed by SCALA/Art Resource, NY (ART372624); **84:** courtesy the Frederick R. Weisman Art Foundation, Los Angeles; **90:** © The Metropolitan Museum of Art/Art Resource, NY (ART403821); **98, 114, 115:** photo by David Smith, courtesy The Estate of David Smith, NY, photo of vintage print by Niel Frankel; **117 (silhouette), 140:** © President and Fellows of Harvard College, by Julius Beebe; **118:** photo by Douglas M. Parker Studio, Los Angeles; **119:** courtesy Christie's, New York; **126:** courtesy Seattle Art Museum, by Paul Macapia; **129:** courtesy Margo Leavin Gallery, Los Angeles, by Douglas M. Parker Studio; **130:** courtesy the Shindler Family Collection; **132, 157 bottom:** courtesy Margo Leavin Gallery, Los Angeles, by Brian Forrest; **145 top, 146:** courtesy the Hirshhorn Museum and Sculpture Garden, Smithsonian Institution, Washington, D.C., by Lee Stalsworth; **148:** © President and Fellows of Harvard College, by Katya Kallsen; **154 middle, 154 bottom:** photo by Jean-Michel Lapelerie, courtesy ENSBA, Paris; **155 bottom right, 166:** © 2011 Museum Associates/LACMA, by Robert Wedemeyer

Index

Page numbers in *italics* refer to illustrations; those followed by "n" indicate endnotes.

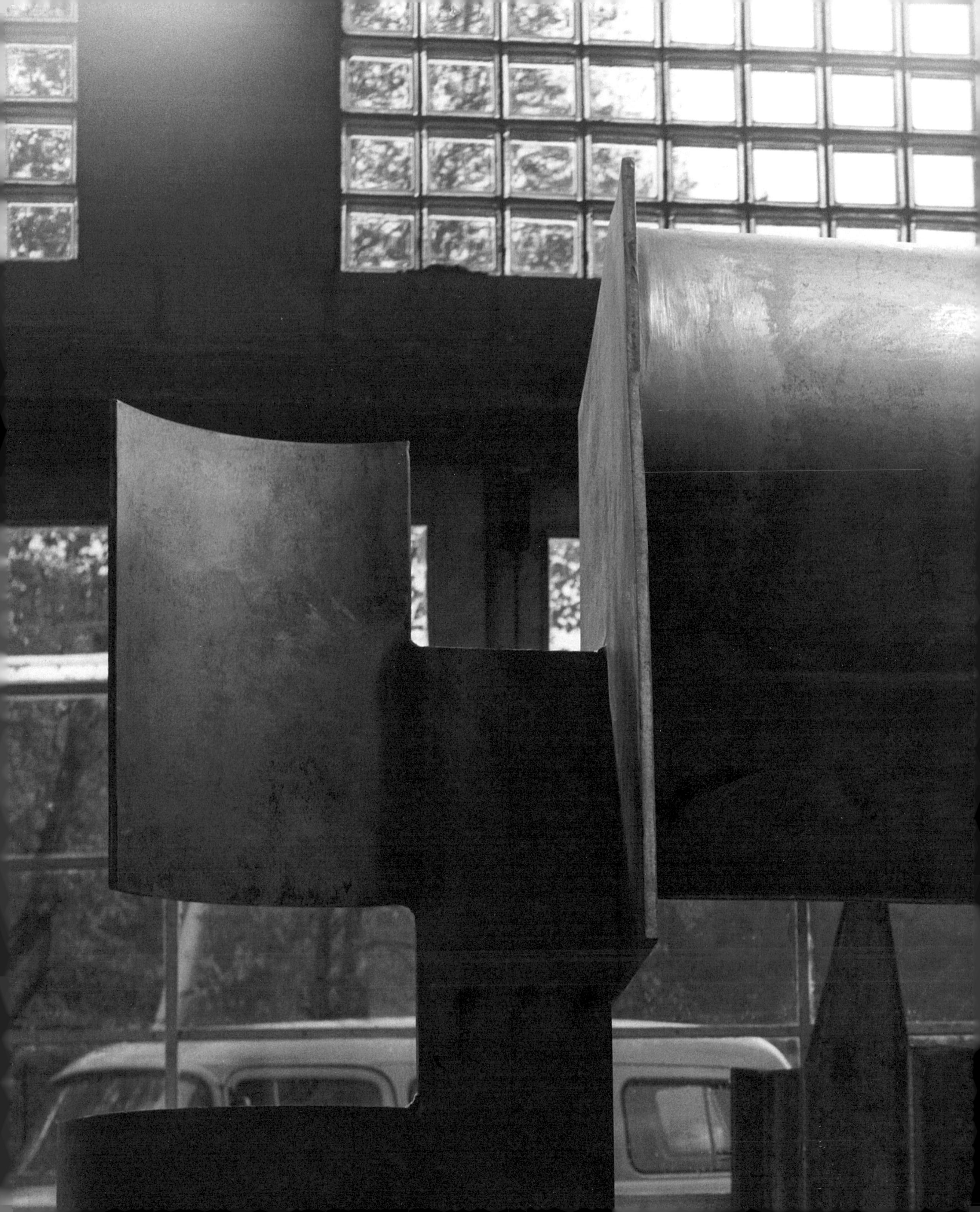